"*Smoke-Free* is an invaluable resource and guide to educate and prepare any citizen who dreams of taking their community smoke-free. This book offers many powerful, poignant lessons about the tobacco industry's typical tactics, and how to respond to them. *Smoke-Free* may even inspire and empower you to become an outspoken advocate. It will arm and prepare you for the adversity you may face on the road ahead. Banning public smoking is an idea whose time has come — but it will only happen with the vision, voices and determination of our citizen-advocates. Read this book and take action now!"

> — Patrick Reynolds, grandson of RJ Reynolds and President, Tobaccofree.org. Mr. Reynolds has been described by former Surgeon General C. Everett Koop as "one of the nation's most influential advocates of a smokefree America." His work has gained him recognition from, amongst others, the World Health Organization.

"I have a reputation for being a critical fellow, but this is a place that did everything right."

> — Stanton Glantz, PhD, Professor of Medicine, University of California, San Francisco. Dr. Glantz is a co-author of *The Cigarette Papers* and has been described in the *Bulletin of the World Health Organization* as a "tobacco warrior."

"A must read for those interested in improving the health of their community."

> — Perry Kendall, MBBS, MSc, FRCP(C), Provincial Health Officer, Province of British Columbia. Dr. Kendall is a public health innovator and a strong advocate for clean-air regulations.

SMOKE - FREE

HOW ONE CITY SUCCESSFULLY BANNED SMOKING IN ALL INDOOR PUBLIC PLACES

Barbara McLintock

Foreword by Jeffrey S. Wigand, PhD, MAT

Preface by Richard Stanwick, MD, MSc, FRCP(C), FAAP

Copyright © Outside the Box

All rights reserved. No written or illustrated part of this book may be reproduced, except for brief quotations in articles or reviews, without permission from the author.

Library and Archives Canada Cataloguing in Publication

McLintock, Barbara

    Smoke-free : how one city successfully banned smoking in all indoor public places / by Barbara McLintock.

Includes index.

ISBN 1-894694-31-7

    1. Nonsmoking areas--British Columbia--Victoria. 2. Hospitality industry--Health aspects--British Columbia--Victoria. 3. Smoking in the workplace--British Columbia--Victoria. 4. Law enforcement--British Columbia--Victoria. 5. Smoking--Law and legislation--British Columbia--Victoria. I. Title.

HV5770.C2M28 2004   362.29'67'0971128   C2004-903446-4

Proofreader: Arlene Prunkl   Indexer: Renée Fossett
Text design: Paul van Hoek   Cover design: Michael Li

All photographs are by staff at the Vancouver Island Health Authority unless otherwise indicated.

First printing: October 2004

Printed in Hong Kong

Granville Island
Publishing

212-1656 Duranleau
Vancouver, BC, Canada V6H 3S4
Tel: (604) 688-0320 Toll free: 1-877-688-0320
www.GranvilleIslandPublishing.com

DEDICATION

This book is dedicated to all those individuals who came together as a team in the development, passage and implementation of the clean-air bylaw in Greater Victoria and to their families, who stood behind them even during the toughest times.

It is also dedicated to all those elsewhere who are considering or have already embarked upon the process of providing smoke-free indoor air in their communities.

ACKNOWLEDGEMENTS

Writing a book like this is, as much as enacting a clean-air bylaw, a team effort. Thanks must go to the many people on my "team" who helped bring this project to fruition.

To Dianne Stevenson, Wendy Boyd and Dr. Richard Stanwick, all from the Vancouver Island Health Authority, for making available to me the thousands of documents that told the story of Victoria's smoking bylaw, and also for sharing their personal memories of times, both good and bad, during the bylaw's development and implementation;

To Jeffrey Wigand, the original tobacco "insider," for kindly agreeing to write the foreword;

To Dr. Stanton Glantz, whose work as a "tobacco warrior" provided invaluable insights into the larger context in which the Victoria story fit;

To Jacquie Drope, whose research on behalf of Dr. Glantz sparked the idea of telling the story in book form;

To Adrian Raeside for allowing the use of his cartoons that capture so well the essence of the smoke-free debate.

To Alan Perry, Michael Li and Claire Battershill for their invaluable editing, proofreading, design and technical assistance.

To Printing Services at the Vancouver Island Health Authority for their efficiency and hard work under tight deadlines;

To the entire team at Granville Island Publishing – Jo Blackmore, Mary-Ann Yazedjian, David Litvak and especially editor Arlene Prunkl – for their patience with, and improvements to, the manuscript;

And most of all, to everyone who was involved in the bylaw process and who freely shared their stories with me. Without you all, it never would have happened.

TABLE OF CONTENTS

Foreword ix

Preface xiii

Introduction xvii

Chapter 1 – The Games Begin 1

Chapter 2 – Taking the Plunge 21

Chapter 3 – Seeking Consensus 39

Chapter 4 – Decisions, Decisions 55

Chapter 5 – Getting Ready 69

Chapter 6 – Home, Sweet Home 97

Chapter 7 – The Big Day 119

Chapter 8 – Media Mania 141

Chapter 9 – Our Day in Court 167

Chapter 10 – Lessons Learned 191

Epilogue 207

Chronology 215

Index 219

About the Author 226

FOREWORD

More than five million preventable tobacco-related deaths occur in the world annually. This epidemic toll is expected to grow within the next decade to the point where tobacco will claim the equivalent in lives of a Holocaust each year. This will be prevented only if the tobacco industry is held accountable for its actions and is substantively transformed through morally mandated regulations and public knowledge.

During the last decade, progress has been made in "denormalizing" tobacco use, which for more than two centuries, has been an accepted part of daily life. Efforts have been made to characterize tobacco products for what they are: products that when used as intended kill not only users but also innocent unborn children and adult workers. Tobacco is now more specifically labeled. Additives are listed. Labeling monikers such as "mild" or "light" have been removed. Prices have been raised. And countries, cities, states and municipalities around the world are creating smoke-free public environments.

Despite these advances, tobacco use is still wreaking havoc across our continent and around the world. In North America, more than 480,000 people, many of whom never chose to smoke, are dying each year from the effects of tobacco use and exposure to its lethal components. More people die from tobacco-related diseases than from many other causes of death, such as AIDS, homicide, suicide and automobile crashes. Tobacco extracts its toll in the form of lung cancer and other respiratory diseases, heart disease, impotence and infertility. Exposure to second-hand smoke before birth causes cognitive impairment in newborn children.

The tobacco industry displays immoral behavior by generating obfuscation and controversy over the scientific and economic issues of personal tobacco use and the creation of smoke-free environments. Taking on the tobacco industry is never an easy task. This became clear to me in 1989, soon after I went to work for Brown & Williamson Tobacco Corporation, part of BAT Industries, which is the world's second largest marketer of tobacco products.

Smoke-Free

When I decided to go public with what I had learned and witnessed while working as the senior scientific officer in such a large tobacco company, I began to understand how difficult it is to challenge this mammoth-sized industry. The tobacco industry has too many billions of dollars at stake to quietly accept any challenges to its power. It is driven to reinvest its enormous profits to further the marketing of its lethal, addictive products. Of course, such behaviour contradicts any industry's moral duty to public health and safety, to the truth, and to widely accepted moral principles such as "do no harm to others."

The elected officials and public health leaders in Victoria, Canada have also understood how difficult it is to challenge the industry. These officials learned this lesson as they struggled for years to pass and implement a bylaw banning smoking in all indoor public places. In their own community, they faced many of the same challenges I faced when I became the most senior former tobacco company executive to address the public health and safety issues involving tobacco products.

The hospitality industry, by directly and indirectly accepting the backing of the tobacco industry, was compelled to warn of economic calamity if the bylaw went ahead. Not surprisingly, the predicted economic disasters never followed. Nor has disaster followed in any other jurisdiction that has had the courage and foresight to pass and implement similar laws. The elected officials and health proponents in Victoria faced the same sort of legal challenges, personal abuse and direct threats that all of us who have taken on the tobacco industry have suffered. But, in spite of these obstacles, the leaders of Victoria held true to their duty and convictions. In the end they won the battle. Now, five years after the bylaw went into effect, more than 99 per cent of hospitality establishments in Greater Victoria are complying with it. Smoke-free indoor public places have become the socially accepted norm in the community. The most important outcome is that innocent lives have been and will continue to be saved.

I have long argued that legislation mandating smoke-free places is one of the three pillars necessary for a full challenge to the

Foreword

tobacco industry. Not only does such legislation protect workers and other patrons from the deadly effects of second-hand smoke, a known human-specific carcinogen, but it is also a key part of the effort to denormalize smoking. A major effort to prevent children and youth from starting to smoke is the second pillar of this strategy. The third is the provision of effective cessation programs for nicotine addicts who are ready to break their addiction. These prevention and cessation efforts benefit when smoking is seen as being outside the mainstream in 21st century North American life. The success of a fully implemented bylaw is shown by the ongoing reduction in the proportion of smokers in Greater Victoria and especially by the reduction of the number of teens that are lured into taking up the habit.

The Victoria experience and this book clearly demonstrate that none of the tobacco industry's arguments are valid. *Smoke-Free* shows that, while passing and fully implementing legislation may not be easy, it *can* be accomplished. The book also contains numerous tips for those jurisdictions now either considering, or in the process of passing and implementing, indoor smoking bans. The lessons learned from the Victoria experiences will be of great benefit both to those elected officials responsible for passing the legislation and those in public health departments charged with making it work.

What is it that will enable someone to persevere, to stay the course in spite of threats, obstacles and challenges? Undoubtedly, knowing that what one is doing is right, and understanding one's duty to protect the innocent plays an important role.

I would like especially to stress the point that a jurisdiction must have sufficient resources in place to go the distance with the tobacco industry before attempting to bring legislation into effect. The tobacco industry still has deep pockets, and it will not hesitate to use its profits to try to deflect any challenges to its power. I have often said that if it were not for the help I received from health groups, the media and some government representatives, the company for which I had worked, Brown & Williamson, would have litigated me to death. In particular, the company would have proceeded with so many lawsuits and charges that the useful information I had in my possession might never have made it into the realms of public debate. Similarly, any jurisdiction proceeding with smoke-free legislation must ensure it has the resources available to fight a court challenge as far as it needs to be fought.

The public health officials and elected officials from Greater Victoria and I share a common bond. We have remained steadfast in our battle with tobacco interests for the benefit of public health and safety. Reading this book should inspire other jurisdictions to pass clean indoor air legislation, knowing not only that it can be accomplished, but that it can be accomplished successfully.

Jeffrey Wigand, PhD

Thou shalt not be a victim.

Thou shalt not be a perpetrator.

Above all,

thou shalt not be a bystander.

Using his knowledge about the tobacco industry, Wigand seeks to educate the public on how the industry uses the media, the entertainment industry, sports events, music and deceptive advertising to introduce children to tobacco — to "hook them young, hook them for life." Eighty percent of today's tobacco users became addicted before the age of eighteen, his website is www.jeffreywigand.com.

PREFACE

Public health officials have seldom experienced such a sustained and high profile as during the past two years. They are being appreciatively recognized in the struggle against new communicable-disease pathogens such as SARS, West Nile Virus and Mad Cow Disease. As well, they have become known through their battles against old infectious-disease enemies such as anthrax, now being exploited as weapons of terror. While no one should underestimate the difficulties or significance of these skirmishes, neither should anyone minimize the efforts of public health workers to combat the scourge of tobacco use — a non-communicable disease epidemic far more deadly than either SARS or West Nile Virus Syndrome.

When public health officials such as myself consider sharing our experience in passing legislation and ensuring compliance in controversial fields such as tobacco control, we most often employ the traditional format of submitting peer-reviewed journal articles. Such articles distill the scientific essence of what transpired, ensure that rigorous methods were employed, use exacting statistics to determine significance and finish with a very measured and conservative discussion and/or conclusions. In fact, such a high quality publication has been produced on the Victoria experience.[1] Unquestionably, such an approach is critical in providing credible new knowledge that others can use and build upon in their own efforts to create healthy public policy.

However, journal articles provide only one part of the story when you are dealing with as politically charged and emotionally laden a subject as tobacco control. I realized this when I was co-presenting a workshop on smoking control at the Pan American Health Organization's 100th Anniversary Health Promotion Conference in Santiago, Chile in October 2002. Many of those who attended — especially those who were at the beginning or in the midst of their own efforts towards comprehensive clean indoor air bylaws — found the "adventures" associated with building public support and achieving compliance in Greater Victoria as fascinating a case study as the levels of statistical significance presented in the formal paper.

Regardless of where they were on their respective journeys on the path to clean indoor air, members of the audience wanted to know "what it was really like for us" to traverse the various stages of bylaw development, implementation and compliance. They wanted not just a recitation of events, rather the emotional colouration of those events. They wanted to hear about the psychological pressures that faced the bylaw protagonists in Victoria, and about the visceral aspects of engaging in a full-fledged tobacco-control battle.

Looking back on the history of the Victoria bylaw, there is no question that it was often a veritable roller-coaster ride for those involved. There were moments of despair and even of fear, but also moments of humour and of unequalled camaraderie. And of course the required happy ending. The need for an accompanying document to record that side of the history of Victoria's smoking bylaw became clear.

The challenge of telling this story was taken up by Barbara McLintock, a well-respected local journalist who had already established herself in writing about public health issues in our community. She also had authored a successful book about Victoria's most controversial eating disorder clinic being stripped of its licence to operate despite being the darling of the American media. The major events in McLintock's book, *Anorexia's Fallen Angel: The Untold Story of the Montreux Clinic* (www.anorexiasfallenangel.com) parallelled in time the evolution of the efforts in Greater Victoria to make all indoor public spaces 100 per cent smoke-free. Since our health region's licensing team was responsible for that investigation, I played a role in those events as well. It was her artful blending of fact and circumstance around the Montreux story that made it apparent she was the right person to tell the tale of our bylaw.

Not one to disappoint, McLintock populates her story of the bylaw with a colourful cast of characters; she details coincidences and reveals alliances that would make even the most diehard soap opera fan skeptical of the plot twists. Her text also provides significant insight on how and why the worst *preventable* epidemic in our country — an epidemic of our own making and one with profits "to die for" — continues to cause misery and suffering.

The primary purpose of this book is to document the story of one team, of which I had the privilege of being a member, that took on the challenge of implementing the first successful 100 per cent clean indoor air bylaw in Canada. Examples of the team's commitment, perseverance and passion are intertwined with stories of the adversities they faced and obstacles they overcame — betrayals, misrepresentations and occasionally even immediate threats to their own health and safety. Big Tobacco is a major if subtle antagonist.

After reading our story, I expect that individuals who have engaged in the creation of healthy public policy around tobacco will recognize scenarios that they too have experienced. A majority of the challenges and opposition tactics do not appear to vary much from community to community; hence, the story of how those obstacles can be overcome may provide a valuable template for others on the journey. Moreover, the promise of eventual success as displayed in this recounting of events may serve to inspire others to take up the struggle against the public health epidemic caused by tobacco — although not without the understanding that a successful outcome requires an unusual amount of dedication, tenacity and resources.

In the end, the question that is most often asked is, "Was it worth it?" A local cardiologist quipped that as a result of the bylaw, our community will likely need one less cardiologist in the future. As our region moved through the process of the bylaw and its implementation, the smoking rate in the general public fell from 22 per cent — already one of the lowest in Canada at that time — to less than 15 per cent last year. As well, the banning of tobacco on school property has left us with a teen smoking rate that is between one-third and one-half that of other, less-regulated, school districts in British Columbia. Those are added benefits on top of the fact that the lungs of every hospitality industry worker in the region are protected from the toxins of second-hand smoke in their workplaces — just the same as those of every other employee in the region. No more second-class lungs.

It is now almost nine years since I moved to Victoria to take up the medical health officer's position, and since I first went to the regional board to propose a speedy move towards 100 per cent smoke-free indoor spaces. Looking back on those eight years and the adventures that ensued, I cannot help but conclude that yes, it is a grand and worthy enterprise, one with the potential for tremendous public health returns, and well-deserving of the efforts put into it to achieve success.

Richard Stanwick, MD

Chief Medical Health Officer

Vancouver Island Health Authority

---

1. Drope, Jacquie and Glantz, Dr. Stanton. "British Columbia capital regional district 100% smoke free bylaw a successful public health campaign despite industry opposition," Tobacco Control, 12 (3) 264–268, 2003.

INTRODUCTION

January 7, 1999. In a nondescript office building in Victoria, the capital city of British Columbia, a small team of public health officials gathers to plan their strategy for the evening. They are well aware that their tactics need to be refined with the precision of a military campaign. The officials need to ensure that their armed backup is in place, in the form of police departments and RCMP detachments, ready to respond instantly if they receive a cell phone call from the team. The team is heading out to various drinking establishments in the Greater Victoria region. Their goal: to enforce the newly proclaimed bylaw that bans smoking in all indoor public places, including the smokers' last bastions of pubs and bars.

It is the fourth day of enforcement, and things have not been going well. During the first three days the officials have already witnessed the entrenched defiance that must be overcome. Although virtually all of the city's restaurants are complying with the new law, at least 50 bars and pubs have vowed they'll never obey it. Earlier that day a trip to one of the most rebellious drinking spots, the Esquimalt Inn, has yet again turned into a virtual circus with yelling patrons and the need for police officers to attend.

"Are we ready?" asks Dianne Stevenson, head of the tobacco control program for the Capital health region. It has been Stevenson's job to put together the implementation plan for the highly controversial bylaw. For the first weeks the bylaw is in place, almost every environmental health officer in the region has been assigned to the enforcement team. Most will visit restaurants and bars that are already co-operating with the legislation, but Stevenson will go out with selected members of the team every night, hitting the places where the defiance appears to be the greatest.

"As ready as we'll ever be," says Miles Drew, a full-time bylaw enforcement officer and the only one of the group in uniform.

Smoke-Free

Drew notes the nervousness of the others and wants to ask, as he's wanted to ask so many times before, if they're sure they want to go on with this. But he doesn't. He already knows the answer: they will tell him that they have no choice, that they've come too far to turn back now.

"Then let's go," says Stevenson. "First stop, back to the Esquimalt Inn." Together they will go to the most difficult stops along the route. There is at least some small feeling of safety in numbers.

The Esquimalt Inn has been the most troublesome spot since day one. Manager Brian Mayzes, who tops the scales at more than 160 kilograms (350 pounds), is the head of the Freedom of Choice Business Coalition, an informal alliance of owners of bars, restaurants and even a few long-term care homes. It sprang up when it was clear that the bylaw was actually going to go into effect. Instead of putting up the required No Smoking signs, Mayzes made his own, which read: "This is a Smoking Establishment. Enter at Your Own Risk." The health officers are never sure whether he's referring to the risk of second-hand smoke or to some other risks for bylaw enforcers.

The bar is hopping by the time the team arrives. Most of the crowd is male, dressed in grease-encrusted jeans and work shirts, drinking jugs of draft beer, shooting pool and listening to a country-western singer whine nasally about her broken heart. The air is a haze of cigarette smoke. At almost every table, at least one person is smoking.

The arrival of the enforcement team does not go unnoticed. The group is only a few feet inside the door when a bartender spots them and quickly grabs the microphone away from the crooner.

"Ladies and gentlemen, they're here again tonight. It's the SMOKING POLICE! Let's give them a good old-fashioned Esquimalt Inn welcome."

Within seconds, it seems the entire crowd is giving Nazi salutes, chanting, "Sieg Heil! Sieg Heil!" Some are goose-stepping up and down the aisles, some are standing up and surrounding the group, yelling only inches from their faces.

Stevenson grabs her cell phone and hastily calls 911, connecting with the Esquimalt police department. The seconds it takes for the first squad car to arrive seem like hours to the officials who are trying to talk calmly to the group but can scarcely be heard over the furore.

The chanting stops abruptly when the first two armed police officers walk in. Most of the crowd sidle back to their seats as if trying to pretend they'd never had anything to do with the ruckus in the first place.

"Go ahead," the younger policeman says to Drew. "We're here to protect your back."

The team moves towards one of the nearest tables, where a man has continued to smoke through the entire incident. The man agrees he's well aware of the bylaw and has no intention of obeying it.

"I'm going to give you a $50 ticket for smoking in an indoor public place," says Drew. "May I please have your name and address?"

But the man refuses to give it. Patiently, Drew tries to explain: "You are required by law to provide your name and address, and if you refuse you can be charged with obstruction of justice." Still, the man refuses.

Only when one of the police officers warns him he's likely to be arrested on the criminal charge, does he give in. He receives his ticket in silence, and the health officials leave for the next bar.

"I have trouble believing that," says Stevenson to fellow tobacco educator Claire Avison as they get back in their vehicle. "I have trouble believing someone would be willing to face a criminal charge just because they hate the bylaw so much."

Smoke-Free

Three and a half years later, on July 6, 2002, Stevenson and administrative assistant Wendy Boyd are the only two out to make checks. Enforcement problems with the bylaw are now so minimal that many nights, no one is assigned to the job. The officials know that if any establishment were to start defying the ban again, they'd quickly hear of it. Patrons would likely object, and if they didn't, the complaints would be sent in by other bar owners, who have finally come to understand the advantages of a level playing field in which everyone is bound by the same rules. Still, Stevenson and Boyd have decided that they will hit the toughest spots they can find tonight to make sure owners know they're still around — working-class bars, nightclubs and cabarets.

The Esquimalt Inn is not so much a working-class bar any more. It has changed owners, changed managers and gone considerably more upscale. The smokers are enjoying themselves on a pleasantly furnished patio behind the building, well away from the noise of traffic on the nearby main road.

The bartender again sees Stevenson and Boyd within seconds of their entrance.

"Hello, ladies," he says cheerfully. "How's business? Can I get you a pop or something?"

Stevenson and Boyd lean against the dark wooden bar. "How's it going with you?" asks Stevenson. "Any problems? Anything we can help with?"

The bartender shakes his head. "Actually," he says, "I gotta tell you ... I mean, I never thought I'd say this ... I hated it when it came in, but I gotta say, your bylaw's been the best thing around here."

"How come?" asks Stevenson.

"Working conditions, I guess you'd call it. I don't go home stinking of smoke every night. My girlfriend sure likes that. And it's way easier to work in a cleaner atmosphere."

Stevenson and Boyd exchange grins as they get back into the car.

The compliance rate throughout the region now is more than 99 per cent, even among the toughest bars and nightclubs. It's believed to be one of the highest rates on the North American continent.

Further, the idea of completely smoke-free indoor air has become the city's new cultural norm. Scientific public opinion surveys show public support for the bylaw at over 80 per cent. No one even questions the rules any more.

So, how did the elected regional board members and health officials make the journey from the wild defiance of 1999 to those new cultural norms? That is the story told in the rest of this book.

1
The Games Begin

"The Public Health is the foundation upon which rests the happiness of the people and the welfare of the nation. The care of the Public Health is the first duty of the statesman."

— *Benjamin Disraeli*

When Greater Victoria won its bid to host the 1994 Commonwealth Games, it sparked dreams for citizens throughout the region. For a metropolitan area of fewer than 300,000 people, hosting the Games would be the perfect opportunity to put the city on the map worldwide. Not only would there be thousands of athletes, cultural performers, officials and spectators coming from around the world to the city at the southern tip of Vancouver Island in Canada, but the television coverage would be seen by millions of viewers in countries from New Zealand to Nigeria. Those involved dreamed of outstanding sporting events, of glorious opening and closing ceremonies and of tens of thousands of people attending music and dance performances on the lawns around the Inner Harbour, long the showcase for Victoria's tourist industry.

Dr. Shaun Peck also had a dream for the Commonwealth Games. Dr. Peck was medical health officer for the region (officially called the Capital regional district), responsible for the public health of the region's 300,000 residents and the hundreds of thousands more who visited annually. His dream was that in time for the Games, all public indoor spaces would be free of tobacco smoke, offering a huge health benefit by eliminating the toxins of second-hand smoke across the region.

It was a bold dream, but perhaps not quite so bold as it looked on the surface. Dr. Peck was not proposing an entirely new policy for Greater Victoria, but rather an expansion of one that had been developing in the region for more than a decade. Since the early 1980s, the Capital regional district (CRD) had been one of Canada's leaders in developing smoking regulations, albeit ones weaker than a complete ban in all indoor public places, including hospitality establishments. By the time Dr. Peck made his Commonwealth Games proposal, all other indoor workplaces had been required to be smoke-free for more than a year.

Across North America, the health problems caused by tobacco to smokers themselves had been known since the 1950s, but it was 20 years later before doctors and scientists began to consider the possible illnesses caused by second-hand smoke or environmental tobacco smoke (ETS), as it was also called. When the first non-smokers' rights groups sprang up in the early 1970s, they were worried not so much about the health effects of the smoke, as about the pure discomfort it caused. They saw no reason why they should be subjected to the odour of smoke, and the headaches and itchy eyes that often resulted from exposure.

It was not until 1972 that the U.S. Surgeon-General of the day, Dr. Jesse Steinfeld, first discussed the potential health problems of second-hand smoke in his annual report. At the very least, he said, the chemical elements in that smoke were certainly a peril to those who already suffered from respiratory or heart ailments. Yet many reputable scientists believed Dr. Steinfeld was going out on a limb because, at that point, very little epidemiological or biological evidence existed to prove any links between second-hand smoke and specific illnesses.[2]

Backed by Dr. Steinfeld's report, the non-smokers' rights groups began to pressure governments at all levels in Canada and the U.S. to, at the very least, insist that non-smoking sections be established in public facilities. They concentrated first on the highly enclosed spaces of public transportation — airplanes, buses and passenger trains. In 1973, Arizona became the first U.S. state to pass a smoking-control law; theirs banned smoking in such enclosed places as elevators, libraries and theatres. In 1975, Minnesota followed suit with a law based on a Swedish model that required most public places to set aside a certain proportion of their space as the non-smoking section.

Chapter 1 - The Games Begin

It was not until 1978 that the first major scientific work began to yield results empirically showing that second-hand smoke could be a health hazard to individuals who inhaled it. Those first studies included the research of physicist James Repace, who showed the patterns of dispersion of the toxins found in the smoke,[3] and Japanese epidemiological studies showing an increased risk of lung cancer and respiratory disease in those exposed to high levels of ETS.[4]

In Canada, the first jurisdiction which implemented a smoking regulation was the nation's capital, Ottawa. In 1976, city council there passed a bylaw that prohibited smoking in specific circumstances.[5] It included patient-care areas of hospitals and health clinics; elevators, escalators and stairways; line-ups for service, such as those in banks; school buses and taxis if either the driver or the passengers objected. Restaurants had to post signs saying whether they provided a non-smoking section or not.

The next year, Canada's largest city, Toronto, followed suit with a similar bylaw. However, these bylaws still allowed for smoking in hospitality establishments and in many other public places.[6]

Moreover, the last years of the 1970s showed non-smoking groups that smoking restrictions of any kind should not be considered an easy victory. Two initiatives placed on the ballot in California in 1978 and 1980, initiatives which would have substantially restricted the places in which individuals could smoke, were narrowly defeated by the electorate — in both cases after substantial lobbying by the tobacco industry and its supporters.

About the same time as Toronto was passing its first bylaw, a small group of advocates for non-smokers' rights was beginning to discuss the possibility of having a similar bylaw enacted in Greater Victoria. Founders of the group were Rhoda Kaellis and her husband Eugene, long-time community activists in the city. The Kaellises had become known in the early 1970s for leading the Victoria opposition to the U.S. government's nuclear test program on Amchitka Island in the Aleutians — a test so large that B.C. environmentalists feared it might cause a tsunami or even an earthquake along the Canadian West Coast. Like environmentalists around the world, they failed to stop the test (which caused neither an earthquake nor a tsunami), but they did make some valuable allies among political and media groups in Victoria.

When Rhoda Kaellis decided that the health hazards of second-hand smoke would be a valuable crusade upon which to embark, she enlisted the help of journalist Ed Gould, who edited a free-distribution weekly known locally as the *Shopper*. Gould agreed to run a story encouraging those interested to attend a public meeting. About 20 people turned out to that first meeting — and agreed to form a community group to lobby for a bylaw. Rhoda Kaellis was elected the group's first president.

"We were trying to decide what to call the group," she remembers. "I suggested 'Air Space something something,' and then someone else suggested just 'AirSpace.' We didn't need the something something.'"

Thus, AirSpace was born. It was British Columbia's first activist non-smokers' rights group and today remains unflagging in its efforts, involved in everything from lawsuits against the large tobacco companies to in-depth research on the links between the tobacco industry in Canada and political decision-makers. On its website (www.airspace.bc.ca), AirSpace describes itself as "dedicated to making tobacco a health hazard of the past."

The Kaellises and their allies began researching what was being done in other jurisdictions and readying themselves to make formal presentations to the politicians involved. Originally, they'd planned to approach the council of the City of Victoria, but their research quickly revealed that their target should instead be the Capital regional district board. The CRD board was legally designated as the local board of health under the provincial Health Act, which gave it legal jurisdiction over public health issues for the entire region. At that time, the CRD encompassed about 250,000 people living in seven separate municipalities as well as numerous "unorganized areas" over which the regional board had direct control. The board was composed of members

Chapter 1 - The Games Begin

directly elected by the residents of the unorganized areas as well as delegates appointed from the elected councils of the municipalities. The regional district was the direct employer of the region's medical health officer and his staff.

As work on the bylaw progressed, the non-smokers' rights groups and the board itself realized the strengths of having the same body responsible for health regulations for the entire region. That averted the problems of other jurisdictions in British Columbia in which individual municipalities were responsible for public health within their own boundaries. That meant the rules could differ from municipality to municipality, even when the two abutted each other with the boundary between them running down the middle of a road.

The first time AirSpace came to the CRD board to discuss its idea, the elected directors were unenthusiastic. Their objections were hardly different from the ones raised when it was first proposed that all indoor public places should be smoke-free, some 15 years later. The politicians told AirSpace that a bylaw would never work. It would be unenforceable. You can't stop people from smoking, they said. You'd need a police officer over everyone's shoulder. Besides, people have the right to smoke; tobacco is a legal substance.

But AirSpace persisted. Different members would turn up at CRD board meetings and argue the need for a bylaw. They continued their research on bylaws that were succeeding elsewhere. Rhoda Kaellis made several appearances on radio talk shows to try to gain more public support for the idea of a bylaw.

"You can't stop me from smoking," one irate smoker told her on one of the radio shows. "You're interfering with my rights."

"No,'" she snapped back. "You're interfering with *my* right to breathe."

When callers worried that no one would obey such a bylaw, that it would be unenforceable, she pointed out that virtually all Canadian residents were law-abiding citizens who would go along with something that had become a new law. Enforcement would be required for only a small minority of defiant smokers, she predicted.

After a few months of work building public support, AirSpace brought forward a petition bearing the names of more than 150 people concerned about second-hand smoke and asking that the issue be regulated. This time, the board's community health and social services committee asked the medical health officer, Dr. Allan Arneil, to research what bylaws had been passed elsewhere in Canada and how they were working. Dr. Arneil and his staff found that at that point, 10 cities in the country had passed some sort of bylaws, although three of them mandated very few restrictions indeed. The other seven were more extensive, although they differed in some respects.

In his report to the CRD board, Dr. Arneil found that all seven had banned or restricted smoking in retail stores, hospitals, places of public assembly, reception areas, as well as service line-ups, school buses and elevators. Six had imposed some restrictions in banks, offices and restaurants; four had mentioned taxis; and two, municipal buses and bus shelters.

"All seemed to attempt to be reasonable in designating smoking and non-smoking areas as far as [is] practical to try to accommodate all concerned," wrote Dr. Arneil, echoing the general spirit of the day. His research had shown that the public appeared to support the bylaws in place across the country, and although several of the councils had worried about the difficulties of enforcement before passing their bylaws, none reported any difficulties afterwards. Foreshadowing obstacles that would arise 15 years later, however, Dr. Arneil warned that enforcement could "be difficult, [although] probably only in extreme cases." Penalties in other Canadian cities at that time varied from a minimum fine of $25 to a maximum of $2,000 and, depending upon the laws involved, could be levied against either a patron who insisted on smoking, or the operator of a premise who allowed it.

"As the medical health officer," Dr. Arneil concluded, "I have no doubt that second-hand smoke is harmful, especially to

Chapter 1 - The Games Begin

certain individuals, but to some degree to everyone. Therefore any reasonable, fair, practical and enforceable steps should be taken to prevent involuntary exposure to second-hand smoke to others who by necessity must be in certain places to carry out the necessities of normal living (social, commercial, transport)." He suggested that the board approve in principle the idea of a smoking regulation bylaw. Beginning a pattern of negotiation with stakeholders which the board continued throughout ensuing bylaw upgrades, he agreed that "to avoid impractical provisions," he would then meet with those whose businesses might be impacted by such legislation.

The regional board concurred. Dr. Arneil and his staff embarked on a number of consultations before coming up with a draft bylaw, which was then sent out for further public comment. More than 95 per cent of those who replied supported the overall principle of a bylaw, although some were concerned about specific aspects of the draft. Some businesses, particularly in the hospitality industry, were, from those first days of consultation, anxious about the potential economic impact of any restrictions.

The regional district's lawyers warned the board that enforcement could be more difficult in B.C. than in other provinces because, at that time, the law in B.C. stated that the operator of an establishment could not be expected to "enforce" a bylaw by ensuring that people didn't smoke in the areas where it was banned. "You can require owners to set aside areas for non-smokers and you can also require them to post the required signs, but you cannot penalize them for failing to stop people from smoking on their premises," wrote lawyer Don Johannessen. This legal problem cropped up repeatedly over the next 15 years. Overall, however, Johannessen saw no legal impediments to the passing of such a bylaw.

In another area that foreshadowed years of problems, Dr. Arneil found that the greatest controversy surrounded restaurants, and the regulations that should govern smoking within them. "As a health officer, I cannot accept that sidestream smoke in a restaurant is any less hazardous than anywhere else," he wrote. In fact, he noted, the hazard is probably greater in restaurants since patrons usually remain in the place for much longer than they do, for instance, in an elevator or a bank line-up, and the tables are often close together.

The bylaw, as finally drafted, took bits from many of those that Dr. Arneil had studied from elsewhere. It banned smoking at service counters; in the public part of retail stores; in seating areas of movie halls, theatres and the like; in elevators, escalators and stairways, and in school buses and public buses. It allowed other areas, such as reception areas, barber shops, beauty parlors and even hospitals to designate smoking areas, but prohibited smoking outside those areas. And it reached an awkward compromise on the controversial question of restaurants. It would, the board decided, be up to the restaurant proprietor to decide whether his establishment would be all smoking, all non-smoking, or divided into smoking and non-smoking areas. However, a sign had to be posted making clear to potential patrons what the rules were. Any proprietor who decided to set up a designated non-smoking section would have to ensure it included at least one quarter of the total seats. The maximum fine for anyone who defied the bylaw was set at $500.

The bylaw finally received all the necessary approvals by the end of July, 1984, and officially took effect on October 23, 1984. It had taken 18 months of study and consultation for that first bylaw to come into effect.

Rhoda Kaellis still remembers that first bylaw as one of the most successful pieces of social activism in which she had ever engaged. "I think it was partly because people realized there was a moral issue here," she says. She also remembers people wanting Victoria to be one of the first jurisdictions in Canada to pass such a law. Eugene Kaellis also notes it was a project that could yield a considerable amount of public support for politicians while costing very little.

That first bylaw was, however, to remain in place for less than two years. In the mid-1980s, evidence on the harmful effects of second-hand smoke began to accumulate rapidly. Throughout 1984, 1985 and 1986, prestigious medical journals in both North

America and Europe published studies demonstrating that those exposed to second-hand smoke could be shown to have absorbed tobacco byproducts into their own bodies. Literature included major discussions as to whether second-hand smoke could directly cause lung cancer in non-smokers.

One study, written by a consortium of Japanese researchers and published in the *New England Journal of Medicine,* summarized their findings: "We conclude that the deleterious effects of passive smoking may occur in proportion to the exposure of nonsmokers to smokers in the home, the workplace, and the community." In 1986, Dr. Everett Koop, who had taken over as Surgeon-General in the U.S., went so far as to specifically link lung cancer in otherwise healthy non-smokers to their exposure to environmental tobacco smoke. Precisely how dangerous second-hand smoke was remained unclear, but, as Richard Kluger pointed out in his history of tobacco, *Ashes to Ashes*, the fact that danger was clear and present was enough for most health professionals. "Their watchwords were preventive medicine," he wrote, "and linking environmental tobacco smoke with direct smoking in order to alarm and mobilize the public against the still widely practised habit served to counter the unstinting drumbeat of denial, distortion and disinformation sounded by the tobacco industry in order to stay in business."[7]

A labour arbitrator's decision in Ontario backed a grievance that had been filed by a Toronto-area public servant who had complained he was forced to work in dangerous conditions because of the amount of smoke in his workplace. The arbitrator agreed that smoke could be identified as a health hazard and a dangerous substance. Moreover, the decision stated that improved ventilation in the workplace wasn't a satisfactory solution. It said the only solution would be to segregate workers based on their smoking behaviour into separately ventilated rooms, or even on different floors of the office building where they worked.

The result was that by 1986, the CRD's health department and many of the local politicians were concluding that workers needed greater protection from second-hand smoke than was provided by the 1984 bylaw. In the spring, the elected officials of the health committee of the regional board began discussions with the new acting medical health officer, Dr. Brian Allen, and with its lawyers. The conclusion was that the bylaw should be split into two separate pieces of legislation. Bylaw 1440 was specifically titled "A bylaw for the purpose of controlling smoking in the workplace," and banned smoking in all workplaces except for "designated smoking areas" that could be established by employers. The other bylaw was entitled "A bylaw for the purpose of controlling the places where people may smoke." It began by banning smoking in all public premises, but then established a lengthy series of exemptions, much the same as those in the 1984 legislation. Shopping malls could designate half their premises as smoking, and even hospitals were still allowed to have designated smoking areas. As before, restaurants could decide how they wished to designate their establishments, provided that they posted clear signs.

Within a few months of the new bylaws, however, the concerns that Dr. Arneil had originally raised about enforcement began to show themselves in the community. One convenience store customer took his complaint to the local media when employees in the store had refused to butt out while working behind the counter. The customer pointed out that it made no sense in a one-room store to say the customers couldn't smoke (because it was a "public premise," a retail store) but the employees could (because the area behind the counter could be a "designated smoking area" in a workplace, as allowed by the bylaw).

Dr. Allen reluctantly admitted that the bylaw could be confusing, and also that the CRD had not established any resources for policing or enforcement. Complaints or requests for information were dealt with, not by someone specifically hired for the purpose, but rather by Wendy Boyd, the administrative assistant to the medical health officer. Soon after the new bylaw took effect, Boyd was dealing with half a dozen calls a day or more, and found herself mainly explaining what the new rules called for. When the complaint of non-enforcement appeared in the local newspaper, the *Times-Colonist*, Dr. Allen suggested that customers should boycott any businesses that wouldn't obey the law, but only a few weeks later he took a recommended enforcement policy to the regional board's health committee. The policy, approved by the board, suggested that a complainant should originally be asked to deal directly with the business, but if this was found to be unsuccessful, the CRD would send a letter to the offending establishment. Further complaints would result in more forceful letters, and then a personal visit from the region's bylaw enforcement officer. If all else failed, the CRD board would agree to refer the case to its lawyer or to Crown prosecutors for possible prosecution for refusing to abide by the bylaw. The policy was hardly different from that adopted for enforcement 12 years later when the board agreed that all hospitality establishments had to go entirely smoke-free.

The board also agreed at that time to hire a temporary public health inspector for three months to monitor compliance with the bylaw, educate businesses about it and try to raise the compliance rates. In the three-month period, the new employee made hundreds of visits to establishments throughout the region. On first visits to businesses, it was found that only about 30 per cent were complying fully with the terms of the bylaw, but most were quite prepared to make the necessary changes when the law was explained to them. When the inspector visited the same premises for a second time, the compliance rate had risen to 92 per cent.

During the next several years, studies continued to demonstrate the harmful effects of second-hand smoke. In 1989, a new medical health officer came to the region. Dr. Shaun Peck had received his medical degree from Cambridge and had worked as medical health officer in other parts of B.C. before moving to Victoria. He was an enthusiastic advocate of tobacco control and, soon after arriving, established a special task force to look for ways to reduce smoking in the region — already down to 22 per cent, a low figure compared to the rest of the country. At the same time, communities across British Columbia were setting up special projects called "Healthy 2000," looking for ways to improve the health of the populace before the new millennium, just a decade away.

Dr. Peck combined these initiatives into the Tobacco-Free Task Force, established with the aim of having Greater Victoria reach a smoking rate as close as possible to zero over the decade. The task force included representatives from the Big Three health non-profits — the Lung Association, the Heart and Stroke Foundation and the Canadian Cancer Society — as well as representatives of the region's doctors and public health groups. Under Dr. Peck's leadership, they quickly agreed that one goal would be to tighten up the bylaw, especially for workplaces. He had concluded that many workers weren't being protected at all from second-hand smoke because their employers had declared the entire workplace a "designated smoking area," something they were allowed to do under the 1986 bylaw. Another frequent problem was that the "non-smoking" corner of an office was filled with smoke from the rest of the smoke-filled worksite. After several months of meetings, Dr. Peck presented his report on the changes should be made to the CRD board's health committee.

(From Left) Dianne Stevenson, Dr. Shaun Peck, and Cindy Scraba from the Restaurant and Foodservice Association at a Trends Food Show (1995)

Chapter 1 - The Games Begin

"The subject matter is very controversial," warned regional district executive director Bill Jordan in an attachment to Dr. Peck's report.

Dr. Peck suggested that in workplaces, designated smoking areas should be permitted only in places where non-smokers need never go. The law should read, he said, that the smoking area "may not be a room where non-smokers need to have access or thoroughfare, including reception areas, lounges, break-rooms, lunchrooms, etc. unless equal and separate facilities exist for non-smokers." An office could set up two separate staff lunchrooms, one for smokers and one for non-smokers. But in an establishment too small for that, the lunchroom would have to be non-smoking.

He also recommended that smoking be banned entirely in places like shopping malls and recreation centres. Under the 1986 bylaw, he noted, "a shopping mall can designate all seating areas for smoking and place these along the entire length of the concourse. Only a complete ban on smoking in such places can solve the problem of smoke crossing imaginary boundaries."

He moved to solve problems like the one found in the convenience store by specifying that the designated smoking areas must not be areas to which the public has access. And he suggested that beauty parlours and barber shops should also be required to be non-smoking. With the rules in place that allowed a barber shop to have nine smoking seats out of 12, "there is clearly no protection for the non-smoking customer." Laundromats and bus shelters should be in the same category.

Perhaps most controversial of all, Dr. Peck also proposed that all restaurants, cocktail lounges, pubs, bars and cabarets, as well as bowling alleys and bingo halls, be required to provide half their seating as non-smoking.

As Jordan had anticipated, the proposals drew howls of outrage, especially from the hospitality industry. By 1990, the tobacco industry throughout North America had begun to recognize the threat posed by the growing number of clean-air bylaws and was mobilizing its various allies and front groups to fight them. The industry was beginning to adopt publicly its policy of "accommodation" under which it would accept bylaws which mandated smoking and non-smoking sections but would fight vigorously those that would ban indoor smoking altogether. It was also beginning to look at what it hoped would be satisfactory ventilation solutions, and to encourage states and provinces to pass what was known as "pre-emptive legislation" — legislation that would ban local governments, such as municipalities or local health boards, from passing tougher legislation on their own. The experience, particularly in California, had been that local councils were often less amenable to industry influence and inducements, and were prepared to pass much stiffer regulations than were state or provincial legislatures.

It took several months of acrimonious debate, but in the end Dr. Peck persuaded the board to pass virtually all of his recommendations. In fact, it was agreed to go even further when looking at workplaces, but in a two-stage process. On January 1, 1992, almost all indoor workplaces in the region would be 100 per cent smoke-free. No designated smoking areas would be allowed. The main exception remained the hospitality industry, which would move to the 50 per cent non-smoking seating figure. Smoking lounges would also still be allowed in seniors' homes and extended care hospitals. At the time, these facilities were viewed as the residents' homes, and those who had smoked for 50 years needed a place indoors where they could continue doing so. This perspective was understandable. Over time these seniors were living for years, on average, in these premises before passing away. In less than a decade, as pressures on the health care system increased, this stay would be reduced to weeks or months instead of years.

The bylaw made Greater Victoria the first region in Canada to mandate entirely smoke-free workplaces. Even before it had been passed, Dr. Peck was well aware that it could not be administered by Boyd while she did all the other work involved in running the office. He persuaded the board to hire a half-time co-ordinator for bylaw

Chapter 1 - The Games Begin

development and implementation, including public education and monitoring for compliance. The first person hired for the job was Linda Brigden, who did much of the research and consultation work to bring the legislation into being. Shortly after it went into effect, she was promoted to head the tobacco control program for the entire province, and later moved to work on global tobacco control issues as executive director of the Ottawa-based group, Research for International Tobacco Control.

In November, 1992, the regional board hired Dianne Stevenson, a nurse and health educator, to take over the job. Stevenson also had an advantage in dealing with businesspeople in that none of them could ever accuse her of not understanding how business worked. Along with her nursing career, she had owned and operated her own and family businesses, ranging from fashion accessories to an elevator firm. She also had a background in tobacco issues from the four years she'd served as the volunteer national public education chair for the Canadian Cancer Society.

Dr. Peck explained that it wouldn't be her job to go out and search for violators. Rather, the new bylaw was administered through a complaint-driven process. Individuals who believed that a business, or even a government office, was violating the new rules would phone or mail in a complaint explaining the circumstances. Stevenson would then respond to those complaints. As much as possible, she would provide employers with education about the new requirements, but if necessary she could issue letters making clear that prosecution would be an option for continued defiance.

Indeed, Stevenson found her first few months so busy that she was working virtually full-time on the project, although officially it was still a half-time position. Despite the bylaw, managers continued to smoke in their private offices, large office buildings continued to have smoking areas, even if they were no longer officially designated, and the people continued to ask questions about every aspect of the bylaw — including some that no one had thought of before. Did the bylaw still apply if staff were not on their official working hours? Why were restaurants and bars covered but not "private clubs" such as branches of the Royal Canadian Legion? What about casinos, which, up to that point, weren't covered at all?

Health care facilities continued to cause a problem. Friends and family of those residents in long-term care homes remained worried that the residents' smoking was being overly restricted. Meanwhile, at the acute-care hospitals in which all indoor smoking was now banned, complaints were beginning to come in about the gauntlet of smoking patients huddled around all entrances with their cigarettes.

But even as Stevenson sent out letters and explained the bylaw over and over again, neither Dr. Peck nor the Tobacco-Free Task Force had forgotten their objective of providing the same protection for workers in the hospitality industry as they had for those in all other forms of employment. Six months after the workplace bylaw went into effect, Dr. Peck first raised the issue of having all indoor public places smoke-free in 1994 in time for the Commonwealth Games.

"The [workplace] bylaw has been very successfully implemented," he noted in his six-month report to the board. Of all the continuing suggestions made by the public, he said, "the strongest demand we have had is for restaurants to be smoke-free … we believe there is considerable public demand for this restriction in the CRD." He noted that restaurants were already warning that whatever restrictions were to be imposed on them should also be imposed on bars and pubs to ensure there was a level playing field from a business point of view.

The health committee suggested Dr. Peck should meet with the stakeholders — both the health groups and the hospitality industry — to see if the proposed time frame seemed realistic. It took one meeting for Dr. Peck to realize it wasn't going to be in place by the Games.

The opposition from both the restaurants and bars reached new heights. Half a dozen representatives of restaurants and bars attended the health committee meeting. Among the opponents was Christopher Causton, who later went on to become mayor of the suburban community of Oak Bay and chair of the CRD board itself. At that first meeting, Causton talked about the unreasonableness of the CRD trying to regulate what happened in private businesses as opposed to public facilities. Like the others, he was especially anxious that a total ban would reduce the number of tourists coming to Vancouver Island.

Gordon Card, a pub owner and representative of the Hospitality Industry Liquor Licensing Advisory Group, warned that bar owners were already having trouble enforcing the new rules of 50 per cent non-smoking seating. He brought up the idea of improved ventilation — the solution that tobacco interests had been touting across the U.S.

Don Monsour, head of Victoria's restaurant association, was convinced that the economic impact on the hospitality and tourism industries would be devastating. He claimed to have talked to 21 travel agents, not one of whom would book tours of foreign visitors to Victoria if indoor smoking were to be banned in all restaurants and bars. He warned that his association was already looking at taking the CRD to court if the bylaw went ahead for 1994, and that they had tobacco industry money to back them up. As well, he said, numerous restaurant owners had told him they were each willing to put up $2,000 to fight the court case. All the same, he acknowledged the restaurants recognized the need for health protection for non-smokers. He proposed a compromise that would ban smoking in restaurants, except for those that had separately ventilated smoking sections, ones in which the smoky air was vented directly to the outside.

One week after the meeting Dr. Peck wrote a letter to the restaurant association, admitting that his time frame was not proving to be workable. "At the meeting the impact of a 100 per cent ban on smoking in restaurants was very clearly and forcefully articulated," he wrote. "It is clear that the [original] proposal is unacceptable to the industry and will not work." He promised to continue consulting with the industry to find a compromise that would make the plan practicable.

The entire group had great trouble coming to a consensus on any aspect of potential bylaw changes. Eventually, everyone did agree on the mission statement that: "there be endorsement of the long-term goal of elimination of exposure to environmental tobacco smoke in all public premises in the Capital regional district by the year 2000." But the delegates to the committee went on to tell Dr. Peck that when they had gone back to their various constituency groups, it had been problematic to get even that generality endorsed. The restaurateurs agreed to it, but the bar owners wanted to make the date either the year 2000 "or as predicated by market demand."

However, Don Monsour and the restaurant association did come forward with a compromise proposal. If Dr. Peck would put the 100 per cent smoke-free idea on the back burner, Monsour said, the restaurant association would agree voluntarily to move immediately from 50 per cent non-smoking seating to 60 per cent in all member restaurants. Monsour also worked with Stevenson and her staff to develop a program by which restaurants that voluntarily moved to being 100 per cent smoke-free would receive an award and public recognition.

Dr. Peck realized that he would never have the staff or resources to police a bylaw if none of the hospitality groups were buying in. He told the regional board that it should try the restaurant association's plan of voluntary self-regulation for a year and see how it worked. If it was working well, he suggested, the percentage of non-smoking seating could be raised by 10 per cent each year until it reached 100 per cent, theoretically in 1997. Six months after the voluntary plan began, CRD sent out environmental health officers to see how many restaurants were actually complying with the new voluntary directive. The results were not particularly encouraging. Although more than 80 per cent of the restaurants checked were complying with the old 50 per cent figure, less than half (48 per cent) had moved to the new voluntary 60 per cent standard.

Chapter 1 - The Games Begin

Dr. Peck stressed again that from a public health viewpoint, a 100 per cent smoke-free atmosphere was the only way to go. "With the increasing evidence for harm of ETS, there can be no other public health objective," he wrote, while admitting the only question was how soon the policy could be effectively implemented.

Recognizing both the importance of and the controversy surrounding the subject, the CRD board took the unusual step of sending Dr. Peck's report out to all its member councils (by that time there were 10 of them, three more areas having legally incorporated in the past decade) for comment before debating the issue. Only one recommended going ahead with the 100 per cent ban. The most common view was that a ban without buy-in from the industry would be unenforceable; it would be better, councillors suggested, to make the 60 per cent "voluntary" figure a mandatory one as a first step. That was what the regional board did.

Only a few months later, Dr. Peck took on a challenging newly created position, that of deputy provincial health officer for the entire province of British Columbia. It would be up to a new medical health officer to try to bring Dr. Peck's dream of a smoke-free Victoria to fruition.

---

2. Kluger, Richard. Ashes to Ashes: America's Hundred-Year Cigarette War, the Public Health, and the Unabashed Triumph of Philip Morris. Vintage Books, 1996. Page 366.
3. Ibid. Page 493-498.
4. Ibid. Page 499.
5. Cunningham, Rob. Smoke and Mirrors: the Canadian Tobacco War. International Development Research Centre, 1996, Page 111.
6. Ibid.
7. Kluger, op cit., Page 504.

Note: Duncan is a city just outside of Victoria. It takes roughly one hour to drive to Duncan from Victoria.

2
Taking the Plunge

"Only those who risk going too far can possibly find out how far one can go."
— T.S. Eliot

The Capital region's new medical health officer arrived to take up his position on the Friday before Labour Day in 1995. Dr. Richard Stanwick had been chosen after a nationwide search, and the regional directors were looking forward to his move to Victoria.

Dr. Stanwick was coming to Victoria from Winnipeg, Manitoba, where he had been the city's medical health officer for the previous five years. He'd also had a distinguished academic career, starting as a Robert Wood Johnson Clinical Scholar at McGill University. At the medical school at the University of Manitoba he rose to the rank of full professor in two departments. He was not only a specialist in community medicine, but also board-certified as a pediatrician in both Canada and the U.S. During his time in Winnipeg, he had always kept up a small clinical pediatric practice, working with children and teens in inner city clinics.

Throughout his medical career, two issues had dominated Dr. Stanwick's interests. One was injury prevention, especially in children. He led crusades on issues ranging from mandatory bike helmet legislation to safer and less flammable children's sleepwear; from regulations requiring children to be in proper restraints while riding in vehicles to better playground equipment standards.

His second great professional interest was in the problem of tobacco-related illness, especially that caused by second-hand smoke. He had taken up the issue of smoking in public places in the early 1980s, about the same time as AirSpace was making its first presentations to the CRD board, but long before the issue was a publicly prominent one. Dr. Stanwick made presentations to conferences on such topics as "Incentives and Reinforcing Strategies to Deter Smoking." In 1982, he made his first presentation to Winnipeg city council's environment committee on the specific dangers of second-hand smoke, proposing for the first time that smoking should be regulated in public places. Almost as early, he'd become convinced that any regulatory strategy needed to include restaurants and bars as well as other places such as shopping malls. In 1983, he again presented to the Winnipeg council committee, this time looking at "Public Attitudes Towards Smoking in Restaurants and Other Public Places." In one of the first smoking-regulation bylaws in the country, the council there had agreed that one-quarter of restaurant seating should be set aside for non-smokers. For the next decade, before moving to Victoria, Dr. Stanwick served on a variety of local, provincial and national committees that were working to develop anti-tobacco policies and to persuade politicians to enact regulatory strategies against tobacco use.

For all that, Dr. Stanwick's arrival in Victoria was a challenging one. Dr. Peck had left for his provincial job more than four months earlier, and Dr. Tim Johnstone, the soon-to-retire deputy, had been holding the fort in the meantime. Dr. Stanwick arrived in town on Thursday and checked into a motel, since he had not yet found a home. On that first Friday, he spent the day meeting the people he would be working with at the regional district, including board members and the regional administrator, Bill Jordan. It was afternoon before he reached Dr. Johnstone's office.

The news Dr. Johnstone had for the new medical health officer was not good. Dr. Stanwick had known that one of his first tasks in the new job would be to deal with an outbreak of toxoplasmosis (toxo), a parasitic disease that can harm pregnant women and their unborn babies. While still in Winnipeg, he'd been following the story of the growing number of Victoria cases, and knew that a team of environmental health officers and biologists from both the region and the province had been struggling to pinpoint a source.

Chapter 2 - Taking the Plunge

Dr. Johnstone had just received new and very disconcerting information. The team had discovered that the source of the outbreak was the municipal water supply, something that had never happened before anywhere in the world. The only time drinking water had been linked to toxo was a case of soldiers drinking straight out of creeks in the Panamanian jungle. If the team was right — and Dr. Stanwick had no reason to doubt the conclusions — this would be a news story of national, if not international, proportions.

Dr. Johnstone explained that a news conference had been scheduled for the next Tuesday, immediately after the Labour Day weekend. Unfortunately, Dr. Johnstone would not be able to attend. He had long been committed to leaving town on vacation once the new medical health officer was in place. He gave Dr. Stanwick a cardboard box filled with the toxo files and wished him luck.

Dr. Stanwick spent the three-day weekend reading files and developing strategy. What did the public need to know? Who needed to be there? How could the citizens be reassured about the quality of their drinking water while still ensuring that appropriate cautions were taken, especially for pregnant women (who are the most likely to have serious consequences from ingesting toxo parasites)? On Tuesday he and the toxo team faced half a dozen TV cameras to explain what was believed to have happened, what steps were being taken to ensure the water supply was safe, and what was being done to monitor and treat those who had become ill, particularly pregnant women and their fetuses. It didn't make for an easy day, but Dr. Stanwick was no stranger to dealing with controversy in the media. During his time in Winnipeg, he'd had occasion to appear on both national and international television to discuss public health issues. Many of his injury prevention initiatives had garnered him time on national media, such as the CBC's *Marketplace* and CTV's *W5*, where he'd had no hesitation in taking both government regulators and industry representatives to task. The toxo news conference went better than he had hoped, and the coverage over the next few days was more sympathetic than he had anticipated.

It had been a trial by fire, but it had allowed him to establish himself in the community early in his tenure. He figured that the worst was over, and he could begin looking at longer-term issues for the region.

Among the imminent concerns was that of smoking in public places. One of the aspects of the Victoria job that had most intrigued him had been the impetus that he had seen building towards comprehensive second-hand smoke legislation. As he prepared for the job interview, he had become aware that regional politicians and the community as a whole were much more prepared for someone to take a firm stance against smoking in public places than was the case in Winnipeg or most other Canadian cities. Perhaps that was in part because British Columbia already had the lowest smoking rates in the country. The city of Vancouver, just across the Strait of Georgia, was also already planning a bylaw that would ban smoking in all indoor public places. In Victoria, although Dr. Peck's dream that the whole city would be smoke-free in time for the Commonwealth Games had not come to fruition, it had brought the idea to the forefront of the public mind. After only a few weeks of private discussions after his arrival, Dr. Stanwick decided he should again take the issue to the regional board.

He had been in his new job for less than six weeks when he wrote his first report on the issue to the board. "All workers and the public in the CRD deserve to have their health protected from the hazards of environmental tobacco smoke (second-hand smoke)," he told the board members. He noted that scientific research in the field was showing the dangers of second-hand smoke ever more clearly, and that the U.S. Environmental Protection Agency had declared second-hand smoke to be a Class A carcinogen, alongside such blatantly toxic substances as benzene and radon gas. Dr. Stanwick had never been able to discern the rationale for the common decisions that all workplaces should be smoke-free except those of workers in the hospitality industry. "Why should people who work in restaurants and bars be considered to have second-class lungs?" he would ask repeatedly. He was insistent

Chapter 2 - Taking the Plunge

that workers and patrons of those establishments be granted exactly the same protection as those in any other business.

Dr. Stanwick's original recommendation was that the 100 per cent ban should come into effect in less than six months, by March 1, 1996. He noted that Vancouver had begun to make plans to implement a similar bylaw on May 1, 1996 and thought it would increase effectiveness for the two jurisdictions to work closely with each other.

As soon as word spread about the recommendations, even before the matter reached the board table, the opposition to the idea started, loudly and vociferously, just as it had when Dr. Peck had made his proposal. Bar and restaurant owners went public, warning of what they feared would be disastrous downturns in their business if the board members were to agree with Dr. Stanwick's plan.[8]

"There's no doubt in our mind that will happen," said Brenda Locke, who was then head of a hospitality group called the Neighbourhood Pub Owners of B.C. (and later elected an MLA in the Gordon Campbell Liberal government of 2001). She said that the anti-smokers were saying the business downturn wouldn't last more than a year, but, she warned, most pub owners couldn't afford a year of reduced business and, consequently, reduced profits.

The hospitality industry opponents also began to produce all the arguments that have been seen repeatedly in virtually every effort to get such legislation passed and implemented across North America:

– Tobacco is a legal product, they argued, and one from which various levels of government make a great deal of money through taxation. That makes it unfair for local governments to try to regulate it to what the industry considered an extreme degree.

– Pubs and bars are places frequented only by adults believed capable of making their own decisions, they said. So while it might be reasonable to ban smoking in places to which children can be admitted, any adults going into a bar or pub should know they're likely to be exposed to second-hand smoke and can decide themselves whether they want to take that risk.

– The bars and pubs quickly raised the possibility of a ventilation solution, arguing that if establishments installed the correct sort of air-cleaning equipment, they could virtually eliminate any health risks to patrons or workers. Hence, they said, legislation actually banning indoor smoking wouldn't be necessary.

– Most of all, they echoed Locke's theme that a complete ban would devastate their businesses. They predicted reduced profits, closed establishments, and hundreds of workers ending up in the unemployment line.

The local tourism industry rushed in to support the hospitality industry, again before the issue had ever made it to the board table. "The proposed bylaw change covers a much broader area of Business than has been discussed," wrote Lorne Whyte, the head of Tourism Victoria, in a letter to the board. "The implementation of this change ... will cause considerable damage and loss of employment to the impacted businesses." Whyte also warned that the process in Vancouver remained controversial.

The regional board members heard the complaints and made two things clear. The first was that they supported the goal of 100 per cent smoke-free indoor public places. The second was that they were not prepared to move quite so quickly as Dr. Stanwick had desired in the face of so much opposition. Rather, they hoped some compromise could be worked out with the hospitality industry so it would accept the proposed changes.

At the first board meeting where the issue was discussed, regional board chair Frank Leonard — a councillor from Saanich (the region's most populous municipality), and arguably the most influential local politician on the board — warned that moving too fast could risk the industry support that the region had managed to build over the years. That support, he argued, had made the various bylaws work as successfully as they had.

Leonard also warned that Victoria politicians shouldn't read too much into the ongoing discussions in Vancouver.[9] He and health committee chair Murray Coell had travelled to Vancouver during the summer to meet with Vancouver regional medical health officer Dr. John Blatherwick, and the impression Leonard got was that Vancouver was unlikely to move as early as 1996 to an all-out ban. The difference, he explained, was that in Greater Vancouver, it wasn't the regional board that was legally responsible for public health. Rather it was the individual municipal councils, all 19 of them, each allowed to make a different decision. Because no physical space separated any of the 19 from their neighbours, a smorgasbord of different regulations governing restaurants, pubs and bars in the various municipalities would be an unmanageable political disaster. It would be quite unrealistic to say that patrons could smoke in restaurants on one side of the street, but would be barred from doing so in other premises less than a block away.

Dr. Blatherwick's dream was for an identical bylaw to be passed by all 19 councils, making the whole Lower Mainland (an area with a population of almost 1.5 million people at that time) a zone where indoor public smoking was banned. He had joined with the Capital regional district to undertake a huge public opinion poll on the attitudes towards a possible 100 per cent non-smoking policy in both Greater Vancouver and Greater Victoria. The poll involved phone calls of almost 5,700 residents, about 10 times the number normally considered necessary for a valid survey. And the results had been, he felt, quite conclusive. Overall, two-thirds of those surveyed said they would support such a bylaw, and it received majority support in every single municipality. "Smokers represent the only group where a majority opposed the bylaw," noted the researchers from the prestigious Angus Reid polling firm, but even 30 per cent of smokers said they would be in favour. The poll also showed that restaurants would almost certainly benefit from increased patronage if they became non-smoking. Even smokers who said they would try to find a place where they could smoke said they wouldn't travel more than half an hour to find such a location.

Dr. Blatherwick figured that meant that if the entire Greater Vancouver regional district adopted a model bylaw, no one municipality would gain a competitive advantage over another through the smoking rules.

Despite these encouraging trends, however, in the last months of 1995, he was beginning to realize an area-wide bylaw wasn't likely to happen. Although some Lower Mainland municipalities were enthusiastically in favour of the new rules, several others had made their opposition clear. In at least two of those cases, the mayors leading the oppositions had financial interests in the hospitality industry, although they were insisting they were not in a conflict of interest when debating the possible bylaws.

When Dr. Stanwick made *his* proposal for Greater Victoria in October 1995, the CRD board members decided to defer their decision for a month while asking him and his staff for more information about the possible impacts of a change. They wanted him to continue to follow the progress of the discussions in Vancouver and also to try to find out what, if anything, the provincial Workers' Compensation Board (WCB) was planning to do about the issue. Numerous politicians in Vancouver had stressed that the best solution to their problem of a potential patchwork of legislation would be for the WCB, or some other arm of the provincial government, to enact regulations that would cover every hospitality establishment in British Columbia.

The CRD board in Victoria also wanted to know what the actual health effects of second-hand smoke were likely to be on hospitality workers in the region over the next few years. Some board members wanted a report on ways of increasing the proportion of smoke-free space more gradually, especially in establishments like bowling alleys and bingo halls, which were still allowed to have a higher proportion of smoking space than were restaurants. Some business-minded directors wanted a realistic assessment of the costs of enforcing a 100 per cent bylaw if it were to be brought in quickly over the objections of the hospitality industry.

Chapter 2 - Taking the Plunge

Dr. Stanwick was neither surprised nor upset by these delays and requests. He had never realistically thought the board would agree to implement the bylaw in only six months, especially one that included every hospitality establishment in the city. He considered his first paper to be an opening negotiating position. He had always assumed that the entire process of having a bylaw discussed, passed and implemented would probably take two or three years. However, he also figured that if he started out with a suggestion of a two- or three-year time frame, the hospitality industry would use that as a baseline from which to begin negotiations. In that case, it might end up being five or six years before the legislation actually came into effect, and he had no intention of waiting that long.

He concluded after the first skirmish that, overall, he had accomplished his objectives. By putting such a strong proposal forward so early after taking up the MHO job, he'd wanted to put both the regional politicians and the hospitality industry on notice. He had sent the message that he considered this one of the most serious and important issues facing the board and that he expected strong and decisive action to be taken. He'd moved the issue onto the front burner in the mind of the public as well, encouraging workers to think about what it would be like to work in a smoke-free atmosphere and customers to consider the benefits of dining out in one. And he'd taken advantage of the public interest in the issue that had arisen because of the numerous media reports looking at the new scientific reports and the EPA declaration.

Even the fact that the Capital regional board was prepared to go so far as to continue studying the issue was enough to alarm the province-wide hospitality groups, which had until then been concentrating their efforts on defeating the plans of Dr. Blatherwick and others for the Lower Mainland. One week after that first meeting, the Victoria board members received their first of many lengthy packages from a loose coalition that called itself the Lower Mainland Hospitality Industry Group. The name alone was enough to make clear that the members had previously focused their interests on the Vancouver area, but were prepared to travel further afield if it appeared anti-smoking bylaws were likely to be passed elsewhere in the province. The coalition included representatives of the B.C. Hotels Association, the B.C. Restaurant and Food Services Association, Locke's Neighbourhood Pub Owners' Association, operators of bingo halls, casinos and billiard parlours, some branches of the Royal Canadian Legion and 88 Chinese restaurants in the Lower Mainland which apparently didn't belong to the larger restaurant association. According to coalition chair Bruce Clark (whose sister Christy in 2001 went on to become deputy premier and minister of education in the Gordon Campbell government), the coalition represented more than 3,000 businesses which in total had about 50,000 employees.

"We are all opposed to the proposed total ban on smoking in hospitality establishments which is currently being advanced by municipal health bureaucrats," wrote Clark in the introduction to the package. The coalition produced various public opinion polls of its own to show that most people were satisfied with current smoking rules and didn't have complaints about air quality in restaurants and bars. The major difference between the coalition's polls and those conducted by Angus Reid for the health department was that the coalition, for the most part, questioned existing patrons of restaurants, bars and neighbourhood pubs rather than the public at large. Stevenson and Dr. Stanwick quickly realized that the poll had, by the way it was conducted, apparently systemically excluded those who might find the air quality unacceptable. If, for instance, asthmatics found restaurants and pubs too smoky to attend without risking an attack, they were unlikely to go there at all, which meant that their views could never be captured in the coalition's polls.

The coalition also put forward an economic study that it had also been using forcefully in the Vancouver debates. The study — enough to make almost any municipal politician nervous — predicted that as many as 3,500 jobs would be lost if the ban went through as proposed on the Lower Mainland. It warned of a net loss of more than $100 million a year to the hospitality industry in B.C. In his letter to the CRD, Clark stressed that

Chapter 2 - Taking the Plunge

the study, undertaken by economist John de Wolf, had taken into account "the increases in spending by some non-smokers who would patronize hospitality establishments more after a ban.... Unfortunately, the increase from those non-smokers ... does not offset losses from smokers who would be driven away from establishments by the ban." That argument was echoed later by Victoria hospitality establishments: the owner of one pub-style restaurant said that during the first few weeks of the ban, his food sales had gone up by more than $1,200, but that had been more than offset by a decrease of $5,000 in liquor sales.

But in looking at de Wolf's study in detail, Stevenson and Dr. Stanwick realized that it had openly used the results of the coalition's own poll to determine what the economic effects would be — and they already had concerns about that poll's reliability, given that it relied solely on current patrons and not on those who might become patrons were the air quality to improve.

The other key point the hospitality group made in this first letter was its proposal for what it called "a clean-air solution that works." Their answer was a ventilation solution, using the ASHRAE (American Society of Heating, Refrigerating and Air-Conditioning Engineers) standards of the day. ASHRAE is an air-quality standard used as the North American norm for various issues of indoor air pollution. A ventilation solution has been repeatedly suggested by hospitality and tobacco industry spokespersons across North America and Europe, who are opposed to any sort of smoking ban. "The total smoking ban," Clark wrote, "is an extreme overreaction to an issue that can be positively addressed by our ventilation proposal." Health experts, though, stress that in relation to second-hand smoke, ASHRAE's standard is one designed for the comfort of those in the indoor space, not protection of their health.

Even as Clark was providing the hospitality industry's arguments to the regional board, Dr. Stanwick, Stevenson and their team were beginning to research the answers to the questions the board had asked. The provincial health ministry was helpful in providing statistics that could be used to look at the health hazards for hospitality workers. The ministry had found that among the provincial population of just under four million people, about 50 lung cancer deaths each year were attributable to environmental tobacco smoke. More tellingly, the ministry's research had found that more than 70 per cent of those individuals had been exposed to the tobacco smoke in their workplace and in public places rather than in their homes. Other studies had showed that hospitality workers were exposed to levels of second-hand smoke that were 1.6 to 2 times higher than even were workers in offices that allowed smoking. For bartenders and servers in bars, the figure was even higher — four to six times higher than the likely exposure in the hypothetically smoke-filled office.

The health department team also retained a top legal expert on the issue of tobacco regulation to provide a report on the legality of the proposed bylaw and what the courts were likely to say about it if it were challenged. David Sweanor concluded that one way of challenging the bylaw might be to suggest that nicotine addiction is a bona fide disability, and therefore, the bylaw would be discriminatory against the disabled. But Sweanor thought even that could be overcome by arguing that the severe impact of tobacco on health would trump that position. He believed the bylaw was constitutional under Canada's Charter of Rights and Freedoms, noting that even if nicotine addiction were to be considered a disability, there are other ways of obtaining a nicotine fix, such as patches, without actually having to smoke.

Meanwhile, Vancouver city council was going through its second round of public hearings on the issue. More than 80 per cent of those who spoke at the hearings there supported a smoke-free bylaw, but the other 20 per cent, mainly from the hospitality industry, were bitterly opposed, just as was the case in Victoria. They were doing their utmost to convince the Vancouver councillors — most of whom came from the right-of-centre so-called Non-Partisan Association — that a 100 per cent bylaw would ruin the city's burgeoning tourism industry as well as cause economic havoc in the hospitality establishments.

Chapter 2 - Taking the Plunge

By the end of October 1995, Dr. Blatherwick realized that, given the amount of opposition generated, it was unlikely that council would adopt his recommendations. On November 8, he reluctantly wrote a lengthy memo to Vancouver's mayor and council recommending a compromise. He noted the huge amounts of fear and opposition in the hospitality industry. "It is not for me to debate whether this consternation is valid, or whether it has been fanned by other interests," Dr. Blatherwick wrote. "The fact remains that the desire for a compromise was expressed by numerous delegations."

He raised the possibility of a two-tier process in which restaurants would be required to be fully non-smoking by May, 1996, but the other hospitality establishments (bars, pubs, casinos and the like) would, be allowed to move to 50 per cent non-smoking seats on that date, and then move to 100 per cent non-smoking by May 31, 1998. The establishments should have to show that their ventilation systems were upgraded, he suggested, but stressed that in the long term, a ventilation solution would not meet the necessary public health objectives. The two-tiered plan, he said, "would still meet the public health objectives of eliminating public and worker exposure to ETS in public indoor environments, albeit over a more protracted time frame." It would allow bars and pubs to "wean" themselves away from their dependence on smoking seats, since few of them had had any restrictions at all on smoking in their establishments previously. It would also give the various municipalities throughout the Lower Mainland the time they needed to ensure the ultimate bylaw was equally applied across the region.

However, Dr. Blatherwick's agreement to compromise did not change Dr. Stanwick's stand on the Greater Victoria case. With the benefit of his own team's research, Dr. Stanwick wrote a lengthy and detailed report to the CRD board's health committee for the November 1995 meeting. It included the provincial statistics on possible deaths and Sweanor's report on constitutionality, as well as a suggestion that all school grounds, inside and outside, should also be covered and declared smoke-free zones.

When the written report was made public, the bylaw opponents started lining up in droves for a chance to address the board personally before a decision was made on the recommendation at the November board meeting.

Some were local. Bar owners Gordon Card and Grant Olson would remain among the most public opponents of the idea for the next five years. Their establishments were quite different. Olsen owned a hotel with a huge complex of bars and nightclubs, a complex so big it could never have been built under 1990s liquor licensing rules, but had been allowed to remain in its oversized state when the regulations had been tightened up more than a decade earlier. Card, by contrast, owned two neighbourhood pubs, much smaller establishments which could legally hold fewer than 100 patrons each. Each, however, was equally concerned about the potential economic impact of a bylaw.

However, many of the speakers who came to present before the board considered themselves representatives of provincial organizations. Bruce Clark from the Lower Mainland Hospitality Industry Group led the charge. He was one of many who wanted to be seen as offering a reasonable compromise, in this case, a much longer time before implementation. He proposed the analogy of smokers who tried to quit by going "cold turkey" as opposed to those who weaned themselves off cigarettes more gradually or with more supports. Most pubs and bars are so dependent on smokers for the large part of their income, he said, that to force them to become non-smoking within a matter of months was the equivalent of forcing them to go cold turkey.

"It just won't work," said Clark. "It can't be done without 'withdrawal' pains."

Equally concerned from the provincial side were representatives of casinos and bingo halls. Because a proportion of gaming revenues in B.C. was legally required to be turned over to charity, the spokespersons for that industry invoked the spectre of youth groups, community agencies and schools losing large amounts of their funding because of drastic decreases in overall gaming revenue.

Dr. Richard Stanwick, Chief Medical Health Officer, Vancouver Island Health Authority. (Photo courtesy of the University of Victoria)

Bill Hutchinson of the Casino Management Council of B.C. told the board that the casinos then operating in Victoria generated about $3.2 million a year for the various non-profit groups. He predicted that the smoking ban would cut that annual amount to as little as $1.2 million a year.

Of all the groups that came out against the proposal, the one that disturbed Dr. Stanwick and Stevenson the most came from the Restaurant Association of B.C. Association president Don Monsour had been actively involved in negotiating the agreement for the 60 per cent non-smoking seating when Dr. Peck had first proposed the no-smoking bylaw back in 1993. He repeatedly said, both in public and in private, that he had reached an understanding with Dr. Peck that the gradual process would continue for the next four years. Only in the year 2000, he insisted, would there be legislation to require 100 per cent non-smoking seating, at least in restaurants. He saw discussion of an earlier date as a betrayal of the good faith with which his association had negotiated previously.

Others involved in the conversations were convinced the problem was nothing more than the result of a misunderstanding. Dr. Peck had certainly consistently said that he wanted to ensure the region was 100 per cent smoke-free "by the year 2000," but he saw that as an ultimate deadline — the last conceivable date if a way couldn't be found to hasten the process along. Monsour, however, had always taken that phrase to mean that "*by* the year 2000" meant "*in* the year 2000," that no changes would be made before that date. It was an unfortunate misunderstanding that caused ill feeling that neither side could afford.

But Dr. Stanwick was not prepared to wait another four years to act on the initiative, especially given the increasing amount of research emerging about the health hazards of second-hand smoke.

The Capital regional board members, though, had been watching the Vancouver discussions carefully. They didn't want to get into the sort of bitter battles that were developing there. After hearing from all the speakers and from Dr. Stanwick, board members decided they should try to find some sort of a compromise

— some kind of a settlement that at least the majority of the hospitality industry would accept. Although most of the board members supported the principle of a move to 100 per cent smoke-free places, few had any appetite for what might become an all-out enforcement war with key segments of the region's economy — the entire tourist industry. They gave Dr. Stanwick two months to meet with the stakeholders and see if everyone could come to some agreement.

---

8. Cleverley, Bill. "Smoking ban fires up business owners," Victoria Times Colonist, October 13, 1995.
9. Wilson, Carla. "CRD would ride Vancouver's smoking coat-tails," Victoria Times-Colonist, July 13, 1995.

3
Seeking Consensus

"The same people who told us that smoking doesn't cause cancer, are now telling us that advertising cigarettes doesn't cause smoking."
— Political columnist Ellen Goodman

In the spring of 1996, Dr. Stanwick and his staff returned to the fray, convening a series of meetings with those who would be most affected — hospitality industry groups and health groups. They wanted to see if there was any realistic possibility that a compromise could be worked out. The March implementation had already come and gone before a time was found when all the stakeholders could come together for discussions. He was neither surprised nor disappointed. Watching similar efforts to have bylaws passed in places like Vancouver and California had shown him that this would be no easy task. Since the tobacco industry and their allies in the hospitality industry recognized the threat that such bylaws would pose if they gained widespread acceptance, they strengthened their resistance.

One of the first tactics that became obvious was the hospitality industry's insistence that a ventilation solution could be found that would satisfy the needs of both the businesses and the health community. Spokespersons for bars and restaurants insisted that if a facility had a powerful enough ventilation system, the second-hand smoke would be banished so quickly that it wouldn't pose a health hazard to workers or other patrons. Documents that have since been made public as part of various tobacco court cases have shown that ventilation solutions had been the brainchild of the tobacco industry starting as early as the first months of 1995. On February 21, 1995, executives from Philip Morris had talked to the Canadian Tobacco Manufacturers' Council about the possibility of developing an international standard for ventilation that could be used as an alternative to smoking bans in public places.

In its fight against the bylaws in the Lower Mainland, Bruce Clark's Hospitality Industry Group had developed a brochure entitled "The Fresh Air Solution" to push for a ventilation-based compromise. When it appeared that the Capital region was heading in the same direction, the brochure quickly started spreading among hospitality industry groups on Vancouver Island as well. "Better indoor air quality without destroying jobs," the brochure promised. Under the proposed plan, all hospitality establishments in the Lower Mainland would have had to improve their indoor air quality to current ASHRAE standards "using improved ventilation or filtration." The hospitality group suggested that every business would have to measure its indoor air quality and post the results publicly for customers. It even proposed that any business that didn't comply could face the loss of its business licence.

The hospitality group argued that the solution was better than a smoking ban, not just because it would let customers keep puffing, but also because "it will guarantee cleaner indoor air — not just a reduction of second-hand smoke." The ventilation system could also get rid of "pollutants": everything from paints and rugs to plant and fungi spores, as well as cooking odours, the group suggested.

Dr. Stanwick had never been enthusiastic about ventilation solutions. He didn't believe that merely meeting the ASHRAE standards would remove the health risks from second-hand smoke. The problem was that second-hand smoke had been shown to contain so many toxic chemicals, many of which had no known safe levels of exposure. ASHRAE itself said its standards were based on providing comfort for those in the rooms, not guaranteeing health. ASHRAE's 1996 documents stated that "the intent of this section is to provide acceptable perceived air quality in the presence of ETS . . . this section does not purport to provide acceptable indoor air quality in smoking or smoke-exposed zones."

Chapter 3 - Seeking Consensus

Even if ventilation could provide acceptable air-quality standards, Dr. Stanwick and Stevenson were concerned it would eliminate the "level playing field" approach which they had promised the hospitality industry. They suspected that ventilation systems effective enough to meet standards were likely to be extremely expensive to install and operate. That meant they weren't likely to be affordable by smaller operators, the mom-and-pop restaurants or even some of the smaller neighbourhood pubs. It wouldn't, Dr. Stanwick thought, be fair if larger or chain establishments were allowed to host smokers because they could afford to install such ventilation systems, while smaller premises would have to go non-smoking to meet the same air-quality standards.

Dr. Stanwick decided that before establishing the "smoking summits," the team should have a reliable answer to the many questions that still surrounded the proposed ventilation solutions. Dr. Stanwick insisted they retain one of the top local ventilation engineers, Rob Hirschfield. He was asked to conduct a detailed study on local ventilation requirements. Hirschfield was familiar with the sort of filtration devices used in hospital "clean rooms" where the air had to be of the highest quality, and knew how a ventilation system to eliminate second-hand smoke would have to work.

Hirschfield immediately ran into the problem of the lack of an acceptable standard for environmental tobacco smoke in the workplace. The American Conference of Governmental Industrial Hygienists (ACGIH) had determined threshold limits for many pollutants, but its standards were for each contaminant on an individual basis, while studies were showing that second-hand smoke included as many as 4,000 of those individual contaminants. The U.S. Labor Department's efforts to try to determine one set standard had been placed on hold. ASHRAE itself was reviewing its air-quality standards and so was just beginning a discussion of how the question of health risks from second-hand smoke might be handled.

Thus, the first question Hirschfield and Dr. Stanwick had to answer was: what might be considered reasonable assumptions of risk for those who might end up working in the ventilated rooms? Although some industry groups were prepared to accept limits that would assume one worker in 7,000 would contract cancer as a result of workplace exposure, Dr. Stanwick considered that far too many workers that would be harmed. For most health and safety regulations, he noted, the standard was one in 100,000 workers for those exposed during a normal daily eight-hour shift. That was what he suggested Hirschfield should use as a starting point. The engineer did his calculations, and concluded that the air flow would have to be more than 4,000 cubic metres per minute for each cigarette smoked per hour to arrive at the level of near-zero toxicity required.

Even the health authorities were surprised at Hirschfield's final calculations. He concluded that in an ordinary 70-seat restaurant or pub, the air would have to be moving at 34 kilometres per hour (21 mph) if it were moving horizontally, 21 kilometres per hour (13 mph) if it were being sucked straight up. For all intents and purposes, the patrons would be sitting in a wind tunnel, often breezier than it would be outside. Clearly the so-called "ventilation solution" was completely impracticable.

Hirschfield calculated the fuel costs required to move so much air so fast. If that same 70-seat restaurant were heated with natural gas, he assumed, and were open seven days a week, 12 hours each day, the fuel costs for the ventilation system would be more than $450,000 a year. Neither he, Dr. Stanwick nor Stevenson could envision even the largest and richest establishments being willing to pay out that much money just so their puffing patrons could continue to smoke inside.

With Hirschfield's study in hand, at the end of March, Dr. Stanwick convened what later came to be known as the "smoking summit." In the course of a week, the summit would consume a total of 15 hours over three different days. Included in all the meetings were members of the public health staff and representatives of

Chapter 3 - Seeking Consensus

the various segments of the hospitality industry, including Bruce Clark, Don Monsour, Gordon Card, Lorne Whyte from Tourism Victoria and Cary Corbeil, who represented the gaming industry. Rob Hirschfield attended one meeting to explain how he'd come to his conclusions regarding ventilation, and members of the region's Smoke-Free Task Force also participated to put forward the views of the health community.

From the first few moments, it was clear these meetings were going to be fractious. It was also clear that the chances of achieving a consensus were extremely remote. Monsour and other members of the restaurant association were still insisting on their agreement with Dr. Peck that smoking wouldn't be banned until the year 2000. The pubs and bars especially were still pushing for their ventilation solution.

Dr. Stanwick suggested a compromise date. He proposed that smoking be banned in all the hospitality establishments effective January 1, 1998. That, he said, would give the industry more than 18 months to prepare itself.

The restaurant operators offered their compromise. They suggested that the size of the required non-smoking sections be gradually increased each year until 100 per cent was reached in the year 2000. They also suggested that rules could be increased to ensure that no minors would be permitted in the smoking sections, and employees wouldn't be permitted to smoke at work. Hospitality establishments wouldn't be allowed to sell cigarettes on the premises.

But Dr. Stanwick objected to that proposal. Experience had shown, he said, that it was just too difficult to keep the smoke only in the smoking section in almost all restaurants and bars. It was, he told the restaurateurs, "like having a peeing and a non-peeing section in a swimming pool. It doesn't work." The restaurateurs laughed — but they still liked their proposal better than his.

The other hospitality groups weren't impressed either. Some of them thought the restaurant association was essentially selling out to the health groups. They said 70 per cent of their revenue came from smokers, despite the studies showing that only 22 per cent of residents smoked. Even if cigarettes weren't on sale there, customers would still bring their own with them, they said. They warned yet again that a total ban would lead to establishments being closed, staff being laid off, and funding being decreased for the community charities that received money from the profits of bingo halls and casinos. They were prepared only to suggest that smoking by employees be banned and that all establishments would ensure their ventilation systems met the current ASHRAE standards within 18 months.

The representatives from Tourism Victoria warned that tourism is such a competitive industry that tour groups wouldn't come to Victoria if a smoking ban were in place. They backed the restaurant association in sticking with a year 2000 date for implementation.

When Hirschfield came to speak to the group, the industry representatives quickly realized it was impossible to argue with his mathematics. Instead, they focused their attention on the standard of a one in 100,000 cancer risk, arguing it was far in excess of standards set elsewhere. Bruce Clark noted it allowed for only one-tenth as much contamination as the current Workers' Compensation Board standards. Some industry spokespersons suspected that even the air quality in restaurants which had voluntarily gone 100 per cent non-smoking wouldn't meet such a rigorous test. They talked again about using the ASHRAE standards, which would require substantially lower levels of ventilation. Others suggested returning to the idea of a one in 7,000 risk, which again would require much less ventilation.

But one of the environmental health officers, Christine Bender, noted that accepting a one in 100,000 risk was normal in dozens of risk-assessment situations, and the health authorities didn't feel they could accept a greater chance of workers contracting cancer. Dr. Stanwick again stressed that the current ASHRAE standards were based on a comfort standard, not a health standard, and were

Chapter 3 - Seeking Consensus

at that point almost a decade old. That meant they weren't based on the latest scientific research about the risk of the chemicals in second-hand smoke.

Between meetings, Monsour polled members of the restaurant association to see what they might be willing to accept. Of more than 550 restaurants surveyed, more than two-thirds agreed they could live with requirements for "acceptable affordable air handling." Unfortunately, no one had actually provided a definition of what would constitute either "acceptable" ventilation from the health authorities' point of view or "affordable" from the restaurateurs'. When asked whether "all restaurants, pubs, bars, lounges, etc. should be smoke-free by Jan. 1, 1998," only 31 per cent agreed.

But Monsour and the other representatives of the restaurants knew their segment of the hospitality industry could have a bigger fight on their hands. In Vancouver, a compromise had finally been reached in February at city council.[10] The council opted for the plan Dr. Blatherwick had devised under which restaurants would have to quickly become completely non-smoking, but bars, pubs and other "adult-only" establishments could move to that standard much more gradually.

Monsour and his fellow restaurateurs realized that were the Capital region to follow Vancouver's example, the threat to their business would be much more serious than if the CRD board decided to advance the date but keep the "level playing field" model. Many drinking establishments, they knew, especially the neighbourhood pubs, provided just about the same services as many restaurants. If patrons were to be allowed to smoke in the pubs but not in the restaurants, the loss of business for the restaurants could be substantial. Already the Vancouver restaurateurs were talking about taking the city council to court to try to overturn the bylaw on the grounds it was unfair and discriminatory.

And already some members of the bars and pubs were putting forward the "adult only" argument in a last-ditch effort to save smoking in their establishments, even while leaving the restaurants

45

out in the cold. The argument, made successfully in Vancouver, was that restaurants should be required to go smoke-free because they were open to children and teenagers, who weren't considered legally old enough to make a decision about inhaling tobacco smoke. Adults, they argued, had the freedom of choice to decide whether they wanted to smoke themselves; they should also have the freedom of choice to decide whether to spend time in an establishment filled with other people's smoke.

In a letter to one municipal council that was dealing with the issue, Card noted that "it has come to our attention that the Restaurant and Food Services Association ... is concerned that the 100 per cent ban will put them in an unequal playing field with neighbourhood pubs. Our businesses are quite different as we are age-controlled."

As Dr. Stanwick pointed out, this argument failed to acknowledge the rights of workers not to have to work on a site that was known to be unsafe or unhealthy. The bar owners argued that since all the staff in their premises were also legally required to be adults to work there, they should also have the right to choose whether they wanted to work in smoky premises or not. When pressed, some reluctantly admitted that if that argument were taken to its logical conclusion, employers would also be able to operate worksites filled with asbestos or other contaminants — and adult workers would have the "right" to decide if they wanted to expose themselves to that contamination.

The final meeting of the "smoking summit" group took place on April 4, 1996. The Tobacco-Free Task Force and other health groups began by expressing their support of the January 1, 1998 date for implementation of the bylaw. As far as they were concerned, the sooner the better.

The casino and bingo operators said that they couldn't support a ban on smoking in indoor public places at any date in the foreseeable future. They were opposed to the whole idea. One of their biggest concerns was that the CRD did not have the power to actually give them a level playing field. For instance, they noted,

Chapter 3 - Seeking Consensus

the region didn't have jurisdiction over native reserves — and elsewhere in Canada and the U.S. many gaming establishments were springing up on native reserves. They feared as well that private clubs would be exempt from the bylaw and could flourish in competition with the government-controlled casinos. In fact, some of the hospitality operators had already been exploring the idea of officially turning their establishments into such private clubs, with customers paying membership fees for the privilege of attending them.

Stevenson and the lawyers had looked at that possibility and could reassure the government-sponsored casinos that it wasn't going to happen. Although private social functions like wedding receptions held in halls would be exempt, there was no way that would be extended to commercial premises, no matter what they wanted to call themselves. They were public places and would be treated as such. The health department staff admitted they couldn't guarantee what would happen on native reserves, which came under the jurisdiction of the federal government and so weren't obliged to obey regional district rules. However, the staff noted that no reserves in the region had been given the go-ahead to set up a gaming establishment and there was no indication that one would be at any time in the near future.

As he listened to such discussions, Monsour realized that the date of implementation would be of much less significance to the restaurants than the need for at least a level playing field between restaurants and bars. He believed a compromise was possible on the date, but there could be no compromise on the position that pubs and bars must be subject to exactly the same regulations as the restaurants. No matter what deal he thought he'd had with Dr. Peck, he realized privately that he couldn't stick to that position with a new medical health officer and newly elected politicians on the regional board. His job now was to get his members the best possible deal vis-à-vis the drinking establishment. Before the meeting ended, he made a tentative suggestion of one more compromise position. It might be possible, he suggested, that if the board would agree to postpone the implementation for one

Smoke-Free

more year — to 1999 instead of 1998 — the restaurant association would accept the decision, and their members would comply with the total ban. But the idea never received full discussion from the summit members.

The group did agree to propose that the provincial health officer for British Columbia should be asked to set up a joint provincial task force that would establish standards for air quality. The standards would deal with how much second-hand smoke could be tolerated and what ventilation targets would have to be met. Hospitality establishments that met those standards could be exempted from the 100 per cent smoking ban, although they'd still be required to keep 50 or 60 per cent of their establishments specifically non-smoking.

At the end of the meetings, no one was particularly happy with any of the compromises suggested. Dr. Stanwick, Stevenson and the health advocate groups still were hoping for the 1998 implementation date. The bar and pub owners said that was far too early, especially if the provincial health officer could work out standards for a ventilation solution — and maybe adult-only establishments should be exempted anyway. The gaming industry wouldn't agree to any date at all. The provincial health officer hadn't even agreed to establish a ventilation task force, let alone devote the time necessary to working out what the standards might be, or even if it were possible to develop such a system. The restaurant association still feared that the board would give in to the demands of the bars and pubs, and force only restaurants to go smoke-free.

As virtually everyone had suspected from the first 15 minutes of the summit meetings, no agreement had been reached. It would be up to the elected politicians on the regional board to decide what would happen next.

Two weeks later, Dr. Stanwick presented his report on the issue to the regional health committee. It was relatively brief. "Unfortunately a consensus could not be agreed upon by the membership of the different constituencies, and the matter is back

Chapter 3 - Seeking Consensus

before the health committee," he concluded. The report did not include a specific recommendation on what the committee might do next, although he repeated his concerns about the growing body of evidence showing the damaging effects of second-hand smoke.

Even before the committee met, the various groups were ensuring that the CRD board members knew their views. The Tobacco-Free Task Force was particularly concerned that the board might agree to adopt some type of ventilation standard.

"The application of any standard is fraught with troubles, particularly if it is administered by the industry," warned task force chair Dr. Peter Coy, an oncologist who had seen too often the costs of smoking. He noted that the standard would need to be monitored by government inspectors, and that would be costly. As well, the task force worried that "facilities, after getting an inspector's approval, will switch off or slow down their ventilation equipment" in order to save money. And rules would have to be established to determine from which parts of a building the air samples would be taken for sampling or even at what time of day.

"Our position remains that all premises should be 100 per cent no smoking as health of customers and employees remains the dominant issue," he concluded.

The bar owners and Tourism Victoria also went public with their concerns about the economic impact a 100 per cent ban would have. Card told reporters that the ban would be enough to virtually kill the bar business in the region.[11]

"They're bureaucrats, so they forget about the economic impact it has on us and the amount of money we have invested," he said of Dr. Stanwick, Stevenson and the other members of the health department. He again pushed for the ventilation solution, insisting that currently available systems could meet Workers' Compensation Board standards. Ventilation systems were not being perceived as a solution only because of the unreasonably high standards that the health bureaucrats had set, he argued.

The tourism group wrote a lengthy letter to health committee chair Murray Coell. The organization backed the restaurant association in insisting that the year 2000 date talked about by Dr. Peck still constituted an "agreement" with the tourism and hospitality industries. "We feel strongly that the Agreement, which has overwhelming support by the tourism industry, is still in effect in spite of the recent unsuccessful fast-tracked negotiations [initiated by Dr. Stanwick]," wrote CEO Lorne Whyte and president Mark Scott. "We believe the negotiating process has been seriously flawed by the insistence of Dr. Stanwick that a new Agreement must be structured to his standards and his timetable in spite of a longstanding Agreement in place."

Tourism Victoria also supported the idea of provincial ventilation standards which, it admitted, might be developed and in place by the year 2000 deadline. Were that approach to be successful, some establishments might not have to go 100 per cent non-smoking even four years later.

The letter quoted Dr. Stanwick when he'd said (in explaining the ASHRAE standards), "What they're seeking is a comfort standard and what we're seeking is a health standard."

Scott and Whyte had no hesitation in stating that "Tourism Victoria is seeking a Business Standard." They echoed the bar owners in their concerns that "CRD jobs and businesses are at risk" if the timetable were to be advanced from the year 2000.

The association called a news conference to make its letter public. Ironically in the *Times-Colonist*, the article was illustrated with a photo of a bar manager having a smoke at her bar, even though the one item the hospitality industry had agreed to in its compromise agreement was that employees shouldn't be allowed to smoke on the job.[12]

Whyte told the news conference that the regional board needed to ensure that whatever plan it developed was one that the industry would support. "It won't work unless the industry agrees," he said. "Enforcement is not the route to be going." One reporter

Chapter 3 - Seeking Consensus

asked if the hospitality and tourism industries had already decided what they would do if faced with a deadline with which they didn't agree. But Whyte said that issue hadn't been raised yet; the industry remained optimistic that the board would take a realistic viewpoint.

The *Times-Colonist* ran a lead editorial strongly encouraging the elected politicians to follow Dr. Stanwick's lead and adopt the 1998 date. "Smoke free workplace policies have been implemented by federal, provincial and municipal governments," the newspaper noted. "Shouldn't the same health protection be extended to waiters and other people working in the food service industry?" [13, 14]

Before the meeting, Coell suggested publicly that the next step should be public hearings. The politicians had heard repeatedly from both the health advocates and the industry, he said, but now needed to hear from ordinary citizens.

The committee adopted that idea enthusiastically at the meeting. Members agreed that two nights of public meetings should be held in early May so that the results could be discussed at the next health committee meeting on May 15. They agreed that as many written comments as possible should be encouraged, but that oral presentations should be limited to 50 on each of the two nights for a total of 100. The various groups involved should all be allowed to make presentations, but so should as many ordinary interested citizens as possible. No oral presentation should be more than five minutes long.

Several committee members also noted that the whole issue would be much more efficiently dealt with on a provincial basis, rather than a regional one. They agreed that the Workers' Compensation Board should be invited to make a presentation to the public hearings as well.

Dr. Stanwick and Stevenson left the meeting realizing they were now in the political battle of their lives. They knew the hospitality industry (and underneath it the tobacco industry) would pull out all the stops to try to convince the board that a full smoking ban would be an unpopular, unenforceable economic disaster. It would be up to them and their allies in the health groups to show the board that the bylaw was not only the right thing to do from a health viewpoint, but would also be popular and accepted by the citizens of the region.

---

10. Munro, Harold. "Smoking ban won't be total," Vancouver Sun, February 1, 1996.
11. Watts, Richard. "Proposed smoking legislation fires up pub owner," Victoria Times-Colonist, April 11, 1996.
12. Bell, Jeff. "Tourism leaders butt into smoking issue," Victoria Times-Colonist, April 17, 1996.
13. Unsigned editorial, "It's time to take firm action on public smoking," Victoria Times-Colonist, April 14, 1996.
14. See Page 14.

PROPOSED CRD 100% SMOKING BAN
(For Public Places)

WHAT YOU SHOULD KNOW:

- **Tobacco Kills**
  - Smoking will kill 40,000 Canadians in 1996. Of those, 500 will be non-smokers killed by the effects of environmental tobacco smoke (more commonly referred to as second hand smoke).

- **If It Doesn't Kill You, It Will Make You Sick**
  - Tobacco smoking causes cancer of the mouth, larynx (voice box) bladder and cervix; heart disease and stroke, emphysema and aggravates asthma and other allergies.
  - Environmental tobacco smoke may result in eye and airway irritation, headache, nausea, chest discomfort, impairment of exercise function, reduced lung function, increased respiratory symptoms and infections like pneumonia and bronchitis, asthma attacks and middle ear infections especially in children and in the long term all of the diseases caused by smoking listed above.

- **Tobacco Costs You as a Taxpayer**
  - The Government collects $450 million per year in tobacco taxes in British Columbia.
  - Government spends over $1 billion per year on tobacco related illnesses in British Columbia.

- **Better Ventilation Is Not Likely the Answer**
  - The hospitality industry has proposed ventilation standards which would result in a 1 in 7,000 risk of employees likely dying of cancer as a result of exposure to environmental tobacco smoke.
  - We believe that ventilation standards should pose a risk to employees of 1 in 100,000 for ventilation to even be considered as an option.

- **Smoke Free is Not Bad for Business**
  - Contrary to information put out by industry, smoking bans have not resulted in negative long term impacts on business in jurisdictions such as California where they have been implemented.

WHAT YOU CAN DO:

- Attend the Public Meetings on either May 1 or 2, to show your support. (City of Victoria Council Chambers - 6:00 p.m. to 11:00 p.m.)

  Or

- Fill in the clip-out section below and mail or fax it to the address/number shown below before May 6, 1996.

- Make a written submission of 600 words or less to the Chair of the CRD Health Committee before May 6, 1996. The submission can be mailed to:

  Chair of the Health Committee
  C/O Capital Regional District
  524 Yates Street
  Victoria, B.C. V8W 2S6

  Fax: 360-3120

THIS HAS BEEN A MESSAGE FROM:

BRITISH COLUMBIA LUNG ASSOCIATION   para·med HEALTH SERVICES BC Cancer Agency

Donald Head Trust   Victoria Medical Society   CRD Tobacco Free Task Force   Public Health Association of B.C.

- I support the proposed 100% smoking ban in all public places.
- I believe better ventilation is not the solution if the health risk to employees is greater than 1 in 100,000.

My name is _____.

I live in the municipality or electoral area of _____.

A form published in April 1996 prior to the Clean Air Bylaw asking the public to fax in a response in order to show support.

4
Decisions, Decisions

*"For success, attitude is equally
as important as ability."*
— Harry F. Banks

Dr. Stanwick and Stevenson were sure that the health committee and the majority of the regional board were convinced of the health concerns posed by second-hand smoke. Murray Coell had said as much to the media, noting that the issue before the board was not whether public places should be smoke-free, but when the law should come into effect.[15] Although some die-hard supporters of the tobacco industry were still issuing reports arguing that the harm caused by environmental tobacco smoke had not yet been well proven, it did not appear this would be an issue of any significance for the elected board members.

Rather, the health team concluded, the hospitality industry seemed likely to focus on the political and economic impacts of fast-tracking the legislation. That was what had happened in other jurisdictions where similar laws had been proposed. The industry would probably try to convince the politicians that an early date would lead to business closures and job losses (although it never was made clear why the situation would have changed so much if the date were to be delayed by two years). As well, a key argument would be that the new bylaw would be ridiculously expensive to enforce — if indeed it could be successfully enforced at all — because defiance would be widespread if the industry didn't agree to abide by the new rules voluntarily.

Some hospitality spokespersons, as well as some talk show hosts, had also already shown that they were going to try to change the focus of the argument from one based on health to one based on the philosophic question of freedom of choice — that in a free and democratic society, governments should not prohibit adults from voluntarily assuming risks if they are prepared to deal with the consequences.

So, when Dr. Stanwick, Stevenson and top environmental health officer Les Potter sat down to plan their strategy for what would be an intensive month-long campaign, they concentrated on ways of defeating those arguments. They wanted to convince the politicians that a move to smoke-free establishments would have widespread public support. They wanted to demonstrate that fears about economic and job losses were groundless, and to show they had devised a system that would make the bylaw enforceable without a huge outlay of extra resources from the region's taxpayers. And they wanted to provide a cogent argument that the need for protection of workers' health and the need for a level playing field should outweigh any philosophic argument about freedom of choice.

Dr. Peck and Dr. Blatherwick had a long-term co-operative relationship, dating from the days when Dr. Peck had served as Dr. Blatherwick's deputy before moving to Victoria. The co-operation had continued when Dr. Peck took over as MHO for the Capital region, and as far back as 1991, the two had joined in undertaking proper scientific opinion polls of residents' views on smoking regulation. In an effort to combat the completely unscientific "polls" put forward by the hospitality industry and others run by newspapers and radio talk shows, they had commissioned their own surveys among area residents. The largest survey, undertaken in 1995, had shown that about 60 per cent of residents of both Greater Vancouver and Greater Victoria supported a 100 per cent non-smoking bylaw.

One of the first steps Dr. Stanwick took as he began planning the campaign, was to commission a new poll from Angus Reid (now Ipsos-Reid), the same firm that had done the work on the 1995 survey. Dr. Stanwick was determined to stick with the nationally known firm to ensure the results would again be seen as unassailable by the elected officials, the general public and even the courts, should the issue ever arise there.

The 1996 poll showed that attitudes had changed very little in the preceding year, despite the increased news coverage surrounding the issue.[16] A total of 61 per cent said they would support a bylaw

Chapter 4 - Decisions, Decisions

"to prohibit smoking in all indoor public places." Of that group, 38 per cent strongly supported the bylaw and 23 per cent supported it moderately. A total of 35 per cent opposed the idea — 19 per cent strongly and 16 per cent moderately.

Among those who supported the bylaw, almost half mentioned health concerns as the main reason for their support. Others said they found it unpleasant, smelly or even "disgusting" to be in a smoke-filled room.

The issue of freedom of choice was the argument that resonated most strongly with those who opposed the bylaw. More than one-third specifically mentioned "smokers' rights" or "freedom of choice," and another six per cent said they disliked government restrictions over such aspects of their lives. About one in eight mentioned the fear that restaurants and bars would lose business.

The pollsters also asked specifically whether people would go more or less often to hospitality establishments if smoking were no longer allowed. For every category of establishment mentioned, more people said they would go more often to a smoke-free place — although in some categories such as bowling alleys and bingo halls, the numbers were very close. (Ten per cent said they'd go more often, eight per cent less often. For the rest, it wouldn't make any difference.) But for some establishments, such as restaurants and neighbourhood pubs, the figures were much more positive. In both cases the net gain in attendees amounted to nine percentage points. And in each category at least 60 per cent of people said it wouldn't make any difference to their attendance one way or the other.

Dr. Stanwick and Stevenson were also delighted to receive the results of a similar poll carried out in the Greater Toronto region just a week before the public hearings. Canada's largest city was beginning to engage in the same debate. The Toronto survey showed that about 65 per cent of the residents there would support bylaws to ban smoking in such places as restaurants and food courts, recreational facilities and other workplaces.[17] (The Toronto-area medical health officers who had commissioned the poll hadn't yet asked about pubs, bars and casinos.)

57

The Victoria health team reasoned that the local figures, backed by the similar results from Vancouver and Toronto, were strong enough that the elected board members wouldn't fear their political careers could be over for supporting the bylaw.

However, they wanted to do even more to try to show the politicians support for the idea across the region. The aim was to try to show the board members that the opposition, as vociferous as it was, represented only a small minority of the region's citizens. In this, they requested the co-operation of the Tobacco-Free Task Force to co-ordinate efforts. Individuals who supported the bylaw were urged to make written submissions, even if they couldn't make it to the public hearings or didn't want to stand up in front of a crowd and state their views.

The health groups that endorsed the bylaw agreed to take out a full-page advertisement in the *Times-Colonist* in support of it. A powerful set of logos was featured at the bottom of the ad. Groups who joined together to sponsor the advertisement included the provincial Lung Association; the Heart and Stroke Foundation; the Canadian Cancer Society and B.C. Cancer Agency; the Victoria Medical Society (representing the region's doctors); the Registered Nurses Association of B.C.; and the B.C. Society of Respiratory Therapists. The text of the advertisement stressed the negative health effects of second-hand smoke and the costs of tobacco-related illness to the health care system. It backed the health department's rationale for the one in 100,000 risk factor to be used as a basis for any ventilation standard. And it particularly offended many of the business groups by including a paragraph headed, "Smoke Free is Not Bad for Business."

"Contrary to information put out by industry, smoking bans have not had negative long-term impacts on business in jurisdictions such as California where they have been implemented," the wording ran.

The ad, which appeared in the newspaper three days before the first evening of public hearings, encouraged people to come to the hearings or to make written submissions (see page 53). It also included a simple coupon for readers to sign and return to express

Chapter 4 - Decisions, Decisions

their support of the proposed bylaw. Although the returns could in no way be considered a scientific sample, it was one of the most successful tactics in showing public support for the bylaw. A total of 1,100 coupons were returned. Only four were opposed; 1,096 urged the board to go ahead with the legislation.

The two-evening public hearing on May 1 and 2 was widely advertised. The hearings were held in Victoria City Hall, a central location with space for a couple of hundred spectators. It was full nearly the entire time. To avoid any accusations of unfairness, the politicians decided they would bring someone in from the outside to moderate the hearings. Their choice was Alan Perry, a well-known reporter for the city's largest radio station. The radio station taped all 10 hours of hearings, and the local community cable TV station also attended on the second night and videotaped the proceedings. These clips of the hearings were shown repeatedly over the next week. Stevenson's office also prepared a brief questionnaire for all those who attended, asking about their views on the bylaw.

As had been anticipated by everyone who had participated in the smoking summit, the hearings were emotional, passionate and tense. The regional health department staff who had organized the speakers' lists had made efforts to try to balance supporters and opponents as well as to ensure that representatives of all stakeholders groups found a place on the agenda. Most of those who were prepared to give up an entire evening or two were also passionate about the issue.

Along with the official spokespersons for the hospitality, tourism and restaurant industries, numerous employees from those industries took the microphone. Many were themselves non-smokers, but said they opposed the bylaw because they feared for their jobs. One pit boss from the city's largest casino predicted that all 120 employees at its location would be laid off if the bylaw were to come into effect, because business would be cut so drastically. She feared that she would either be forced into personal bankruptcy or would have to leave the region in order to find another job. As well, she noted, the 365 charities that received a share of funding from the casino would also be facing financial problems because of the loss of gaming revenue.

"The majority of our customers are smokers," she noted. "They want to smoke while they play. If they cannot smoke in our casinos, we will lose most of our business to private home and underground games. Games which are played in poorly ventilated rooms. Games which support the underground economy and not the charities of Victoria."

Others spoke passionately about the right of all adults to be able to choose whether to expose themselves to second-hand smoke or not. Another manager from the same casino said the proposal would not only cause the job losses and charity revenue cuts previously mentioned but would also infringe upon "our personal rights and freedoms. Those freedoms include our rights to choose."

He stated that: "This ban is not a win-lose proposition, but rather a lose-lose proposition. Charities will lose. Governments will lose. Jobs will be lost. But worst of all, our rights to make an adult choice will be lost."

The restaurant association also moved back to a strong freedom-of-choice argument in its presentation. If tobacco is really such a problem, argued Monsour and local official Frank Bourree, then the government should be banning its sale altogether, not targeting the hospitality industry specifically. They noted that the "Smoke-Free Lobby" (their name for the consortium that had sponsored the full-page advertisement) included such influential groups as the Cancer Society and the Heart and Stroke Foundation.

"With this backing and the clout these organizations carry, they are striking at our livelihoods, but are not forcing the federal and provincial governments to ban the sale of this deadly substance," Monsour and Bourree said. "We are very frustrated by their proposals and feel we are being attacked for something our governments sell and condone. If there should be a forced smoking ban, it should start at the top, not the bottom."

The restaurateurs urged the board to allow the marketplace to dictate what would happen as far as smoking in their

Chapter 4 - Decisions, Decisions

establishments. "The non-smoking lobby fails to see that if the restaurateurs of this city saw the potential to increase business by going non-smoking, they would," they said. They noted that some restaurants had voluntarily moved to become 100 per cent non-smoking and had been highly successful while others had found that the experiment had not worked for them.

All the same, the restaurant lobby group was much more cautious about the potential effect on its business than either bar operators or casino managers. "We do not pretend to know for certain if the 100 per cent ban would in fact cause business losses," Monsour admitted frankly, "just as the smoke-free lobby does not know for certain that it would not. We simply are stating that the possibility for losses is there [so] the market forces should be allowed to dictate change."

But what remained most important to the restaurateurs was the creation of a genuine level playing field with the same rules applying to bars, pubs and cabarets as to restaurants. That, they noted, was why the health advocates shouldn't be making a comparison with what happened to business in California. In California, they noted, restaurants were still allowed to have "lounge sections" in which smoking was permitted, as well as outdoor patios where liquor could be served.

"In Victoria we are not allowed fully licensed patios or lounges, nor could we use them anywhere near to 300 days [as is the case in many places in California]," Bourree noted.

Again, they never explained why or how the situation would have changed so drastically by the year 2000 such that all the same problems would not continue to plague the passage of a bylaw.

Tourism Victoria reiterated the same points it had made in its news conference a few days earlier, and again suggested the issue should be dealt with on a provincial level, rather than a regional one. Again, they said the date should be delayed until 2000 without saying why the hospitality industry would be prepared to accept a ban then, rather than in 1998 or 1999. But they insisted that a 2000 date would be acceptable.

"Voluntary support by the tourism industry is essential for the successful implementation of the smoking ban as well as an open mind on an approach for better ventilation," CEO Lorne Whyte argued.

The freedom of choice argument was a strong one for many of the bylaw opponents who didn't work for a hospitality establishment and wouldn't be impacted directly — the ordinary citizens that the regional board had hoped to attract to the hearing. These individuals insisted that they should be free to smoke where they wanted to, at least in adult-only establishments. "This is not really about smoking versus non-smoking," argued local lawyer Natexa Verbrugge. "It is about personal freedom to choose. What will be next? A ban on your favourite junk food? No more hiking in public parks (you might fall off a cliff and fall on someone else)? No talking or laughing above a certain decibel level in all public places? Whether you smoke or not, take a stand on the greater issue: do not let the state assume responsibility for your life."

On the other side, most of those who supported the bylaw stressed the health aspects, many from a personal point of view. Several individuals who suffered from asthma or other respiratory difficulties came to the hearings to say how much they would enjoy being able to go out for dinner or a drink without becoming ill because of second-hand smoke.

Others, including the Tobacco-Free Task Force, the Lung Association and other health groups stressed the health concerns for the bartenders, waiters and other staff in the hospitality industry. They cited studies which demonstrated that hospitality workers were much more likely to be exposed to second-hand smoke in the workplace than almost any other group of workers — with commensurate health consequences.

One mother made a heartfelt plea: "My greatest fear is that I will lose my son, a restaurant worker, because he is exposed to cigarette smoke in his workplace," she said. "A non-smoker, he has been a restaurant waiter for 15 years, and now he has a severe and chronic bronchial condition and often has to use a bronchial

Chapter 4 - Decisions, Decisions

dilator in order to breathe. ... He has always been a hard-working, taxpaying citizen who through no fault of his [own] is constantly exposed to a known carcinogen at his workplace."

Other passionate supporters of the bylaw were students from several local high schools. They urged the board to implement the ban in hospitality establishments as early as possible, but also to move on the issue of abolishing smoking pits at area high schools. One young woman described the adults as "hypocrites" for continuing to permit the outdoor smoking pits even though they knew full well that nearly all students were too young to buy tobacco products legally. Another student pointed out that at one area school at least, the smoking pit was right outside the windows of the elementary school classrooms. It was, she pointed out, setting a horrendous example for the younger students to watch the "big kids" as well as some young "hip" teachers smoking outside their class.

While emotional moments disrupted the hearings from time to time, halfway through the second evening the entire building began to shake and vibrate. It was obviously an earthquake, not an uncommon event on the Pacific Northwest coast. Bruce Clark led the dive to get under the tables in the hopes of finding safety if the old building began to crumble or the skylights above the crowd fell in. Others fled down the stairs for the exit. It turned out to be a quake that had struck just outside Seattle with a Richter scale rating of over 5.0 — just below the level at which actual damage would occur. Within a few minutes it was obvious that the building was still safe and stable, everyone returned and the presentations continued.

After the hearings were over, written submissions continued to pour into the health department offices from both individuals and agencies. Those who wrote in support ranged from children to senior citizens, from restaurant operators to asthmatics looking for cleaner air.

One 12-year-old girl told the department that: "I would like to see smoking banned from public places because I have a lot of trouble breathing when there is cigarette smoke around. ...

Smoke-Free

I don't like going into restaurants where smoking is allowed because even though the non-smoking section is away from the smoking section, the smoke still drifts over."

One man included a note from his doctor in which he was diagnosed as having "a chronic debilitating cough" as a result of sensitivity to cigarette smoke. "Because of this, I have advised him that he should try to avoid a work situation that exposes him to cigarette smoke," the doctor wrote.

Of the writers opposed to the ban, most again cited the freedom of choice argument, some in polite terms, some less so. One "Victorian restaurant owner," who didn't care to give his name, wrote Dr. Stanwick to say: "As all you have done since coming to Victoria is to rant on and on about cigarettes, and try to sell tin helmets for children [he was apparently referring to a campaign to have children wear bike helmets], we would be most grateful if you would go back to Winnipeg. ...Perhaps you could go to medical school there and try to learn a little more about all the germs that can hit us."

Another frustrated smoker wrote: "It appears to be the year for fanatics, bureaucrats and the politically correct. They are in their element now that they can vent all their anger and frustrations on a visible minority. The focus of all this wrath are [sic] the smokers."

Others worried about possible job and business losses, and some were still prepared to doubt the scientific evidence on the health risks from second-hand smoke. "The hype and hoopla about the dangers of second-hand smoke are grossly exaggerated and greatly unproven," wrote one woman.

But some hospitality establishments were prepared to buck the industry trend and express their support for the bylaw. "The Stonehouse Pub supports a total ban on smoking," owner Philip Charland wrote. "But why wait until Jan 1/98? If smoking is killing us now, let's stop it now."

Chapter 4 - Decisions, Decisions

Charland noted that he'd taken a straw vote among pub patrons and found most supported the ban, even a majority of the smokers. "We believe that any loss in business will be compensated by new customers who avoid going to pubs because of the smoke," he concluded.

When the deadline for all public submissions had passed, more than 600 people had provided comments, either in writing or orally at the hearing. Dr. Stanwick, Stevenson and the rest of the health team began preparing their report for the next meeting of the board's health committee. All board members received an individual binder with copies of all the correspondence enclosed, so they could read each letter at their leisure.

They also received a copy of the information provided by the Workers' Compensation Board (WCB), attempting to answer their questions about the provincial stance on the issue. Staff from the board explained that it was in the process of drafting regulations to cover the hazards of second-hand smoke in the workplace, but the regulations were not yet complete.

"The consensus among subcommittee members [working on the issue] was that workers who do not smoke should be entitled to a smoke-free workplace, and that smoking should be prohibited in all workplaces at some point in the near future. In the meantime, they recommended that employers be required to provide a smoke-free environment by implementing administrative controls." Those controls could introduce policies prohibiting smoking or restricting smoking to designated areas with separate and suitable exhaust systems. But at the same time, the subcommittee believed it would be too difficult to implement those rules in "workplaces which are public service and entertainment facilities," such as restaurants and nightclubs. Those areas should be given "special consideration," the WCB suggested, and it was looking at whether a workable ventilation solution could be found.

The response was not of much help to the regional board members faced with the decision.

In his summary report, Dr. Stanwick again recommended to the health committee that its recommendation to the full board be that the 100 per cent smoke-free policy go ahead on January 1, 1998 as originally proposed.

The health committee agreed without a single dissenting voice. In fact, the committee members suggested a couple of ways of tightening up the bylaw even further. Following the level-playing-field analogy, they suggested that pubs and bars (which were still allowed to have half their seats in a smoking section) should have to move by September 1 to the same standards as restaurants, with 60 per cent guaranteed non-smoking. The same 60 per cent rule should apply to bingo halls, casinos and bowling alleys, in the same four-month time frame, the committee said.

They also endorsed the suggestion of the high school students at the public hearings that all school grounds be made smoke-free zones. They added a clause to Dr. Stanwick's recommendation to prohibit smoking anywhere on school property, also by September 1.

But then it was almost a month before the full CRD board met to consider the committee's recommendations, and the hospitality and tourism groups spent those weeks lobbying the board members as intensively as possible to get them to change their minds. Half a dozen bylaw opponents asked to speak at the board meeting before a final decision was made, and others packed the room. The points made were virtually identical to those made by the same organizations at the public hearings — the fears of loss of jobs and business closures, the freedom-of-choice argument, and the suggestion that the issue should be tackled provincially and not regionally. And despite the problems that the Lower Mainland was having in trying to come up with a unified solution, another suggestion made was that the issue should be handled by individual municipal councils, as was being done on the Lower Mainland, rather than at a regional level.

However, when Monsour addressed the board, he formalized the final compromise position he had first tentatively brought up during the last meeting of the smoking summit. If the regional board would delay implementation just one year until 1999, he said, and if it would ensure all establishments were treated equally, the restaurant association would give its word that its members would abide by the bylaw. Indeed, Monsour said, he would personally take responsibility for ensuring full compliance by members of the association.

When Dr. Stanwick was invited to address the board, he emphasized the health risk especially to the workers in the hospitality industry. "What you are looking at is economic interests versus health interests," he said.

Debate among the board members was passionate. Some wanted to support the health advocates' view that 1997 would be an even better date than 1998. Others wanted a compromise for the hospitality industry by giving them until 1999. Several said they'd been swayed by the promise from Don Monsour that if the board gave the restaurants that one extra year, the restaurant association would promise full compliance from its members. Others noted that the extra year would give the health department itself more time to work with establishments to help them make the changes necessary, and to run major public education campaigns to explain the new legislation.

In the end, those arguing for the one-year delay won the day. Greater Victoria would, it appeared, become the first city in Canada to have a 100 per cent smoke-free policy in place — but not until January 1, 1999.

---

15. Young, Gerard. "Smoking issue thrown to the public," Victoria Times-Colonist, April 12, 1996.
16. Angus Reid Group Inc., "Support for Proposed No Smoking Bylaws in the Capital Regional District," May 1996.
17. Moloney, Paul. "Diners favour smoking ban: poll," Toronto Star, April 25, 1996.

5
Getting Ready

*"The problems of victory
are more agreeable
than the problems of defeat,
but they are no less difficult."*
— *Winston Churchill*

Even though implementation of the bylaw for the hospitality industry wouldn't take place for another 30 months, Dianne Stevenson and her team realized after the CRD board meeting that they had one project that needed immediate work: to make all school property smoke-free. It would mean the abolition of the "smoking pits" which were a part of daily life in many schools, the places where the smokers among the students — and even a few teachers — would congregate for a cigarette at lunch time, between classes, or before and after school. Although the issue had been on the tobacco team's agenda for several years and had been specifically mentioned by students who spoke at the public hearings, the health department hadn't originally proposed it as part of the 1996 bylaw changes. Because it had been added on by the health committee and endorsed by the entire regional board, the health department had not previously devised a plan for its implementation.

It posed problems for Stevenson and her staff. The bylaw didn't receive formal approval until mid-June, and the change was scheduled to go into effect on September 1, at the beginning of the new school year. That proved an extremely short time frame in which to work with the schools to develop policies to bring in the new rules, to provide the necessary education for everyone from parents to principals, and to devise a workable enforcement program. It was made worse because the schools were all in the process of closing down for summer holidays. Principals and other administrators weren't likely to return to be able to even start planning for such a program until about the middle of August. And from the moment the change was publicly announced, numerous principals and administrators were complaining loudly that it was an impossible task for them.

It shouldn't have been as much of a surprise to the school administrators as it appeared to be. The issue had been raised with superintendents of the three school districts over the previous couple of years at regular meetings that they held with Dr. Stanwick in his role as the school medical health officer. The superintendents had personally supported the change, but had told Dr. Stanwick and Stevenson that they didn't want to be the ones initiating the new policy because of potential backlash from the schools under their jurisdiction. They had suggested to Stevenson that if smoke-free school grounds were included in the regional bylaw, it would greatly simplify their job. They could then tell the reluctant administrators that it wasn't the school districts' decision but rather one that they had no choice but to implement.

However, many of the principals didn't see it that way. They complained that there had been no consultation with them, no discussion about how best to make the new policy work, let alone discussion about a reasonable time frame for implementation. They couldn't see why the regional board had put so much effort into consultation with stakeholders and the public while dealing with the hospitality industry, but none at all into the issue of the smoke pits.

Unlike the students at the public hearings, the reluctant principals didn't want to discuss the issue of the legality of the students even buying cigarettes. Instead, they worried about the consequences of shutting down the smoking pits. They worried that the elimination of the smoking pits would put the students at even greater risk. They feared the smoking students would sneak away from the school grounds to grab their cigarettes, leaving them prey to everything from traffic mishaps to drug dealers.

Chapter 5 - Getting Ready

They suspected that many of the students, especially those who were only marginally attached to school anyway, wouldn't return to class, leading to an upsurge in truancy and absenteeism. They worried about relations with their neighbours because they feared the students would hang out in neighbourhoods just off school property, creating noise and litter. Several talked to the parents' advisory councils at their schools and pointed out these perceived risks, enlisting the parents as allies in their battle against the new rules.

Listening to their complaints, Stevenson realized it would be impractical to try to have a full-blown enforcement program in place by September. Instead, she, Dr. Stanwick, and her staff agreed that the first term would be spent in educating stakeholders about the change, in visiting schools to work with administrators and staff to ensure the new system would be practical, and in monitoring compliance. Only in January would staff begin considering enforcement actions against students or schools who refused to abide by the bylaw.

As they visited schools, the team soon realized that there were various opinions among students, staff, parents and administrators on the value of the new law. Some schools embraced it, using it as a catalyst for programs to discourage students from taking up the habit and to help existing smokers to quit. Others remained more distressed about the logistical problems it was causing for administrators.

The parents' advisory council from Stelly's Secondary School wrote to the regional board, urging it to reconsider the law. The council, PAC chair Lynn Lewis wrote, "objects to our administrators using their valuable time walking parking lots and fields looking for students who are smoking. Those students who do go off school property to smoke are now on Stelly's Cross Road, which is a narrow road, and we are concerned for the increased risk of an accident." The parents were convinced that the rules wouldn't actually discourage smoking among teens, but only move it to a less controlled area.

But other parents wrote the board urging it to stay the course with the regulation. The parents' association at Parklands Secondary School told the board that "we believe schools need to be places that exemplify healthy living as well as promote healthy choices." The Parklands parents recognized the logistical difficulties involved for administrators, but concluded "we still think it is worthwhile to prohibit smoking in a controlled area on school grounds despite these challenges."

The CRD board had little difficulty in deciding to reaffirm the new regulations. Stevenson and her team went from school to school, working with principals to design policies that would ensure the bylaw was obeyed while not causing trouble with the neighbours. Victoria High School, for instance, instituted a "bubble zone" around the school grounds, stating that students not only couldn't smoke on the grounds themselves but also were banned from doing so within one block of the school building. The school established policies stating that students who repeatedly violated the smoking guidelines would not only face the possibility of a fine from the regional district but also a suspension from the school itself.

Stevenson found that schools that adopted such strict policies achieved quicker and higher compliance with the bylaw than did those in which the school administration took little responsibility for managing the situation. In the spring of 1997, the team wrote some "warning tickets" to students who were flagrantly disobeying the bylaw, but waited until the next school year before taking enforcement actions that would lead to fines for the students.

But from the first day of school in September 1997, the team made it clear that the period of grace was over. They would be regularly monitoring compliance at area schools and ticketing students who weren't obeying the bylaw. By the end of September, they'd written their first half dozen tickets for students from four different high schools. By the end of the fall term, the number had risen to 37. If the students didn't pay the $50 fine, enforcement procedures were taken against them.

Chapter 5 - Getting Ready

Many of the students were unhappy about receiving their tickets, and the team got a first glimpse of the unnerving lengths to which opponents would go to show their displeasure. One afternoon in September, tobacco educators Claire Avison and Michael McKinley were visiting Parklands to talk to the principal about the problems the school was having making the new system work. Despite the parent council's endorsement of the rules, neighbours had complained students were still smoking on the property, and the enforcement teams had caught some doing so. The day before, they had issued $50 tickets to some who were blatantly defying the bylaw.

When they came out of the meeting, they found their car — clearly identifiable through the CRD logos on the doors — pelted with eggs. As Avison went back inside to discuss this with the principal, McKinley got into the car and began writing up his notes. Suddenly the car was surrounded by at least half a dozen teenagers, who began rocking it back and forth with increasing ferocity. Just before McKinley was sure they were going to succeed in tipping it over, Avison and the principal came back outside. As suddenly as they had appeared, the students disappeared back into the woods that surround Parklands.

"We were just incredulous when we heard about it," Dr. Stanwick remembers. "We couldn't believe anyone would go that far just because they opposed a bylaw." Fortunately the violence was never repeated in a school setting.

February 1998 saw several of the students in small claims court at the Victoria courthouse, at least trying to work out payment schedules. In B.C.'s court system, fines that aren't paid on time increase, so some of the students by then were owing as much as $150 on their original $50 ticket. Stevenson was prepared to be extremely flexible about payment schedules. One girl agreed to pay five dollars a week from her allowance until the debt was paid off. Others admitted they could use some of their earnings from after-school jobs to pay the fines. Several complained they couldn't afford it, but on that point Stevenson was adamant: if they could afford five dollars a pack for cigarettes, they could afford the fine.

Some even had the backing of their parents in their complaints. "Why target the kids?" grumbled one father who had brought his son to the courthouse for his appearance. "They don't have any money."

Word that the health department was serious about the bylaw began to spread, and, as with many other changes the bylaw brought, defiance began to dwindle. For several months, occasional complaints surfaced from neighbours about the problems of students smoking and littering. One of the problem areas was Victoria High, where the courtyard of a community theatre was just outside the bubble zone, and became the student smokers' favourite gathering place. The school's principal continued to complain about the bylaw, saying it was better to have the smokers in "a controlled environment in a controlled area" under direct supervision.[18]

"It was much easier to control the situation when we knew where the area was, who the students were, and the situations they were in," said principal Dennis Harrigan. But eventually the school deputized a supervisor to monitor and clean up the courtyard if necessary. As well, individuals performing community service work as part of a criminal sentence would come once a week to the courtyard to ensure it was clean.

Though Harrigan and other opponents of the bylaw were sure the changes hadn't discouraged student smoking, statistics over the next few years proved otherwise. Ironically, one of the biggest success stories was Stelly's, where the parents had originally opposed the regulations so strenuously. A new principal at the school embraced the bylaw and started various prevention and cessation programs. Over a period of three years, the smoking rate amongst students at the school decreased from 21 per cent of students to just seven per cent, one of the lowest rates in the province. The success there was so outstanding that when Jeffrey Wigand — the former high-ranking tobacco executive who was the real-life hero of the Disney movie *The Insider* — came to Greater Victoria, it was Stelly's where he chose to deliver his lecture.

Chapter 5 - Getting Ready

At the same time that the team's main public activities involved the schools, Dr. Stanwick, Stevenson and the regional board were watching bylaws that were being tried in other parts of Canada with interest. The results were not particularly encouraging. North York, a suburb of Toronto, tried the innovative approach of not allowing smoking in restaurants until after 9 p.m. daily, presumably after all or nearly all the children who might be customers had headed home. But only three weeks after implementation, the city council there reversed its decision by an eight to seven vote. As well, they decided that only 25 per cent of restaurant seating needed to be set aside as non-smoking seating, rather than the 40 per cent they'd originally mandated.[19]

An even greater public relations disaster for proponents of clean-air bylaws occurred in Toronto, Canada's largest city, in the spring of 1997. Like Victoria, Toronto had been willing to include bars as well as restaurants in its tough anti-smoking bylaw that had essentially banned indoor smoking throughout the hospitality industry. The bylaw went into effect March 3, 1997, but the outrage and defiance that greeted it overwhelmed enforcement resources. The vehement opposition of restaurant and bar owners went so far that some had to be arrested at a city council meeting which they disrupted and refused to leave.[20] Weeks later, city council and public health authorities admitted defeat and changed the regulations.[21] Seven years later, Toronto is still moving slowly towards 100 per cent smoke-free status for bars, with the complete smoking ban now scheduled to take effect in 2005.

As Dr. Stanwick and Stevenson watched the problems the Ontario cities were having, they became even more convinced that a careful and detailed pre-implementation process was essential to ensure the same thing didn't happen in Victoria. They knew they already had one big advantage over Toronto and North York. That was the commitment from Don Monsour that his influential restaurant association would be on board with the changes and would do its best to ensure that all its members among the region's 1,200 restaurants abided by the law. That commitment reduced the number of problem establishments that the Victoria team could expect to be faced with. Restaurants formed the greatest proportion of hospitality establishments in the community. Enforcement teams in Victoria would have fewer than 100 bars and pubs to deal with, even if every one of them was non-compliant.

Some of the news they received was more encouraging. California was set to become the first U.S. state to ban indoor smoking in bars beginning January 1, 1998, one year before the Victoria date. In July, a huge public opinion survey undertaken there by the Field Research Corporation showed that the economic disasters being predicted by the hospitality industry were unlikely to materialize.[22] The survey found that 60 per cent of bar patrons said they'd prefer smoke-free establishments and 17 per cent said it wouldn't make any difference. Only about one in five preferred bars that allowed smoking. The poll also contradicted claims that patrons would stay for a shorter time in smoke-free bars because they couldn't smoke inside. In fact, 27 per cent said they'd probably stay longer in a smoke-free bar compared to only 13 per cent who said they'd probably leave to smoke elsewhere. The CRD health team put that in its files along with its own Angus Reid surveys as ammunition for reassuring anxious politicians that smoke-free laws continued to have widespread public support.

When the California statewide law did take effect on New Year's Day in 1998, it was greeted with the predictable howls of protest from the industry there. Several pro-tobacco politicians, most of whom had taken campaign donations from the large tobacco companies, promised they would try to ensure the law was repealed by the California House of Representatives or Senate. In Victoria, local opponents, such as pub owner Gordon Card, leapt upon the California tumult to tell reporters that the problems there showed the Greater Victoria law wouldn't work either.[23] But with implementation still a full year away in Victoria, his comments attracted little attention.

By early 1998, however, Dr. Stanwick and Stevenson were becoming aware that resistance within the hospitality industry was already beginning to build. The leader at that point was Don Rittaler, an hotelier who owned the Sooke River Hotel, an idyllic

Chapter 5 - Getting Ready

riverbank property in the westernmost part of the region, about 35 kilometres (20 miles) from downtown Victoria. Rittaler knew better than most how the regional district worked. He had actually served four years on the regional board in the early 1980s, having been elected as the director from Sooke.

Rittaler also had a long history of taking on government regulatory authorities — and winning. As far back as the 1970s, he had challenged rules imposed by the Liquor Control and Licensing Board which had, at that time, banned dancing and taped music in hotel beverage rooms. He won. A few years later in the 1980s, he again took on the LCLB, arguing it was unfair and discriminatory that a hotel drinking establishment classified as a "lounge" could serve hard liquor to its patrons but one classified as a "beverage room," like his, was restricted to just beer and wine. He won again.

Rittaler was one of the strongest opponents of the 100 per cent smoke-free law, but he decided to begin his opposition by refusing to obey even the law in place at that time — the one that required that 60 per cent of the seating be set aside for non-smoking customers. Rittaler began urging the board to repeal even that law, and pushed hard for a ventilation solution instead. He insisted that air quality standards should be used (often creating laughs with his play on words of the "Ashtray Standards," rather than ASHRAE), instead of a smoking ban or even smoking and non-smoking sections. He had installed a smoke-eater ventilation system in the beverage room, and told reporters "we've done everything we can in here to make sure the air is good to breathe, and our patrons are comfortable. We'd be fools not to." The health team immediately realized that Rittaler was virtually making their case for them. He was talking publicly about a "comfort" standard without addressing the health issues raised by second-hand smoke.

Environmental health officers paid several visits to Rittaler's pub to try to persuade him to change his ways, but he refused. His defiance was so blatant and so public that Dr. Stanwick felt he had no choice but to ask the regional board to authorize taking Rittaler to court for breaching the existing bylaw. On March 25, the board agreed. Jody Paterson, an editorial writer for the *Times-Colonist*, wrote, in a moment of prescience, that the experience with Rittaler showed that "it's plain that clearing the air in Greater Victoria pubs and restaurants won't be as simple as marking January 1 on the calendar." [24]

Long before the regional district's suit against Rittaler could be heard, Rittaler struck back. In early May, he launched his own lawsuit, challenging the constitutionality of the 100 per cent smoke-free bylaw that was scheduled to go into effect seven months later. The petition Rittaler filed in B.C. Supreme Court sounded more like a political polemic than a standard legal document. He argued that the bylaw "constitutes a serious infringement of the liberty of adults . . . who choose to smoke either at [his] hotel" or in other establishments that admit only legal adults. Those legal adults, he said, have the right to accept whatever risks the second-hand smoke might produce, and "wish to be able to smoke in places where minors are prohibited entry, as it is lawful conduct which provides them with great pleasure and constitutes for them . . . a fundamental personal decision and lifestyle choice."

The petition stated that most of Rittaler's patrons were smokers and that they had told him that they wouldn't come to his bar if they couldn't smoke there. That, the petition claimed, was enough to make the bylaw unconstitutional because it effectively "prohibits the operation of a pub such as that in the hotel because the ability of patrons to smoke therein is an integral component of business."

Rittaler went even further in his public comments, stating: "What is really going on is that the CRD is pandering to some anti-smoking zealots — but for political reasons, not health reasons." He again stressed the need for a ventilation solution, adding, "government just cannot regulate our lifestyles." [25]

Despite the political-sounding nature of the petition and Rittaler's comments, no one from the regional district or the health regions across the province took the lawsuit lightly. Rittaler had hired

Chapter 5 - Getting Ready

one of the top constitutional lawyers in Victoria, Joe Arvay, to represent him. A Harvard graduate, Arvay had served as a law school professor and a senior lawyer for the B.C. government before setting up his own law firm. In most of the high-profile cases he'd taken in private practice, he had represented individuals who were challenging a variety of government actions. In the few months before Rittaler hired him, Arvay had hit the headlines defending an ex-cabinet minister accused of sexual harassment; a small community agency accusing the government of corruption in its running of bingo programs; and a gay and lesbian bookstore accusing federal customs officers of discriminating against them by refusing to allow their books into the country. Any lawsuit launched by Arvay had to be taken very seriously.

What the regional board members and health authorities didn't know at the time was that Rittaler was the sole bylaw opponent in Greater Victoria who received direct funding from a program run by Big Tobacco. The program was called "Courtesy of Choice" and was run by the tobacco companies worldwide.

Big Tobacco used the program to provide money and resources to hospitality industry groups that were working for "accommodation" rules which allowed both smoking and non-smoking sections in restaurants, bars, pubs and hotels. The program, which was supported by both Philip Morris and British American Tobacco globally, had already made great inroads into some second and third world countries, where health authorities were trying to prevent tobacco from gaining the foothold it had found in North America and Europe. Courtesy of Choice was well-supported in places like Slovakia, Kenya and Uganda. One of its proud members was the *Yak and Yeti Hotel* in Kathmandu, Nepal.

In Canada, the Courtesy of Choice program was more low-key. It was administered by the Canadian Hotels' Association, at arm's length from the tobacco industry itself — and that was how the industry wanted it.[26] They did not want to be seen as putting any controls on the money; it would be up to the hospitality industry itself to decide which establishments should receive funding and how it should be spent. The tobacco money that funded the program amounted to about $800,000 a year.

Rittaler and other opponents of the Victoria bylaw had hoped the tobacco industry would provide the necessary funding for a constitutional court case. But Dave Laundy, the vice-president of the Tobacco Manufacturers' Council of Canada for the western provinces, told the dissident bar owners that would be counterproductive. From the view of politicians, taxpayers and even judges, it would be horrendous, he explained. They would see all opposition to the bylaw as stemming purely from the greedy motives of the tobacco industry, something many people were quite willing to believe anyhow. The industry itself didn't want to be seen as giving money directly to businesses that wanted to take on bylaws or similar regulatory schemes across Canada. It would simply mean the arguments against restrictions would lose all credibility.

However, tobacco money from the Courtesy of Choice program, paid for Russ Clifford, a former TV camera operator turned media consultant, to help Rittaler get his message out to the public. Rittaler's various programs of defiance also got widespread support in communications that were sent out to the network of Courtesy of Choice supporters. Three other Victoria-area hotels also joined the program, but none of them ever sought or received the sort of profile that Rittaler did.

An internal Canadian Tobacco Manufacturers' Council memo dated June 2, 1998, stated that: "After discussions with Don Rittaler at the Sooke River Hotel regarding his court challenge, we are offering to provide media training and support for his upcoming interviews. According to Don, he has hired one of the most competent lawyers in Victoria, but he is feeling somewhat 'alone' in this battle.

"In order to boost the public awareness of local hotels' support for a 'choice and ventilation' solution, each hotelier has been provided with an oversupply of communications materials . . . . It was also requested and agreed that we prepare a Response Coupon that

Chapter 5 - Getting Ready

each hotelier could request patrons to complete and then forward to the head of the CRD."

Six weeks later Rittaler turned up at the CRD board meeting with about 3,000 signed postcards gathered at his own and other hotels, all opposing the move to 100 per cent smoke-free spaces. It is questionable if any of those who signed them ever realized they had been provided courtesy of Big Tobacco.

The launching of the lawsuit was not a great surprise to Dr. Stanwick and Stevenson, nor to CRD lawyers Guy McDannold and Kathryn Stuart. They had been expecting some sort of court challenge to the validity of the bylaw. It did, however, add an extra dimension to planning for implementation. Every step as well as every public pronouncement by Dr. Stanwick or Stevenson, had to be viewed in the light of how it could appear if cited during the court case. Key advice provided by the lawyers was that it was now more important than ever that every decision must be made solely through the "public health" lens. The bylaw had been passed under a section of the provincial Municipal Act which stated specifically that a local council or regional board was permitted "to regulate persons, their premises and their activities, to further the care, protection, promotion and preservation of the health of the inhabitants of the municipality."[27]

McDannold explained both to regional directors and to Dr. Stanwick and his staff that the key word in that clause was "health." If the elected or appointed officials were to make decisions on any other basis, such as business or compassionate grounds, it would significantly weaken their ability to defend the bylaw. Lawyers for those opposed could argue that the board had exceeded its jurisdiction because it was adding other considerations to a "health" regulation.

The legal processes themselves took up hours of valuable time that could otherwise have been used in planning the implementation process. From the beginning, McDannold and Stuart warned the health department that a court challenge was likely, so it was important that they kept all their documentation. Arvay wanted to see every piece of paper that had anything to do with decisions surrounding the bylaw's passage. In the end, he was given copies of more than 1,200 documents — from scientific studies on second-hand smoke to copies of all the letters individuals had written during the public hearing process. As well, countless hours of time were spent meeting with the lawyers, drafting affidavits, and responding to those from the other side.

Only a few weeks after Rittaler launched the suit, however, the team had to worry about a legal problem much more immediate than Rittaler's court case. The municipal council of Burnaby, a suburb of Vancouver, had passed a bylaw similar to the CRD's although it covered only restaurants, not bars. The restaurant association there had challenged the bylaw in court on the grounds that the same Municipal Act gave councils power only to "regulate" an activity, not to prohibit it altogether. In June 1998, a provincial court judge (a lower court than the B.C. Supreme Court) agreed with that argument. If the decision were to be upheld, it would make the CRD bylaw invalid and the whole process would have to begin again. Even if Burnaby council or the government appealed the decision to a higher court, it was doubtful whether the appeal would be completed before January, when the CRD bylaw was scheduled to go into effect.

This, perhaps more than any other time, was the occasion when the tacit support of the provincial NDP government for the bylaw became essential.

Throughout the pre-implementation period, Dr. Stanwick had wanted to keep informal links between the health officials and the provincial government as strong as possible. In early 1997, he had approached Elizabeth Cull to see if she would consider taking over the chair of the Tobacco-Free Task Force from the retiring Dr. Coy. To the surprise of some, she accepted. Cull's credentials were impeccable. A former school trustee for Greater Victoria, she had in 1989 been elected MLA for the riding of Oak Bay-Gordon Head. In her seven years in government, she'd served in several key portfolios, including environment minister and health minister for the NDP. By 1996, she had risen to the position of finance minister and deputy premier. In the provincial election that year, she lost her seat to a Liberal opponent and returned to work as a consultant in the private sector.

Cull had a personal and passionate interest in tobacco issues, having watched several close relations die of smoking-related lung cancer. She described the health ministry as "my first true love" among the several provincial portfolios she had held. She had been a driving force behind the NDP's battles against Big Tobacco. She agreed to take on the new role with the task force, and realized that for several months one of her biggest undertakings would be the necessary political strategizing to ensure the bylaw stayed on track right up to January 1.

"There was always a fear," she remembers, "that the board would start to lose heart," when faced with so much rowdy public opposition. As someone who was neither an elected board member, nor a member of the health bureaucracy, she was free to manoeuvre among the different groups and ensure enough directors remained on side to guarantee that each vote taken would uphold the bylaw.

Cull didn't necessarily want to be seen as being a high-profile spokesperson for the bylaw or to take the floor at regional board meetings, as Dr. Coy had often done. The bylaw's supporters thought that was a good idea. Some of the directors who remained in lukewarm support were strongly anti-NDP — and Cull's open support might have been like waving a red flag in front of them. Instead, she met behind the scenes, one on one, with various board members to assess their position and try to discern what would be needed for them to stay in full support of the bylaw. Not all of her allies on the board were NDP supporters. She remembers getting strong support from Sheila Orr, a Saanich council member who, in 2001, became a Liberal MLA in the Gordon Campbell government.

Cull's NDP history gave her the advantage of direct access to the provincial NDP government. She remained on first-name terms with the new premier and health minister, and could easily arrange to talk to them, rather than being shuffled off to some lower layer of bureaucracy. When she spoke at a regional board meeting in February 1998, she stated openly that the task force had been working closely with the provincial government to ensure that the health ministry understood the importance of a successful implementation of the bylaw.

When the Burnaby court decision was made, Cull was among those who could use political clout to ensure a legislative solution was quickly found. Within days, municipal affairs minister Jenny Kwan and her staff grasped the magnitude of the problem and agreed to speedily introduce the necessary legislative amendments. B.C. had long had in place a relatively easy mechanism to fix such glitches, the Municipalities Enabling and Validating Act — MEVA for short. However, a MEVA did require a specific bill to be passed by the legislature. It took less than six weeks for Kwan to introduce and have passed in the legislature a MEVA bill which specifically stated that "regulation" could include total prohibition, and that any bylaws passed in the past were deemed to be valid despite that problem.

The change did not go through smoothly, though. Gordon Wilson, then the leader of the opposition Progressive Democratic Alliance, complained that the NDP was taking away too many rights from hospitality businesses. "It seems to me," he told the legislature, "that the government surely recognizes that this is an extremely high-handed action, to bring in an enabling bill that essentially forecloses on the rights of people who are operators of businesses." He wasn't happy with the idea that municipalities could decide to ban smoking in hospitality businesses "which actually cater to people who choose to go in there and have a beer and smoke a cigarette and do whatever they do."

But Kwan reassured him that anyone who believed he or she had a valid constitutional challenge to a smoking bylaw would still be allowed to proceed. Thus, the legislation did not kill Rittaler's lawsuit.

Chapter 5 - Getting Ready

With that issue settled, Dr. Stanwick, Stevenson and their team could begin to prepare for the bylaw's implementation. If they had ever dreamed that the challenges would be minor, they had long been disabused of that idea by the actions of Rittaler and his supporters. It had become clear that the bars and pubs had dissociated themselves from the restaurant association once Don Monsour had agreed to go along with the 1999 date. They were prepared to embrace an uneven playing field, sacrificing restaurants so they could find a way to retain smoking in their premises.

But by mid-summer, Dr. Stanwick and Stevenson were worried that even Monsour was wavering in his support. Hospitality industry trade papers were reporting widespread problems with the California law, including uneven enforcement and a loss of business for many establishments. Those reports were troubling Victoria restaurateurs, even though they were mostly collections of anecdotes from unhappy operators, not backed up by any hard evidence.

Monsour was still convinced that his member restaurants would experience few problems if a genuine level playing field were put in place as promised. But he was being pressured by many of his members who were hearing and reading second- and third-hand reports from California that they found horrifying.

Dr. Stanwick and Stevenson had long thought it would be worthwhile for them to travel to California for a few days to see how the law there, by then in effect for eight months, was working. Officials there could give them a heads-up of the problems to expect in implementation and tips on how to solve them. Now, Dr. Stanwick insisted, prompting consternation on the part of the team, they should invite Monsour to go with them. Dr. Stanwick was convinced Monsour would not believe information about the California experience from the health officials' site visit, but if he could see for himself that the law in the most populous U.S. state was not bad for business and that a genuine level playing field could be created, he could answer his members' concerns from first-hand observation. Also invited on the trip was Maxine Marchenski, one of the region's environmental health officers, chosen because she would be responsible for monitoring and enforcement in the downtown core where the highest proportion of restaurants and bars was located.

The group left on August 18, 1998 for four days in California. Their first stop was San Francisco, where welcoming officials showed them a wider variety of entertainment facilities than they had ever imagined existed. They visited mainstream bars and restaurants; bars that thrived by showing old cartoons; even gay "cowboys and Indians" bars. The people they met ranged from middle-aged businesspersons to transvestite nuns running harm reduction programs involving clean needles and condoms. But what they found — across the board — was that the clean-air law was working. The bars were uniformly non-smoking. Some were packed with patrons, and some almost empty, but the difference didn't appear to have anything to do with the smoking law. The busy ones were crowded both inside and on outdoor smoking patios, the quiet ones were empty in both areas. "What they told us," says Dr. Stanwick, "is that if you're offering a product that people want, they'll come — whether they can smoke inside or not."

Maxine Marchenski and Dr. Richard Stanwick fact gathering in San Francisco's lively club scene.

Chapter 5 - Getting Ready

As they toured various establishments in San Francisco, Oakland and Sacramento, Monsour sometimes stayed with the group, but other times he disappeared on his own to talk to owners and managers with none of the health professionals around. Dr. Stanwick and Stevenson encouraged that. They wanted Monsour — who had insisted on paying his own way to California

(From Left) Dr. Richard Stanwick, Dianne Stevenson, and Don Monsour during their scouting trip to California

— to be entirely free to ask his own questions and form his own impressions. And Monsour was won over by seeing so many establishments where the law was working successfully. He agreed it was possible to create a level playing field. Provided the CRD followed that same system, he said, he was prepared to continue his backing of the bylaw.

A highlight of the trip for Dr. Stanwick and Stevenson was meeting with Dr. Stanton Glantz, who provided them with both encouragement and advice. Dr. Glantz proved to be a critical resource for Dr. Stanwick, serving as a sounding board for strategy from time to time, as well as a mentor for practical issues such as dealing with reluctant non-government agencies.

As summer became fall, the team found itself working on three main fronts. The first was making it as easy and positive an experience as possible for hospitality establishments to comply. They printed up napkins and coasters to distribute to all the restaurants and bars along with the signs the establishments would be expected to post. They developed a kit for each establishment, which included everything from a copy of the bylaw to hints as to how to make it work best. They conducted a series of open forums in which anyone affected by the bylaw was invited to come and ask questions or make suggestions.

The second front was dispelling the myths about the bylaw that were being put forward by opponents. In October, the various bars and pubs that were fighting the change came together to form the Victoria Age of Majority Business Coalition. Co-chairs of the coalition at that point were pub owners Gordon Card and Grant Olson. A few weeks later, Card and Olson said about 50 members of about 90 that would be eligible to join the association had enlisted. The group started making regular presentations to the regional board, predicting economic catastrophe if the board allowed the bylaw to go ahead as planned. At one point, based on self-report figures from 33 members, the group predicted that the hospitality industry would lose $12.5 million a year in revenues, and at least 250 jobs would be lost. No one ever explained how they could make such predictions before the bylaw had even gone into effect.

Chapter 5 - Getting Ready

In early November, it became apparent that the coalition's main thrust would be its political actions at the regional board level, rather than Rittaler's lawsuit. Rittaler's suit had been scheduled to be heard in court beginning on January 4, 1999, the first day of enforcement for the bylaw. But on November 2, he went to court and asked for an indefinite adjournment. "We just couldn't get our work done by that time," he said publicly.

But in fact, the lawsuit was falling apart because of a lack of funds. Arvay didn't come cheap, and the number and complexity of the documents that regional district and health officials had handed over had shown him that a full-blown constitutional lawsuit would undoubtedly be a lengthy and time-consuming process. A full trial and appeal could well have cost as much as $100,000 in legal fees. That was money that Rittaler, as an individual, just didn't have. When he launched the suit, he had expected he would have all sorts of help in paying for it, but that help never materialized.

The tobacco companies and their Courtesy of Choice program agreed to provide media relations, but wouldn't contribute to the lawyers' bills. Rittaler and some of the other militant anti-bylaw operators also requested funding through some of the large breweries. They were turned down there as well. Representatives from the brewery houses explained that they personally didn't have any financial stake in the outcome of the bylaw. They saw no reason to believe that overall beer sales would decrease. Even if they accepted the opponents' arguments of business loss in the beer parlours, they assumed the patrons would simply buy the same amount of beer and take it home or to house parties to consume. As far as the breweries were concerned, it was a non-issue.

The greatest disappointment for Rittaler, though, was how few of his fellow bar operators were prepared to contribute money to help fund the legal challenge. He had figured that as much as $100,000 was an affordable sum if it were divided up among 40 or 50 bar owners. Everyone, he thought, could afford $2,000 or $2,500 for the lawsuit. But only a handful stepped up to the plate. Rittaler was never quite sure why. Some told him they didn't think the economic impact was going to be as severe as he and the other opponents were predicting. Some told him they were worried that if they were too publicly opposed to the bylaw, they'd become targets for additional enforcement from the CRD or even the local police. Others just didn't want to get involved. By the time Rittaler asked for the indefinite adjournment, Arvay had demanded a guarantee that substantially more funding would be available, a guarantee that Rittaler could not give. Throughout the implementation process, the health authorities continued to worry that the lawsuit would at some point be resurrected, but it never was.

In an effort to calm the fears that the coalition was raising, Stevenson arranged to have two of the California bar owners whom they had met on their August trip come to Victoria for a couple of days to talk both to the media and to hospitality establishment owners. One of them, Carol Brookman, who owns a bar called Heinold's First and Last Chance Saloon in Oakland, admitted she'd had all the same fears she was hearing from Victoria establishments when the California state-wide ban was due to take effect in 1998. However, she'd found no trouble enforcing the law, and virtually all of her smoking customers had returned after only a couple of months. As well, she said, there had been secondary benefits she'd never thought of — she herself was healthier, her employees were healthier, absenteeism was down and her fears of a devastating fire in the historic wood structure where her pub was located were much reduced.

The health department team not only produced figures from California showing that no economic disaster had occurred, but also a study that showed bartenders' respiratory health had already improved.

As well, they commissioned one last Angus Reid poll to give the elected board members a final dose of confidence before implementation day. The poll, made public only a few days before Christmas, showed that the proportion of area residents who supported the bylaw had risen even further, and now stood at 65 per cent.

Chapter 5 - Getting Ready

The third task was to take care of internal planning for implementation and enforcement. Much of this work fell to Les Potter, the region's chief environmental health officer. Potter realized the need for sufficient resources to undertake the project, more than could easily be provided through the regional district and health authority. He and Stevenson began working with the health advocacy groups who had so strongly supported the bylaw back in 1996 — groups like the Heart and Stroke Foundation and B.C. Lung Association. Those groups didn't feel that their mandate included enforcement actions, but did include public education. Indeed, they'd been given money from the provincial government to use on campaigns dealing with, among other things, second-hand smoke issues. The groups confirmed that they were prepared to use some of that money to help the CRD provide the necessary educational materials to both the general public and the establishments affected. That, in turn, freed up the regional district money for enforcement work.

Potter found that even small grants from many of these organizations, just $5,000 or $10,000 at time, would provide the money needed for such items as printed napkins and coasters, (see page 139) and for development of a public education campaign around the bylaw. As well, staff needed enhanced training. The original plan had been that, at least for January, every environmental health officer in the region would be taken off his or her regular duties (except for emergencies) and put on bylaw monitoring and enforcement. Shifts would need to be rescheduled so people were freed up to work evenings and weekends, since most activity in bars didn't tend to occur from nine to five, Monday to Friday. A special phone line was designated to take the complaints of non-complying establishments that Stevenson was sure would be phoned in, and staff were assigned to monitor and respond to those calls.

It didn't work out quite that way in practice. When Potter and other senior officials started meeting with the individual EHOs, most were enthusiastic, but a few were decidedly cool to the idea. A couple simply declined to work overtime, for either personal or political reasons. Several simply thought the CRD was moving too far too fast in trying to reach a universal 100 per cent ban in 1999. Others had developed good working relationships with the hospitality establishments in their neighbourhoods when they inspected them for cleanliness, food safety and the like, and didn't want to jeopardize that relationship by having to play the heavy in tobacco enforcement. In the end, Potter concluded that it would be better for all concerned if about half a dozen of the EHOs were never assigned to the tobacco team, not even for those first few weeks.

A similar problem arose with local police forces and RCMP detachments, to Potter's great frustration. He and Dr. Stanwick had discussed an approach by which some of the enforcement money would go to pay overtime costs for uniformed police officers to accompany EHOs and bylaw officers on their visits to the most difficult and potentially violent bars during the first weeks of implementation. There was ample precedent for such a use of officers. The provincially owned auto insurance company, ICBC, regularly paid police overtime costs for roadblocks to catch drinking drivers. Organizers of other special events also often paid for a uniformed police presence. Sometimes local councils even required them to hire full-fledged officers before granting a permit for an event to proceed.

When Potter first broached the subject to local police officials, he found most of them happy to co-operate. In some cases, they even suggested that the teams travel in marked police cruisers to reinforce the appearance of legal authority. A couple of chiefs, however, were less than enthusiastic about the idea, saying they didn't want to set a precedent for helping enforce bylaws that weren't in their mandate.

Somehow in the last days of December, the naysayers won the day. When it was far too late to devise a new plan, the police chiefs told Potter the idea wouldn't work. The EHOs and bylaw enforcement officers would have to go out on their own. They could call the various police departments for help if they

Chapter 5 - Getting Ready

ran into trouble they couldn't handle on their own — just the same as any other citizen could. To this day, Potter still doesn't know just what happened to make the departments change their collective mind.

The health team could also never forget the ongoing political machinations of the bylaw's opponents. Only a week before Christmas, the issue was raised one last time at the Capital regional district board. During the fall, word had got out that the Workers' Compensation Board was ready with its regulations but they wouldn't take effect until January 1, 2000 — one year after the CRD bylaw. The Age of Majority Coalition and other opponents launched a last-ditch heavy lobbying effort to try to persuade board members that the CRD should delay implementing its bylaw until then as well, allowing every place in the province to go smoke-free at the same time. Indeed, they argued, it would be a duplication of effort to have two similar laws, so perhaps the regional district could scrap theirs altogether.

Before making a decision, the regional board invited the WCB to send representatives to its Dec. 17 meeting to explain the WCB position, and how they thought WCB regulations would mesh with a regional bylaw. Policy director Rex Eaton and communications director Scott McCloy were clear. The WCB saw regional or municipal bylaws as complementary to its own regulations, they said. They noted that the WCB's mandate was only to protect workers, not customers or members of the general public. Hence, there were many places where local government would have jurisdiction to ban smoking, but the WCB would not. They cited elevators and the corridors of shopping malls as examples. They also stated that in any case where a local government had a stricter bylaw than the WCB rules, the WCB would still expect any employer to abide by the local rules.

That was enough to convince a majority of the directors. By a vote of nine to seven, the board agreed that the CRD would proceed with its own bylaw and implementation day would remain January 1, 1999 — just two weeks away.

18. Soodeen, Jeanine. "Non-smoking bylaw causing 'nothing but grief,'" Victoria News, Nov. 18, 1998.

19. Ferens, Leslie. "Council snuffs smoke ban; North York reverses stand on controversial butt bylaw," Toronto Star, Jan. 23, 1997.

20. Wanagas, Don. "300 bylaw protesters bring City Hall to a halt," Toronto Sun, March 25, 1997.

21. deMara, Bruce and Moloney, Paul. "Smoking 10% solution. But critics say compromise bylaw won't work either," Toronto Star, April 15, 1997.

22. Field Research Corporation, Survey Highlights, July 1997

23. Cleverly, Bill. "Pub owner predicts smoke ban will fail," Victoria Times-Colonist, January 31, 1998.

24. Paterson, Jody. "Losing battle," Victoria Times-Colonist, March 11, 1998.

25. Westad, Kim. "Hotel owner files lawsuit over ban on smoking," Victoria Times-Colonist, May 9, 1998.

26. Rick Cluff, in interviews with David Laundy and Tony Pollard, Early Edition, CBC Radio, June 13 and 14, 2000.

27. Section 513 (1)(a), Municipal Act, Revised Statutes of British Columbia, 1996, Chapter 323.

We are making Smoking History in 1999

Greater Victoria goes smoke-free in 1999

 for more information call 360-1450

SMOKE FREE BYLAW
Capital Regional District

On Monday, January 4, 1999, the Capital Regional District (CRD) will start enforcing the Clean Air Bylaw. The Bylaw bans smoking in all restaurants, licensed premises (pubs, lounges, caberets), bingo halls and casinos.

The Bylaw is designed to help protect workers and the public from the health risks associated with second hand smoke. Smoking has been banned in other work places and public premises since 1992.

- *Tobacco Smoke Kills:* Smoking will kill approximately 40,000 Canadians this year. In the Capital Region over 300 people die from tobacco related illness. Many are the victims of second hand smoke.
- *Effect on Business:* This Bylaw will not result in a long term loss of business to restaurants, pubs or cabarets. Eighty per cent of residents in the Capital Region do not smoke. Other jurisdictions have found that smoke free environments actually increase the number of non-smoking customers.
- *An Even Playing Field:* This Bylaw applies equally to all businesses in the Capital Region. All businesses are treated fairly and equally under the Bylaw. No one will have an unfair advantage.
- *Ventilation is not the Answer:* The Workers Compensation Board has confirmed that there is no ventilation system currently available that eliminates the dangers of second hand smoke.

For more information regarding the Smoke Free Bylaw, please contact us at 360-1450, or at our INFO-LINE 370-8999

6
Home Sweet Home

"Smoking does seem to have an effect on nursing home admission. It kills most people before they get to that age."
— Prof. John McCallum,
University of Western Sydney

Throughout the debate on the bylaw, controversy had centred on the decision to make all hospitality establishments 100 per cent smoke-free. The main speakers, both for and against, had concentrated on the likely effects on restaurants, bars, pubs, casinos and bingo halls. However, these were not the only places that would feel the impacts of the new bylaw, come 1999. Significant adjustments were also needed in long-term care facilities and nursing homes for the frail elderly. Hospitals themselves weren't a problem; several years earlier all the hospitals in the region had agreed that all smoking should take place outdoors. Extended care hospitals, whose patients were even more frail than those in the nursing homes, had gone smoke-free in 1993.

Nursing homes, of which there were 16 in the region, didn't allow residents to smoke in their individual rooms. That practice had been banned years ago, as much because of the risk of fire as much as the risk of second-hand smoke to staff and other residents. But almost all the nursing homes had some sort of indoor "smoking lounge" for their residents. Those rooms would have to go, just as much as the smoking sections in bars and restaurants would.

As Dr. Stanwick pointed out, it wasn't as if hundreds of people in the nursing homes were going to be affected. Only a small proportion of smokers actually lived long enough to require nursing home accommodation. In most of the homes, the percentage of residents who smoked varied between eight and 10 per cent; in none did it exceed 15 per cent. As well, the length of stay in most of the homes was sufficiently short that, given the 30 months' time for implementation, few of the current residents who smoked would need to change their habits. New residents could be informed of the coming change before they moved in, so it would not be a big surprise for them. Still, some residents and staff were going to see the move to outdoor smoking as a big adjustment. Steps needed to be taken early to ensure as smooth a transition as possible.

Although the nursing home debate had never attracted the public profile of the hospitality industry, some concerns had been raised from quite unlikely sources during the 1995 and 1996 debates about the problems that might arise in nursing homes. The provincial health ministry's own officials who supervised nursing homes were far from happy about the bylaw — even while their New Democrat government was launching its own all-out attack on the tobacco industry. In a memo sent to Stevenson in 1996, the ministry admitted that smoking "constitutes a health hazard to both staff and residents of long-term care facilities," but still proposed that "smoking should be allowed in facilities which have, or are developing, enclosed segregated smoking rooms that are separately ventilated away from the rest of the facility." The ministry put forward the idea that requiring residents to smoke outside would be more of a health hazard than an indoor smoking lounge, and that to ban smoking entirely "would unfairly discriminate against a segment of our population, including the elderly."

Stevenson and Dr. Stanwick had been surprised that a government ministry that was supposed to be promoting health was so willing to compromise the health standards around second-hand smoke. However, they remained firm in their belief that they could work with the nursing home operators to design and develop outdoor spaces that would pose no serious health hazard and would be acceptable to residents and staff.

At the beginning of January 1997, Stevenson pulled together a committee to begin work on the long-term care issue. Along with staff members from the health region, the provincial ministry and the regional district, the committee included representatives from management and staff of long-term care homes, and even a resident from one of the homes, a smoker.

The first meetings of the committee weren't easy. The managers from the homes were worried that a decision to move all smoking outside wouldn't be popular with residents. Some feared the most obstreperous residents would try to sneak cigarettes secretly in their own rooms or in washrooms if they could no longer use the smoking lounges. Some complained about the cost of setting up suitable outdoor facilities when the homes were already thinly stretched for money. They cited the case of one patient who had died at an extended care hospital from pneumonia, apparently brought on or exacerbated by going outside in bad weather to smoke.

Stevenson and her team were sympathetic but implacable. The bylaw would work only if it applied to every workplace in the region, be it a bar, a bingo palace or a nursing home. The point of the meetings, she stressed, was to help the homes find the easiest possible ways of abiding by the bylaw, not to help them find ways to get around it. The health region sent out packages to all the facilities, offering the latest research on the effects of second-hand smoke, as well as details of how the bylaw would work. Stevenson and the team emphasized that it was never too late for someone to quit smoking and realize health benefits from doing so, and that quite a large number of elderly people actually did quit each year, even if they'd been smoking for decades.

The health region agreed to provide not only information, but also all aids possible, such as nicotine gum or patches, for any residents who wanted to take the opportunity to quit. The regional district agreed to provide the services of a building designer to any homes whose managers wanted help in developing their new outdoor smoking areas, or deciding what to do with their former indoor smoking lounges. Stevenson and the team made plans to provide necessary support to management and staff of homes when it was needed, and to work with the homes to develop responses to potential resident aggression.

One by one, the homes came on side. They began to look at areas to be used as outdoor smoking spaces and necessary provisions to provide suitable shelter and heating in winter. Some realized it would probably be easier for residents to make the transition in milder weather, and decided to shut their indoor lounges down in summer, rather than wait for the more blustery days of January. One of the first to make the change was Mount Edward Court, a nursing home located just a few blocks from downtown Victoria. It moved all smoking to an outdoor patio on May 15, 1997, in an effort to allow its smokers to have all summer to get used to the outside location. It also tracked the results of the change, and its experience bolstered the courage of several other operators who were considering how they would cope with the bylaw.

Manager Gerry Anderson concluded that about 10 per cent of Mount Edward Court's residents were "serious smokers" with another five per cent having an occasional cigarette. After a full year's experience, he summarized the home's findings in a report: "Our smokers have accepted the change . . . we have not detected any health problems that could be attributed to the outside location . . . I do not feel that residents' rights have been seriously compromised by the change." In fact, Anderson said at one meeting that he suspected the overall health of smokers at his facility might actually have improved somewhat because of the fresh air they were getting each day.

In 1997, Stevenson started regular surveys of the homes to find out how many had made the change, how well it was working for them, and how far along the others were in their planning. In July 1998, with six months to go until implementation day, she was delighted to find that 10 out of the 16 homes had already banned indoor smoking altogether.

Still, she suspected all was not going to go smoothly. The largest long-term care home in the region, Oak Bay Lodge (OBL),

Chapter 6 - Home, Sweet Home

had not closed its smoking room and was not expressing any intention of doing so.

Dr. Stanwick was aware of Oak Bay Lodge's potential to be difficult, for reasons that had very little to do with the bylaw itself. By the summer of 1998, Oak Bay Lodge had long made clear that it intended to oppose Dr. Stanwick in all ways possible. The 273-bed lodge had, in earlier years, been seen as a leading light in progressive care for the frail elderly. But about 18 months earlier, licensing staff for the health region had begun to find problems in the operations of the lodge — a succession of small complaints that, taken together, reached the point of putting some residents' health and safety at risk. And the licensing division came under Dr. Stanwick's bailiwick: he was the person delegated to make the final decision in the case of a facility accused of breaching minimum standards of health and safety.

At the same time as Stevenson's committee was working on co-operative solutions with other long-term care homes in the region, Oak Bay Lodge management and staff were battling with licensing officers over such issues as the lack of care plans and nutrition plans for residents, and food safety. In the spring of 1997, Dr. Stanwick found it necessary to hold a two-day public hearing into the problems the licensing staff had found. On the basis of the evidence from that hearing, he wrote a judgment that gave the facility five months to get its operations back up to standard.

The licensing staff had been severely critical of the long-time lodge administrator, suggesting Dr. Stanwick should find that she didn't have the necessary temperament or skills to be managing such a facility. Dr. Stanwick wouldn't go that far, but he did agree that the manager needed to take some personal accountability for the facility's shortcomings. That finding infuriated not only the manager but also other members of both the management team and the volunteer board at the lodge. In the spring of 1998, a bitter and hostile appeal of the judgment was held before the provincial Licensing Appeal Board. It ended with a compromise — the lodge admitted all the specific breaches of the regulations and standards, and Dr. Stanwick agreed to remove the references to the manager

Smoke-Free

personally. But Oak Bay Lodge's dislike of Dr. Stanwick and his whole department had not diminished in the intervening months. The lodge's lawyer during the entire process had been Joe Arvay, who was also handling Don Rittaler's lawsuit.

As a result, Dr. Stanwick was disappointed but not unduly surprised when the lodge chose the smoking bylaw as its next battleground with him and the public health authorities.

The lodge's determination to remain outside the bylaw blew up publicly in August 1998. Instead of going directly to the regional board, Oak Bay Lodge's volunteer board went first to the municipal council in the toney suburb of Oak Bay. It wanted the council to take the issue forward to the regional board to try to obtain an exemption from the bylaw for not just OBL but all the long-term care homes. From the first night when the issue came before the council, it was obvious that the OBL board and management had been carefully crafting their political strategy behind the scenes.

Aside from its history with the public health department, Oak Bay Lodge was more frustrated with the bylaw than some of the other nursing homes because of the unique status of its smoking lounge. The lounge had been built as recently as 1992, with a grant of more than $90,000 provided, ironically, by the provincial health ministry. At the time, it had been considered to be state-of-the-art as far as ventilation systems went, with efforts made to vent it separately so the second-hand smoke didn't seep into the rest of the building. (Licensing inspectors and other visitors often said it wasn't as efficient as promised, however, and the smoke could often be smelled in the lobby.) From Dr. Stanwick and Stevenson's viewpoint, the only thing the lounge's existence demonstrated was how far the research into the dangers of second-hand smoke had come in the intervening six years. The lodge's board and management, however, wanted to use the ventilation system as one of their key arguments in favour of the lounge remaining open.

Chapter 6 - Home, Sweet Home

Before approaching Oak Bay council, the lodge board had made sure it had what appeared to be as overwhelming a case as possible. It had a letter from the municipal fire chief, concerned about the possibility of a devastating fire if residents tried to sneak cigarettes in their own rooms once they couldn't use the smoking lounge. (Two similar fires had proven fatal at the lodge several years earlier, before the smoking lounge had been built.) It had a letter from the Workers' Compensation Board agreeing that the lounge met the current WCB standards for air quality — even though those standards were expected to become much stricter within the next 18 months. And it had a thick file of letters from the smoking residents, their friends and family members, waxing eloquent about how much the loss of the smoking room would mean to them.

Some were angry. "Those pompous asses at the CRD want to control everyone's life," wrote one woman whose mother was an OBL resident. "If they don't like something, they expect everyone

The exterior of Oak Bay Lodge (2004).

to do as they do. It would be a real shame to take this last pleasure from those who have smoked all their lives."

But many more expressed a sense of loss. "The smoking room is the one thing that has allowed me to accept OBL as my home and not an institution for the infirm," wrote one resident. "I can sit with my friends and have a cigarette just like it was my living room. It is one semblance of a normal life that I wish to maintain."

That was the whole thrust of OBL's argument. Its key point was that the bylaw still allowed for smoking in private homes and residences, and that the lodge, and similar long-term care facilities, were the "private homes and residences" for their patients, although they were institutional settings. Therefore, the lodge board members argued, the residents should be entitled to smoke within them. With the help of a lawyer on the OBL board, they drew up a specific proposal for an amendment to the bylaw, changing the definition of "residence" to include smoking lounges in facilities that functioned as the homes of individuals.

From the first night the OBL delegation went to Oak Bay council, it was clear they were going to have a champion in the municipality's mayor, who was Oak Bay's representative on the regional board. It was the same Christopher Causton who, then as a restaurant owner, had been one of the bylaw opponents from the hospitality industry at the smoking summit in early 1996. As well, his wife worked at Hospice, the region's facility for the terminally ill, which was located just a few blocks away from Oak Bay Lodge and was also required to make adjustments to comply with the bylaw. It was just another example of how small a city Victoria really was, politically speaking; everyone always seemed somehow to be related to everyone else.

Oak Bay council had no trouble unanimously passing a motion that asked the regional board to reconsider the bylaw only as it applied to long-term care facilities, and Causton promised to bring it as soon as possible to a regional board meeting. Manager Joyce Westcott, board chair Andrew Maxwell and board lawyer Ken Walton went away delighted. They agreed to make a presentation

Chapter 6 - Home, Sweet Home

to the regional board at the same meeting at which Causton made his motion for the exemption.

Less than 48 hours later, news of the moves afoot became public. The *Times-Colonist* and other local news outlets were made aware of the story. Lodge management was happy to have reporters come out to OBL to view the smoking lounge and talk to the two dozen or so residents who were still smokers.[28] The residents were vocal about their fear of the new regime. Somehow, the standard interpretation became that the new bylaw would force them to give up smoking altogether, even though, as the lodge said repeatedly, many of them had been smoking for more than half a century — before the health dangers of tobacco were publicly known. The public perception became that the residents would be forced to quit in the last days of their lives — not as was really the case, that they were just being asked to move outside, in fact only a few metres to an area that many of the smokers already enjoyed during the milder summer weather.

It immediately became obvious to Dr. Stanwick and the team, and also to the strong supporters of the bylaw on the regional board, that, politically, this was going to be a much more difficult fight than the one over bars and restaurants. It was far easier for politicians and the public to sympathize with frail seniors, perhaps war veterans, than with regular folks who just happened to want to keep the traditional smoky taverns where they drank their beer. From the first time the issue arose at the regional board, it was clear that a significant minority of the directors were at least interested in the possibility of exempting the long-term care facilities. The strongest supporters of OBL on the regional board were those directors who were opponents of, or weak supporters of, the bylaw as a whole. Some, like Esquimalt councillor Jim King and Saanich councillor Bob Gillespie, had always been supporters of smokers' rights and had never believed that the regional board should try to enforce the 100 per cent ban. They realized that their arguments were highly unlikely to win the day overall, but saw the long-term care issue as one where they could perhaps drive a wedge into the board to weaken the bylaw. Others, like Causton and Victoria councillor David McLean, had cautiously endorsed the overall bylaw, but were not prepared to push the point with the long-term care issue.

Frank Leonard, who by this time had taken over as mayor of Saanich, also quickly realized the potential for the long-term care issue to cause major political problems for the bylaw as a whole. Citizens were regularly telling him that while they supported the bylaw overall, they just couldn't accept forcing such drastic changes, as they saw them, on 90-year-olds and war veterans. Fair or unfair, he knew that some residents were going to accuse Dr. Stanwick and the health authorities of being out to get Oak Bay Lodge because of the past history surrounding the licensing issues. Leonard realized the first problem was to ensure that an emotional vote wasn't held during the first meeting. He feared that Oak Bay Lodge could win the day, without the board ever having had a chance to look at how it would affect the bylaw as a whole or what alternatives might be developed. His immediate proposal was that the board defer the issue until it had received detailed reports from both Dr. Stanwick and from lawyers McDannold and Stuart. Most of the directors understood the value of that, and the motion to postpone a decision passed easily.

As Dr. Stanwick and the two lawyers began work on the issue, OBL didn't let up on the pressure. They hired a professor of ethics from the University of Victoria to write a report on the ethical problems that might be caused by imposing the bylaw in long-term care facilities. Dr. Eike Kluge was probably B.C.'s best-known medical ethicist, but the area of specialization where he'd made his name was that of the ethics of modern medical technology, such as cloning and gene manipulation. However, on September 4, Kluge forwarded to Westcott his three-page report to be sent on to CRD board members.

"I cannot escape the conclusion that such an action would be indefensible from an ethical perspective," wrote Kluge. He agreed that smoking is harmful to health, but wasn't even prepared to admit without qualification that second-hand smoke itself posed a health hazard.

Chapter 6 - Home, Sweet Home

In any case, he said, it would be unreasonable to close the smoking lounge because "Oak Bay Lodge functions as the home of the residents . . . to interfere with their smoking is to interfere with their right to do as they please in their own home. This is an unacceptable intrusion into their private lives." Interestingly, Kluge didn't mention the fact that the residents were already banned from smoking in their individual rooms, a place that could be considered even more their own home than a room near the front door. Neither were they allowed to smoke in the dining room or other public areas of the facility. All that the bylaw would actually do would be moving the one spot where residents were allowed to smoke from one place to another, but this perception was never reflected in Kluge's analysis.

Most of Kluge's other arguments appeared to be based on the premise that residents were to be forced to give up smoking altogether, not just to move the place where they had their cigarettes. He suggested that residents were going to be "deprived . . . of the possibility of meeting their social interactive needs" through associating with their friends while smoking. They were, he wrote, going to be "required, without choice, to give up an addiction without being offered an effective and guaranteed way of achieving release from that addiction." They were going to lose "the right to make decisions for themselves, using their own values."

Kluge commented on the harm-reduction model for heroin addicts, wherein they received help through needle exchanges and even controlled injection sites "so as to minimize the collateral harm of the addiction itself." A similar approach for the smoking residents would be to allow them to maintain the smoking lounge, he argued — although just as good an argument could have been made for saying the outdoor smoking area would be the equivalent of a "controlled injection site" for nicotine addicts.

At one point Kluge did discuss the idea of moving smoking outside, writing that "I would also venture to say that being forced to go outside, into a different environment, would alter the socializing aspect of smoking so profoundly that the social and mental health needs of the affected residents would be impaired." He never gave an explanation of why he thought that would be so.

However, the paragraph that most upset McDannold and Stuart was one in which Kluge suggested that moving smoking outside at OBL might be prohibited under Canada's Charter of Rights and Freedoms. He argued that since only those who were old and frail were admitted to the facility, it would be discrimination on the basis of age and disability to require them to smoke outdoors when other citizens could smoke indoors in the privacy of their own homes. This was a particularly worrisome argument for the lawyers because the lawsuit launched by Don Rittaler was, at that time, still expected to go to trial within the next few months, and one of Rittaler's main arguments was that the bylaw was contrary to the rights guaranteed Canadian citizens under the Charter. If the board were to agree that long-term care facilities deserved an exemption based on Charter rights, McDannold, for one, was convinced that the region's defence in the court case would be substantially weakened.

Analytically, Dr. Stanwick found Kluge's argument to be full of false assumptions and contradictions in logic. Legally, McDannold and Stuart saw it as a nightmare. But politically, they were aware that it gave fresh ammunition to those regional board members who wanted, at best, to grant OBL an exemption and, at worst, to weaken the entire bylaw. Kluge had a good reputation among the public, the media and opinion leaders in the community. It was going to be tough to go up against his opinion stating that what the board was doing was unethical.

Methodically, Dr. Stanwick began to put together a report to the regional board in which they would challenge the arguments made both by the lodge board itself and by Kluge in his report. By the end of September, they had a preliminary presentation ready. They outlined the efforts they'd made to help long-term care facilities come into compliance with the bylaw and noted how well most of the other nursing homes were doing at meeting requirements. What, they wondered aloud, made OBL so different that it couldn't

Chapter 6 - Home, Sweet Home

successfully follow the same path as the others? They stressed that while OBL met current WCB regulations, those regulations were poised to change on January 1, 2000, so the facility was likely to get only one year's respite anyway. Overall, there were too many issues that needed to be examined for the regional board to make a precipitate decision. They asked for a further extension to prepare more detailed reports on "the legal, health and ethical issues" that had been identified. The regional directors agreed. It would be mid-December before regional directors would debate the issue.

The next step was to prepare a more detailed report, trying to rebut Kluge's points one by one. Dr. Stanwick and the team reviewed literature from other jurisdictions and from legal cases from across North America, trying to learn as much as possible about other ways of tackling the question of "smokers' rights" in the nursing home. They talked to other health authorities across the country to see what policies had been put in place elsewhere. They talked to the operators of other nursing homes within the region to try to ensure that the shift in policy had not caused them any catastrophic difficulties. They did find that one other home had been forced to evict a resident because of his persistent (and dangerous) habit of trying to sneak cigarettes in his room. However, the facility's operators quickly reassured Stevenson that this was not primarily a problem with the bylaw — the resident in question had been posing problems long before that because of his desire to smoke in his own room and not in the designated smoking lounge even when the lounge was indoors.

With the results of all this research in hand, Dr. Stanwick put together a lengthy and detailed report to be circulated to the regional board. In it, he stressed that even though a long-term facility is the residents' "home," "numerous aspects of the lives of long-term care residents are subject to public scrutiny, rules and policies" — not just their smoking behaviour. When someone moves into Oak Bay Lodge, he noted, they have to share a room, "give up hobbies that cannot be accommodated within the limited confines of their new quarters, give up any pet they may have had, minimize their personal wardrobe and downsize entertainment devices and furniture to fit the modest size of their new accommodations." In fact, he noted, these rules differ only in degree from health and safety rules that apply to the entire community and often deal with issues of what someone can, or cannot do, in their own home.

He admitted there could occasionally be a problem with inclement weather making it difficult for the frail to venture outside, but noted that Victoria is very fortunate in its climate. This would likely be a problem for only a few days each year; smokers would probably be prevented from smoking for no longer, in total, than was already the case based on the rules OBL had in place governing its smoking lounge.

He noted that the literature showed the U.S. had not considered the right to smoke one of the rights that nursing home residents should be guaranteed, and that many long-term care facilities were actually going fully smoke-free, not even allowing smoking outside on the grounds. He acknowledged the risk of a catastrophic fire in any nursing home, but stressed that the literature "shows that the occurrence of these fires is not associated with having a designated smoking area, be it indoors or outdoors. Rather, the problem arises with a confused or obstinate resident who wants to smoke in their own room, rather than go to a smoking lounge of any description."

Dr. Stanwick knew that this was a decision that would have to be made by the politicians. His final recommendation was simply "that this report be received for information" before the board made a decision.

While Dr. Stanwick and the team were preparing the report, an unlikely alliance was springing up among the bylaw opponents. Oak Bay Lodge was suddenly found to be a member of the Age of Majority Coalition, alongside the bar and pub owners. Board chair Andrew Maxwell turned up at some coalition meetings, and the coalition embraced OBL with open arms. On the surface, it was obvious the coalition would enjoy the added public support that was being shown to the veterans and other seniors at OBL.

Chapter 6 - Home, Sweet Home

The more cynical of the bylaw supporters wondered if this wasn't a carefully considered strategy aimed at helping both groups. Winning an exemption for the long-term care homes would, as McDannold and Stuart warned, weaken the court case and perhaps allow the bars and pubs to win their exemptions as well, this time in court.

Dr. Stanwick's report was circulated more than a week before the board meeting was scheduled, and Oak Bay Lodge hastily sent its copy back to Dr. Kluge for his reply. Thus, when the board met on November 25, they had before them both Dr. Stanwick's report and the debating points back from the other side.

Kluge took strenuous exception to the suggestion that restrictions on smoking should be considered in the same light as other restrictions imposed on persons entering long-term care facilities. "To the best of my understanding," he wrote, "hobbies are not addictions, as neither are pets. Smoking is an addictive lifestyle that penetrates to every aspect of the individual's life on a somatic as well as a psychological basis." Therefore, he argued, it should be worthy of greater consideration by the authorities.

Dr. Stanwick figured that argument should be turned around exactly 180 degrees. After all, he said, pets and hobbies have been found in most cases to enhance the health of people, especially those in institutions. Entire pet-therapy programs have been developed as well as clubs and classes for a variety of hobbies. Would it not make greater sense to offer more protection for factors in a resident's life that would enhance their health, rather than one that would harm not only themselves but also others around them?

Kluge didn't like comparisons with other jurisdictions in either Canada or the U.S. Other Canadian jurisdictions "may have made errors" in deciding how to tackle the problem, he suggested, and "the U.S. is notorious in ethical circles as having the most unethical health care system in the Western world." (Most such criticisms of the U.S. system are actually aimed at the extreme difference in access for the affluent and the poor, not the rights of those in institutions.)

Again, however, McDannold and Stuart were the ones most distressed by Kluge's response. At least half of the report dealt solely with the Charter of Rights and Freedoms and how Kluge believed that the bylaw violated the Charter for long-term care homes. Moving smoking outside would, he said, be "a curtailment of liberties and rights" of the residents, and such curtailment under the charter can occur only if it can be proved to be "demonstrably justified in a free and democratic society." He wrote that "the objective in undertaking any such limitation must be sufficiently important and pressing in a free and democratic society as to warrant overriding constitutionally protected rights and freedoms." Some jurisdictions, he noted, had ruled nicotine addiction to be a disability, and society was required to make all possible efforts to accommodate disabilities. He suggested that OBL's indoor smoking lounge was a reasonable accommodation and therefore should be required to be allowed under the Charter. As with David Sweanor's report years earlier, Dr. Stanwick and his team were prepared to argue that even if "nicotine addiction" were to be considered a disability, it could be better and more safely accommodated through the provision of nicotine in other forms, such as patches.

Laid out so clearly in Kluge's report, McDannold and Stuart saw that here again was the thin edge of the wedge. If the board were to agree to an exemption based on such an argument, the court challenge for the whole bylaw would be at significant risk. After all, how could you argue that smokers at OBL were any more or less addicted (or disabled, if you wanted to call it that) than smokers at Joe's Bar and Tavern? If one group was entitled to protection under the Charter, why wouldn't the other be? If one class of business (the operators of long-term care homes) gained an exemption under the Charter, why should another class of business equally likely to suffer not be entitled to the same changes?

The issue again came back to the clause of the Municipal Act under which the bylaw was permitted. The only grounds on which such regulation could occur were those of "health." Changes based

Smoking seniors deserve right to puff indoors

If you've been smoking for the past 50 years, you're unlikely to quit now

THERE'S A FAMOUS joke about the condemned man, tied to a post and waiting to be shot by a firing squad, who's asked if he wants a last cigarette. "No thanks," he says. "It's bad for my health."

The Capital Regional District might ponder this today as councillors debate the weighty issue of whether to allow smoking rooms in seniors' lodges, and specifically the Oak Bay Lodge.

About 25 seniors there are fighting to keep their ventilated smoking room, in the face of a CRD bylaw banning smoking everywhere but in private residences as of Jan. 1.

Sure, there are health concerns. Smoking can kill you, and in an ideal society, nobody would smoke. But there are other concerns, too.

If you've been smoking for the past 50 years and somehow made it to age 70 or more, you're not likely to quit now.

For most of the lifetime of seniors, smoking was actively promoted as an individual stress reliever and a social activity. Why deprive seniors of that individual and social pleasure in the twilight of their lives?

Seniors forced to go outside in blustery weather for a puff are at greater risk of pneumonia or flu than tobacco-related illnesses.

Finally, seniors are consenting adults. If they want to smoke, and no one else is harmed, surely that's their business.

Our seniors will be gone from us soon enough. Let's not bury them in red tape while they're still alive.

Times-Colonist, November 1998

on Charter rights, or on anything except strictly health grounds, would leave the entire bylaw open to a challenge of being ultra vires — beyond the regional board's jurisdiction to pass. The lawyers wrote the board a strongly worded legal opinion stressing the risk to the entire bylaw, should board members give in to the OBL lobby.

In retrospect, Oak Bay Lodge would have done better not to tie its cause so clearly to that of other bylaw opponents. The lodge's obvious affiliation with the defiant bars and pubs and their insistence on use of the Charter, similar to Rittaler's court case, gave the bylaw's supporters plenty of ammunition. The lodge would probably have garnered more sympathy from regional board members had it said straight out that the board had every legal right to insist on outdoor smoking at OBL, and appealed for a break for its aged smokers on purely humanitarian grounds.

The days leading up to the key vote on the OBL exemption were tense ones for the bylaw's supporters. In their heads, they repeatedly tallied which board members were sure to support standing pat, which ones were sure to support an exemption, which ones couldn't be considered a guaranteed vote by either side. As the date for the meeting became closer, Leonard and other bylaw supporters believed they would have enough support to carry the day, but it was too close for them to be sure. Bylaw opponents were also publicly cautiously optimistic that, at the least, the board would agree to the long-term care exemption.

The meeting to decide the issue was long and tortuous. It was the last board meeting at which changes could be made before the bylaw would go into effect on January 1. The Oak Bay Lodge delegation and the hospitality industry coalition were in the audience to make their final presentations, pleading for and demanding changes. Maxwell and the rest of the OBL delegation again stressed the ethical issues as outlined by Kluge. Maxwell insisted that workers would be protected from second-hand smoke because they'd never have to go into the lounge while smoking was taking place; the residents could cope by themselves. No one, he

Chapter 6 - Home, Sweet Home

insisted, would ever need to be subjected to second-hand smoke except the smokers among the residents.

In the end it fell, as it so often had in the past, to Leonard to make the key motion. He moved that the bylaw remain unchanged. Leonard had carefully studied the points of law made by McDannold and Stuart, and he stressed the legal difficulties likely to arise if the board started trying to grant exemptions to one group or another.

"We passed this bylaw with a philosophy based on public health," he noted. "We are not trying to pick and choose among the groups to whom it will apply." He reminded the board that Dr. Stanwick had already said enforcement wouldn't start against OBL immediately, that the health authorities were quite prepared to wait for milder weather for the lodge to make the switch.

Not surprisingly, the lodge had strong advocates on the regional board. Esquimalt council member Jim King described a decision to force OBL to comply as "unethical and unjustified."

When the vote was finally taken, however, Leonard's motion passed, by a vote of nine to seven. It was the closest vote of any ever taken by the regional board on the smoking bylaw issue. Even before the room was cleared, OBL was making it clear they still weren't about to accept the decision. Maxwell said he didn't think the board had understood the full impact of what it had done, saying lodge management would still try to persuade board members to change their minds.

OBL's next strategy was to try to get the issue taken back to the local councils that made up the regional board. The lodge hoped that if enough council members backed the exemption, they would order their delegates to the CRD to vote the wishes of the majority of council, rather than their personal beliefs. Oak Bay, where the lodge was located, had already come on side. Jim King agreed to take the issue back to Esquimalt council; David McLean did the same for Victoria. In both cases, the other members of council were voting with no real understanding of the background of the issue or of the legal implications of any change. King and McLean both got support for their stands from their councils relatively easily. Causton agreed to try to bring the matter back to the full regional board for reconsideration.

It still wasn't enough. By the time the issue was back before the board it was January, and the bitter battles over implementation in bars and restaurants were already breaking out. Regional board members could see more clearly the need to hold firm in the wake of such overt defiance, and realized that any willingness to make changes would be seized as ammunition by the other side. It was also clear to them that the struggles to enforce compliance in the hospitality industry were likely to be severe, thus it was going to be months, at best, before anyone had the time or inclination to force OBL to abide by the bylaw. The motion to hold firm on the bylaw passed even more easily than it had the month before.

Leonard also realized that some tactful compromise was going to have to be worked out for OBL. He watched the high drama unfold as the enforcement officers issued tickets in the bars and bingo halls. He led the politicians in making changes to the bylaw to hold defiant bar and pub operators responsible for what went on in their establishments. He realized that the media spectacle of the bars and pubs would be nothing compared to what would happen the first time an enforcement officer tried to write out a ticket for an 87-year-old war veteran sitting in his separately ventilated smoking room at OBL.

"I was prepared to go to the wall on the issue of the restaurants, the bars and the pubs," Leonard says now in retrospect. "But you just couldn't go to the wall on the issue of those senior citizens and the dying."

He began to consider a compromise that could satisfy OBL without risking the whole bylaw, and held quiet behind-the-scenes conversations with McDannold and Stuart.

By the time OBL returned to the fray, it was May. The bylaw had been strengthened for the hospitality industry to ensure

Chapter 6 - Home, Sweet Home

that defiant operators, not just individual smokers, could face penalties. Rittaler's lawsuit was showing no signs of proceeding. Summer was on its way, and still OBL was not ready to move all its smoking outside.

This time, though, the lodge asked for something much simpler: not an amendment to the bylaw, but just a policy change to ensure the bylaw still wouldn't be enforced in their case. This time, Leonard agreed that would be a reasonable compromise. The bylaw wouldn't be changed, but as a matter of discretion, the board would agree to allow long-term care facilities to apply for special permits. A facility that received a permit wouldn't be subject to enforcement proceedings as long as it strictly maintained the conditions of the permit. McDannold stressed that this was an idea that could work, as long as it involved only the use of discretion and not any formal change to the bylaw. Legislation and court decisions allowed a council or regional board to exercise discretion in deciding how strenuously to enforce one of its own laws, provided that discretion wasn't used maliciously or unreasonably. When Leonard agreed with the compromise, the board, long exhausted with the fight over the long-term care homes, readily went along with it.

In the end, Oak Bay Lodge was the only facility that ever bothered applying for the permit. Enforcement action has still never been taken against it.

---

28. Bell, Jeff. "Seniors fight for their smoking room," Victoria Times-Colonist, August 19, 1998.

7

The Big Day

"The best thing about the future is that it only comes one day at a time."
— *Abraham Lincoln*

New Year's Day, 1999. No time remained for preparation. The health team had announced it would not begin enforcement until January 4, the first Monday of the new year, so as not to begin on a weekend, especially one full of New Year's Eve parties and celebrations. From all of the conversations with operators, the team's best guess was that most of the restaurants would comply with little difficulty. Many of the bars and pubs were also expected to go along with the new rules, especially those attached to higher-class hotels and located in the city's better neighbourhoods. But they knew they were going to face a significant amount of rebellion. Some of the members of the Freedom of Choice Coalition had made that abundantly clear.

Coalition members had also made no secret of the fact that — covertly or overtly — management and staff at those bars would support the actions of defiant patrons. If Gordon Card and Grant Olson had led the coalition's political forays, another bar manager named Brian Mayzes had made it clear he'd be leading the active rebellion. Mayzes himself was a non-smoker and a diabetic, but, along with most of his patrons at the working-class Esquimalt Inn, he was passionately devoted to the cause of smokers' rights.

From what they had learned of opposition tactics in California and other jurisdictions, they expected that the non-conforming establishments would try to make it appear that the bylaw was essentially unenforceable and that the defiance was extremely widespread. That would then be used as a rationale to return to the regional board to try to get the bylaw abandoned or amended. Thus it was important from the beginning that the health team get the message out to the community that most establishments were in fact abiding by the bylaw, that it could be and would be enforced, and that the long-promised level playing field would in fact be established.

On New Year's Eve, Dr. Stanwick sent out the last pre-implementation "fact sheet" to the media, focusing again on the health benefits of the new legislation and the "level playing field" that would be provided for all hospitality establishments. Over the long weekend, he conducted his last pre-enforcement media interviews, making the same points again. Even though teams weren't out in the field, over the weekend the information started filtering through to public health about places where defiance was already overt. To no one's surprise, the most blatant was Mayzes' Esquimalt Inn, which had posted its own signs. Instead of the No-Smoking Zone signs provided by the CRD, the ones there read: "This is a smoking establishment. Enter at your own risk." In fact, the air quality at the Esquimalt Inn and many of the other defiant establishments decreased substantially the first day the bylaw went into effect. Previously, almost all operators had made at least some effort to comply with the former rules and have a smoking section and a non-smoking section. Now they weren't bothering to do even that much. The air throughout the Esquimalt Inn was blue with smoke.

By January 4, everyone on the enforcement teams was on edge. Reports from the community had confirmed that their job would be difficult. Still, they all agreed they should stay with the plan they'd developed. From day one, they would pressure bars that were deliberately disobeying the law, especially those that were bragging about their defiance in the community and to the media. However, Dr. Stanwick decided that inspectors would also visit restaurants and bars where they believed they'd find no problems. Part of that strategy was to give the environmental health officers (EHOs) a break; they were going to have a tough time being thrust into a purely enforcement role; it was important they got to see that in many establishments the bylaw was being obeyed without problems. Part of it was also to assure these premises that their compliance and good behaviour was appreciated. And part was to provide Dr. Stanwick with first-hand evidence that hundreds of establishments were obeying the bylaw to

Chapter 7 - The Big Day

counteract "unenforceability" arguments that were made publicly by opponents.

They knew that they had to hit the most openly defiant premises early and firmly so no one would get the impression they were nervous about enforcing at such places. The Esquimalt Inn was the obvious first target, and the first visit was scheduled for Tuesday afternoon, January 5. Dr. Stanwick, administrative assistant Wendy Boyd and Stevenson decided they should all be part of the team that made the first visit there. They were curious to see what would happen in the first tough enforcement visits, but they also felt it important to send the message that they were strongly backing up the environmental health officers and bylaw enforcement officers. In part, based on the advice of the Esquimalt police department, the afternoon was chosen for the first visit because the crowd was likely to be somewhat smaller and more sober than later in the day, and thus the atmosphere perhaps a little less highly charged. The police were less likely to be busy during the afternoon and could therefore provide better and quicker backup should it be needed.

The afternoon visit proved to be more of a symbolic gesture than an effective enforcement technique. Not only did the team grow to six before arriving, but three Esquimalt police officers also turned up, perhaps out of curiosity. The team did note the absence of proper signs and wrote Mayzes the necessary ticket for that. They didn't try to ticket individual smokers, but talked to customers and staff members to try to get a feel for how enforcement activities would play out. They concluded that the bartenders and wait staff were more overtly hostile than many of the customers. Somewhat reluctantly, their other conclusion was that it was important to return that evening when the bar was busier — as Mayzes and the staff were implying that the team wouldn't dare to come then.

"We needed to show them right off that they weren't going to get away with anything," Stevenson remembers. The team that went that night was smaller. It was agreed that Dr. Stanwick shouldn't be along; he was seen as the public face of bylaw enforcement; his very presence was enough to increase hostilities.

Smoke-Free

Stevenson returned along with a member of her staff and Miles Drew, the head of bylaw enforcement for the CRD.

When they arrived about 8 p.m., they found, as they expected, that the bar was much busier and louder than it had been earlier and the atmosphere even more smoke-filled. What they had not expected was that Mayzes wasn't there; his shift was over for the day. For the first time, but not the last, they realized that Mayzes actually had a calming influence on the place. He was verbal and strenuous in his opposition to the bylaw, but he always somehow managed to keep his crowd's behaviour more or less in check. Without his presence, the crowd was much rowdier and more prone to abuse and violence.

The team had discussions with the bartender on duty, but he told them he had no intention of telling the patrons to stop smoking. Instead, an announcement came over the loudspeaker that "The CRD is here" and that patrons might want to put out their cigarettes. As Stevenson and the others easily guessed, the announcement had exactly the opposite effect. All attention was focused on them, and they were greeted by a chorus of shouts and boos. One patron got up from his seat and belligerently started goose-stepping up and down the aisles between the tables, yelling "Heil Hitler! Heil Hitler!" The team hastily called police from a cell phone and asked for urgent backup. Officers were there within three minutes.

With the backup available, the team figured they should issue a ticket to at least one of the defiant patrons, and chose a man who had deliberately continued to smoke directly in front of them in the midst of all the clamor. However, they found they again needed police help, because the man refused to give them his name or identification information so that they could actually write him a ticket. It took the police officers to explain that he was legally required to provide the information and that the other option would be a criminal charge for obstructing a peace officer.

Eventually the man, Geoff Jackson, did agree to give the police officer his name; it was the first in a series of ongoing

Chapter 7 - The Big Day

confrontations the team would have with Jackson, who proved to be one of the most defiant individual smokers in the region.

The enforcement team breathed a sigh of relief as they left the smoky atmosphere of the inn for the cold air of the parking lot. It hadn't been easy or pleasant, but they realized it could have been much worse. The thing that worried Stevenson the most had been the urgent need for police backup. They were going to be at a constant disadvantage because of the last-minute decision of the police to respond only after trouble had broken out rather than agreeing to go along with the teams in a proactive role.

It was obvious that in the more difficult bars, one team member was always going to have to be ready to dial 911 to summon backup. The various police departments were also going to have to be notified of who was going to be heading out in their municipalities each night. Stevenson didn't much want to think about what might happen if enforcement troubles broke out when the local police officers were already tied up at a major crime or disaster. However, the rapid-response system was all they'd managed to negotiate, so they were just going to have to make the best of it.

Even though they didn't want to be a regular part of the bylaw enforcement team, the chiefs of several police forces weren't too keen about the health department employees enforcing it on their own either. They questioned whether the EHOs were actually legal "peace officers" with the power to write tickets. Had the chiefs prevailed in that argument, the ability of the regional district and health department to enforce the bylaw would have been severely compromised. There were too few full-time bylaw enforcement officers working for the district to cover the number of establishments needing visits during the first weeks of implementation. The health department had therefore chosen to put nearly every EHO on the enforcement team for those critical initial weeks. Eventually a legal opinion put the issue to rest. The EHOs were indeed peace officers with all the rights and obligations that entailed.

Smoke-Free

As the reports began to come in from the enforcement teams during the first two weeks, it became clear that the Esquimalt Inn was not the only place where management and staff were actively encouraging patrons to defy the bylaw and to verbally abuse the enforcement teams. The first Friday evening of enforcement, a team of six RCMP officers was needed to provide backup at a bar in the working-class suburb of Langford when it appeared that the patrons were ready to riot at the first sign of the team. Other enforcement teams reported regular instances of heckling, harassment and shouting when they visited some of the publicly rebellious bars.

Although Dr. Stanwick and Frank Leonard didn't go out on the enforcement ventures, they weren't immune from the abuse. Many of the bylaw opponents still saw them as the architects of what was going on, and realized that the enforcement teams were little more than foot soldiers in what they perceived as a just war. Both Leonard and Dr. Stanwick started getting phone calls at home in the early hours of the morning, often just as the bars were closing down. The callers would rage about the unfairness of the bylaw, accuse each of them of various political agendas, and occasionally resort to threats of harm or death. Dr. Stanwick was advised by more than one caller that he should return to the practice of clinical medicine and treat worthwhile diseases such as cystic fibrosis if he wanted to remain healthy. Others told him to leave town or else.

The calls exasperated them, and occasionally worried them, but neither ever thought of backing off enforcement because of them. Leonard in fact became more convinced that it was important he remain the politician leading the charge, because it was obvious he had the least to lose politically. Callers would rant and rave and tell him that they were never going to vote for him again. When he asked questions about their whereabouts, he'd realize that they lived not in Saanich but in Langford or Colwood or Esquimalt, had never been able to vote for him before, and were very unlikely to ever be able to vote for him — or against him — in the future. It would, he figured, have been much tougher to take those calls if

Chapter 7 - The Big Day

you were a mayor or council member who lived in a municipality where strong opposition from the anti-bylaw lobby might actually cost you your job in the next election.

Dr. Stanwick found himself frequently besieged by abusive calls because at the same time as the smoking bylaw was coming into effect, he was in the middle of two other major controversies. He was about to conduct a licensing hearing to consider shutting down an eating disorder clinic that had previously been featured in the most positive terms on top U.S. talk and news television shows. He was also battling with environmentalists who wanted him to ban the spraying of a biological insecticide against a threat of gypsy moths. He was only half-kidding when he considered putting a new message on his office answering machine: "If you're calling in a death threat and it's about the smoking bylaw, press one; if it's a result of my stance on the Montreux Clinic, press two; if it's due to my not banning the gypsy-moth spray program, press three."

The enforcement had been underway for exactly a week when the bylaw opponents first went public about what they described as a "devastating" loss of business in many bars and some restaurants.[29] The manager of a 400-seat beer parlours in Victoria said his business was down an average of 40 per cent — 20 per cent on weekends and 50 per cent during the week (with exactly one weekend on which to base his comments). Other pub owners described business losses ranging from 25 to 60 per cent. In Esquimalt, the manager of the Tudor House pub, chief rival to the Esquimalt Inn, said he'd already cut the number of staff hours per week by 16 because business was down as much as $1,000 a day. Ironically, most of the bars complaining the most loudly were ones which were defying the bylaw and still allowing smoking in their premises.

When the *Times-Colonist* conducted its own mini-survey, it discovered that several other bars, which were complying with the bylaw, had found business hadn't changed or had even improved.[30] At the Bird of Paradise pub on the northern edge of town, staff said they had seen numbers of new customers in the first week of the bylaw. Several, they said, had commented that they were happy now to be able to come to the pub, something they previously had not been able to do because of sensitivities or allergies to cigarette smoke. Several bartenders and other hospitality staff also commented that they already felt their health had improved, now that they didn't have to spend eight hours a day in a smoky fog.

From an enforcement point of view, the second week wasn't all that much different from the first. With more calls coming in on the complaint line and more reports in from the enforcement teams, it became clearer that about half of the region's bars were the hotbeds of resistance, whose employees were openly or covertly supporting patrons' insistence on continued smoking. The atmosphere remained extremely hostile in those bars when the enforcement teams came to call, and teams called for police backup several more times. On the other hand, almost no problems had been found in any restaurants, and numerous bars were complying satisfactorily and apparently without difficulties.

The number of problem establishments, though, prompted Stevenson and Dr. Stanwick to provide extra training to their enforcement teams. Sergeant Darren Laur was the Victoria city police department's expert on the use of force and on handling particularly difficult situations. He came in and gave the enforcement officers tips on such techniques as "verbal judo," in which nothing but words are used to defuse potentially violent episodes. As well, he offered tips on how to avoid being placed in a physically dangerous situation, such as keeping a safe distance away from the most hostile patrons.

Two weeks after enforcement began, the dissenters went public again. They called a news conference at the Esquimalt Legion, another of the most blatantly defiant establishments. The air in the legion was so smoky that some of the reporters began coughing and getting headaches even during the short time of the presentations. The Freedom of Choice Coalition had brought

Chapter 7 - The Big Day

the reporters together to announce that it was again planning a court challenge of the bylaw, provided it could find enough in donations to pay a lawyer to take the case. Mayzes said the court challenge was essential because of the downturn in business that the bylaw was causing.

Thursday's Sports Bar — the bar that would later struggle on its own to take on the bylaw in court — said its business was down at least 25 per cent during the first two weeks of the bylaw. Even though the bar wasn't trying to enforce the bylaw, said manager Stewart Logan, the thought of being fined for smoking was driving the patrons away. Logan and Mayzes admitted that even were they to win such a court case, they might end up having to fight it all over again one year later when the planned Workers' Compensation Board rules came into effect.

But Logan made no secret of the fact that he thought the WCB shouldn't be interfering in the issue either. He said it should be up to workers to decide whether they were willing to work in a smoky atmosphere. Asked by reporters whether the same logic should apply to other dangerous situations, such as working in asbestos-laden buildings where working is clearly banned, Logan agreed it should. If workers were willing to go there to take a job, he said, it shouldn't be up to government to say they couldn't. One reporter considered asking whether this philosophy should apply even to sites contaminated by radioactivity, but restrained himself. "It would have been too much like shooting fish in a barrel," the reporter recalled later. "Logan had made it clear that profit, not health, was the motive for his group."

One of the only bylaw opponents who ever produced hard numbers was Malcolm Palmer, the manager of the Elephant and Castle, a pub-style restaurant in the largest downtown shopping mall. Palmer told the news conference that in the two weeks since the bylaw went into effect, the total number of customers in his restaurant had actually risen. So had the sales of food, up $1,327 over the average of the same two-week period for the previous three years. But what he found devastating economically, he said, was that the sales of alcohol had decreased by more than $5,000 in the same time. It was exactly the same argument as had been predicted by economist John de Wolf in his study for the Lower Mainland bars four years earlier.

The same day the coalition announced its plans, one downtown café announced it would be closing its doors, citing the bylaw as a key factor in the decision. The owner of Johnny's Café admitted that business had been steadily declining in the six years she'd owned the place, but said the bylaw was the final straw.[31] An old-style diner with the original look of the 1950s, Johnny's had been known downtown as a place to go for a coffee and a smoke. Many of its customers were older people who had grown up in the era when a smoky atmosphere was a normal part of a diner. Johnny's was one of only two businesses that ever cited the bylaw as a reason for actually closing their doors.

Neither the politicians nor the enforcement teams were happy about the extensive media coverage of the businesses claiming to be suffering such significant losses, nor about the ongoing confrontations between enforcement personnel and patrons and bar staff in some of the pubs. However, they remained convinced that this was to be expected in the initial shakedown period. Bar managers and staff would realize that the bylaw — and its enforcement — were in Victoria to stay and the vehement opposition would gradually dwindle away.

It was the end of January before they began to fear they were wrong.

By that time the team had divided the non-complying establishments into two groups. There were what Stevenson called the "continuous non-compliers." They were the bars which, on the surface, showed signs of co-operating with the bylaw. If not friendly, staff and management were polite and civil when enforcement patrols showed up at their establishments. They escorted the teams around the premises. They didn't post any rude or defiant signs of their own, and they didn't make announcements over the loud-speaker systems that might incite

Chapter 7 - The Big Day

the patrons to abuse the staff or have a riot. They didn't object when the teams went to give out tickets to individuals who were smoking. They tried to calm down unruly patrons, and warned them that they did indeed have to give their names to bylaw enforcement officers. On the surface, they seemed to be going along with the bylaw, albeit reluctantly. But when the team would go back two or three or four days later, there were always just as many people smoking as there had been the time before. Clearly the management of those establishments was taking no initiatives to ensure compliance except at those precise moments when the enforcement teams were on the premises. Of the 50 or so non-compliant bars in the region, about half fell into that category.

The other half were what Stevenson called the "actively defiant," and they were the ones the teams dreaded visiting. The actively defiant bars were usually sprinkled with literature encouraging patrons to defy the bylaw and to come to a variety of meetings and fundraisers for purposes of opposing it. Every time a team went into an actively defiant bar, the message would come over the loudspeaker system: "The CRD is here." Some bartenders added, "You might want to put your cigarettes out," but the patrons never did. What they wanted to do was to find the enforcement teams and yell at them, berate them, and offer as much resistance possible without actually getting arrested.

What worried Dr. Stanwick and Stevenson as January became February was that the active defiance wasn't diminishing, as they had hoped. Rather, the battle lines seemed to be hardening. The hostility of the bartenders, waiters and patrons in those actively defiant bars was, if anything, increasing. The verbal abuse was getting worse. Those bars appeared determined to show the regional board that the bylaw was never going to be enforceable, that the protests and "civil disobedience" (as they called it) were so widespread and profound that the board and the health authorities could never win. It reached the point where every evening Stevenson worried she would be awakened in the middle of the night by a phone call informing her that one of her staff had been assaulted, injured and was in the hospital.

Her fears worsened in early February when she received a report of the wildest evening yet, this time at Thursday's bar. Thursday's had been a problem bar from the beginning. The Logan brothers, who owned and managed the pub, were enthusiastic members of the Freedom of Choice Coalition. Stewart Logan was the one who had told reporters that businesses should be free to operate asbestos-laden premises. The brothers had told enforcement staff on an early visit that they were expecting the bylaw to be overturned by the courts, and in the meantime were prepared to do only the absolute minimum required by the law. Complaints to the CRD's hotline, as well as visits by inspectors, had made it clear they weren't doing even that much. The CRD No Smoking signs were posted, but were dominated by Freedom of Choice Coalition signs. Bar staff gave out "candy dishes" for smoking patrons to use as ashtrays. The pub had been a venue for some of the coalition's meetings and fundraisers.

Only 10 days after the bylaw went into effect, the pub had put out a "newsletter" for its friends and supporters, warning that Thursday's — and doubtless other hospitality establishments as well — were going to go out of business because of the loss of revenue resulting from the bylaw. "Make no mistake about it," read the key article in the newsletter. "This bylaw is going to result in lost jobs and closed doors. Perhaps Richard Stanwick considers this a small price to pay in the course of his crusade — will he explain that to the bartender's landlord when the rent comes due?" Ironically, the article complained that non-smokers weren't rushing in to take the place of the nervous smokers who were staying away from bars like Thursday's. What it didn't say was that the air was so smoky in those defiant bars that most non-smokers would hate to spend even a few minutes in them.

On the first Friday evening in February, a team of four enforcement officers arrived at Thursday's just before 11:30 in the evening, always one of the busiest times for any bar. Although the teams normally worked in pairs, they often had taken to combining into groups of four for weekend visits to the most hostile bars. It allowed them greater safety and also a better ability to observe

Chapter 7 - The Big Day

the entire premises. Despite the Logan's concerns that business was greatly reduced, they found the bar jammed, with many of the patrons appearing to be drunk. Indeed, the enforcement officers suspected that many of the customers would be considered to have been "over-served" had a liquor inspector checked the premises.

Almost as soon as they walked in, one of the female enforcement officers found herself confronted by an older man who began screaming, "F***ing Nazis, f***ing Nazis!" at her, waving his arms around wildly. She asked him to step back, but instead he kept pushing against her, still yelling as she began to try to write a ticket for a man who was smoking at one of the tables. Despite her training in maintaining a safe physical distance from anyone she was attempting to ticket, she found it impossible as more seemingly drunken patrons moved over to the scene, all crowding into the narrow space and screaming similar abuse. The other EHOS who had stayed in that area of the bar hastily called police.

Meanwhile, the other two enforcement officers had moved through to the rear area of the bar and walked down a few steps to a lower lounge. They spotted a young, ponytailed man smoking obviously and publicly and approached him to write a ticket, but he completely ignored them, walking straight by them to the pool tables. The officers followed him and explained that they were designated peace officers and that he was required to provide his name, address and birth date, so they could write the ticket. Still he ignored them, refusing to say a word. "Is there anything I can say or do to gain your co-operation, sir?" asked the officer in a loud voice, following the verbal judo techniques he'd been taught. But the man still pretended they weren't there. The EHO went to phone the police, but was quickly told by the others that police officers were already on their way.

As they waited for the police, patrons crowded around the officers in the lower lounge, joining in the screaming of "F***ing Nazi smoke-cops!" and "F***ing CRD!" The downstairs team kept an eye on the man who had ignored them, but became increasingly worried about the noise and disturbance in the upper part of the bar. They realized that the man who was leading the shouting against the officers there was the same fellow whom they had run into a few days earlier at a different bar, where he had also shown the potential for physical violence. It was a nerve-wracking wait until the police showed up, less than 10 minutes later.

The crowd quieted when the police entered the bar, but the man who had ignored them still wouldn't provide any identification, even to the uniformed officers. They took him to a quieter corner of the bar, near the washrooms, for conversation. Then, much to the bylaw officers' surprise, they saw him being arrested, handcuffed and led out to a waiting police van. As they waited, the police came and showed them why. One of the officers on the call was Sergeant Laur, who had provided the training for the enforcement teams, and he had recognized a gadget that looked like a penlight that the man had on the zipper of his jacket. It was not a penlight at all, but rather a dagger that opened with the push of a button. When they'd searched him, Laur had found another dagger concealed inside his jacket — both highly illegal weapons in Canada. Even though the man had made no attempt to use the daggers on the enforcement officers, the incident left Stevenson and Dr. Stanwick, as well as the team, shaken. They were all aware of how easy it would have been for someone to have been seriously injured in a scuffle with those sorts of hidden weapons present.

Constable Rick Anthony, who was Sergeant Laur's partner that night, still remembers the confrontation. "I couldn't believe that guy we arrested," he says. "Here all he was going to get was a $50 ticket under a bylaw, no criminal charge, and instead, he waits until we get involved. He must have known he had those weapons on him, and now he was under arrest, heading to jail and facing all sorts of heavy-duty criminal weapons charges."

For the health team it was the final straw when the bar's manager on the night in question complained that the EHOs had phoned

Chapter 7 - The Big Day

police before first speaking to him about the problems they were having.

Les Potter, who had been instrumental in putting together the financial and administrative structure for the early enforcement days, was away from Victoria during the first weeks of implementation. When he returned to the office in mid-February, he was told of the harrowing events that had occurred. Potter immediately decided that he too wanted to see for himself, and headed out one dark and rainy night to visit some of the downtown Victoria drinking spots with one of the teams.

Their first stop was at the Swiftsure Lounge, a bar which looked straight out onto Victoria's famous Inner Harbour. In the summer, with its outdoor patio, it was a mecca for tourists, but in the rainy winter season, it was taken over by a harder-drinking crowd of locals. Potter and the team arrived before 7 p.m., but even then, the crowd was drunk, raucous and hostile. The bouncer on duty made it clear he wasn't going to help them enforce the bylaw, and rapidly got into a heated argument with the young female uniformed bylaw enforcement officer from the CRD. Potter watched in some horror as the 140-kilogram bouncer eventually grabbed the diminutive woman and slammed her up against the wall. Hastily, he gathered the team and they made as decorous an exit as possible, waiting until they were outside to call the police. When officers arrived, the team demanded the bouncer be charged with assault. To Potter's amazement, the bouncer said he also wanted to charge the female officer with assault. There were several days of telephone conversations with senior police officials before it was finally agreed that no one would face criminal charges.

To add to the surreal quality of the evening, the team headed on foot to the several bars and clubs located in Grant Olson's Strathcona Hotel, about four blocks away. But they never made it. As they reached the street in front of the hotel, they were among the first to see two pedestrians lying critically injured on the pavement, without a vehicle in sight. Within seconds, paramedics and police officers arrived and hastily cordoned off the scene. (The two were later found to have been victims of a hit-and-run tour-bus driver; the young man died; his wife, though badly injured, survived.)

Potter and the team then headed north, out of the downtown core, to the Tally-Ho, another working-class bar that had been causing problems. Again the crowd and the bar staff were so hostile that Potter had to call the police for backup — even though he knew every available officer had been sent to try to track down the hit-and-run vehicle.

By the time Potter finished that one night on the street, he agreed with the opinion that was forming in the mind of everyone on the team — a different enforcement system was needed. In growing desperation, the team, including lawyer Kathryn Stuart, pressured Dr. Stanwick, as medical health officer, to issue an order deeming the non-compliant bars to be a public health hazard. That would have given them the legal power for substantially greater penalties, but Dr. Stanwick saw problems with that route and resisted the team's desire for a seemingly quick fix. One was logistical: the health hazard existed only at the moment the patrons were smoking; within minutes of their stopping, the health hazard was gone. Dr. Stanwick couldn't figure out how he would be able to write hundreds of health hazard orders each and every day to cover each time the smoking started up again.

The second problem, which worried him more, was his concern that for him to go that route would be to take control of the agenda away from the community and its elected officials, and put it into the hands of himself, a non-elected civil servant. The whole process, he noted, had been community based and community driven from the beginning, even from the time AirSpace had first approached the regional board more than 15 years earlier. He did not want to take steps that could be perceived as the crusade of one person or even just the public health department.

While the team was still grappling with the problem, word of a possible solution came to them in the form of a judgment from the B.C. Supreme Court. As far back as 1996 when the bylaw was

Chapter 7 - The Big Day

first being drafted, Stevenson and Dr. Stanwick had considered the possibility of including a section that would provide a penalty for facility operators who refused to co-operate with the rules. At that point, however, they had been discouraged by Stuart, who told them that if such a section were included, it might make it easier to challenge the legislation in court. She had explained that the operators would doubtless argue that such a clause delegated the authority to enforce the bylaw to the owners and managers. It wasn't, she said, at all clear that the provincial laws which established regional governments and regional boards of health allowed them to delegate authority. They had conceded the point, and the legislation provided penalties only for those who were smoking, not for operators, no matter how defiant they were.

The City of Vancouver, however, had taken the other route in drafting its bylaw, which had come into effect in 1997. Although it applied only to restaurants, and not to pubs or bars, it did include a clause which stated that "No proprietor of a restaurant . . . shall permit a person to smoke in their establishment" except as specifically allowed, such as on an outdoor patio. In the beginning, it had appeared Stuart's concerns were well founded. A restaurant known as Doll & Penny's Café in Vancouver had challenged the bylaw on exactly the same grounds as Stuart had foreseen and had won their case in the first instance in court. A magistrate ruled the section was invalid because "in this case it is clear that council expects Doll & Penny's to put this bylaw into effect by carrying out their commands." That, the magistrate wrote, amounted to improper delegation of enforcement authority.

Vancouver city council, however, continued to disagree. It argued that the section being challenged created a separate offence on the part of a restaurant proprietor which didn't involve any delegated duties of enforcement. It appealed the magistrate's decision to the B.C. Supreme Court.

On February 2, 1999, Justice Allan Thackray handed down his decision.[32] It was in the city's favour.

Even better for the CRD, the judge drew parallels in the case that matched almost exactly with the problems the enforcement teams were having with the defiant bars. He noted that Doll & Penny's agreed that staff enforced other health and safety laws in the restaurant — they wouldn't serve drunk or abusive customers, nor customers who wanted to bring their dogs inside. Those bans had all been established by provincial liquor or health legislation. No one, the judge said, would argue that a restaurant should be convicted if its staff had taken all reasonable steps to prevent smoking, including cutting off service to the recalcitrant customer.

However, he wrote, that was clearly not the situation at Doll & Penny's, where "the policy of [the restaurant] . . . was designed to defeat the bylaw and to allow smoking in its premises . . . . They saw no problem in complying with their obligations to deny service or hospitality to customers who were in contravention of restrictions regarding animals or alcohol. However, when it came to a smoking customer the proprietors found themselves immobilized. No doubt this was caused by economic trauma." The Vancouver bylaw was valid, he ruled.

With that ruling to back them up, Stuart, Stevenson and Dr. Stanwick all agreed they should propose to the regional board that the Victoria bylaw be amended to include a clause with wording which would parallel the Vancouver law.

However, before they had time to draft the new proposal, the bylaw opponents took their case back to the regional board. Esquimalt councillor Jim King and a few other board members proposed a motion that would send the whole bylaw back to individual municipal councils for debate. The behaviour of the 100 bar staff and patrons who packed the meeting was so rowdy and unruly that the board members got a taste of what the enforcement teams had been facing. Heckling of "Gestapo!" and "Hitler!" punctuated the debate. While Dr. Stanwick was addressing the board, one man repeatedly used his finger to mimic a gun pointed at him, like small children playing shooting games.

Chapter 7 - The Big Day

The board members weren't impressed. Mayor Wayne Hunter of the suburb of Central Saanich complained that the meeting was disintegrating into a group of people "acting like we're in a beer parlour drinkathon," instead of a normal political discussion. He and others said that the bylaw had to be given a chance to work, and couldn't be up for discussion every meeting. King's motion went down to defeat 12 to 8. Some of the spectators suggested they were going to hold a sit-in, and briefly refused to leave, again requiring the politicians to follow in the footsteps of the enforcement teams and call the police. However, cooler heads prevailed. By the time officers actually arrived, the group had departed.

The outburst was enough to show many of the directors just how solid and difficult the opposition from the small minority of bars was becoming. It made them more willing than they might otherwise have been to accept the idea of a bylaw amendment when the staff put it forward at the end of February.

But if the politicians were accepting, the bylaw opponents were even more vehemently opposed to the change than they had been to the original law. A staff report from Dr. Stanwick to the board made clear the approach that would be taken, a step-by-step policy based on the one the regional board had first established in the late 1980s. A business shown to be encouraging its patrons to defy the bylaw would receive three separate warning letters. If non-compliance remained a problem, the region would be able to apply to the Supreme Court for an injunction that would require an establishment to comply with the bylaw. The penalties for breaching an injunction — a common-law offence known as contempt of court in Canada — were far more severe than anything that could be written into a regional bylaw. They could involve fines in the tens of thousands of dollars, removal of a business's licence, or even a jail term for a particularly recalcitrant individual. The members of the Freedom of Choice Coalition knew that their tactics would be severely restricted if the change were to go ahead.

The regional board meeting to discuss the change was even more raucous than the one a month earlier. Security guards had been hired by the regional board to try to keep matters in line, and even that was barely enough. The operators and staff threatened a "smoke in" right there in the regional board offices, but in the end cooler heads did again prevail. The change sailed through the board with even less opposition than the month previously, although a few directors spoke out strongly against it.

One was Oak Bay mayor Christopher Causton, who continued his long-held opposition to the bylaw, agreeing with the operators that it was unfair for them to expect to enforce a bylaw that was causing the official enforcement teams so much difficulty. "What we've done is we've stirred this pot up, we've brought it to the boiling point, and now we want the owners to take the pot off the stove," he said. He feared that "until we have greater education and greater acceptance of this bylaw, then the hostility is going to still be in the community."

But other directors said it would be easy enough for the owners to "take the pot off the stove" by simply refusing to serve smokers in the same way they refused to serve drunks or those with dogs. When the vote was called, it was 11 to 6 in favour of the change.

The decision totally outraged the coalition. "The gloves are off, war is declared," said Mayzes immediately after the meeting. He vowed that none of the enforcement teams would ever again be allowed in the Esquimalt Inn, and he suspected other owners would take the same tack.

The coalition began planning a campaign to try to discourage tourism to Victoria on the basis of the bylaw. They planned to put an open letter to travel agents up on the Internet. "Don't take a chance on ruining your client's holiday," read the draft they showed reporters. "Avoid the ashtray police and book your clients elsewhere."

Chapter 7 - The Big Day

But the threats didn't much worry Stevenson, Dr. Stanwick or the teams. They were already planning their new strategy based on the amended bylaw.

---

29. Harnett, Cindy E. "Bylaw cleans air in pubs but servers fear for jobs," Victoria Times-Colonist, January 12, 1999.
30. Ibid.
31. Gidney, Norman. "Smoking law forces café to butt out after 88 years," Victoria Times-Colonist, January 19, 1999.
32. Judgment of B.C. Supreme Court Justice Allan Thackray, City of Vancouver vs. Doll & Penny's Café Ltd., Docket #CC981051.

8
Media Mania

*"Facing the press is more difficult
than bathing a leper."*

— *Mother Theresa*

Long before that most controversial of bylaw changes, even before "the big day" for implementation had arrived, the team knew that one of their major challenges would be handling media coverage of the issue. Experience in California and Toronto had shown that during the first days of smoke-free legislation, the media would focus on the places that were defying the bylaw, enforceability problems and anything that looked like an exciting confrontation. Dr. Stanwick and the team had seen a lot of that during the first two weeks of January.

Dr. Stanwick realized the media had hit a new low on the morning of Saturday, January 16, when he picked up his morning newspaper. Blaring at him, eight columns across the top of the front page in the size of type usually reserved for election results or major disasters was the headline: "Victoria's Smoke Enforcers Take Aim at the Dying." [33]

The first sentence showed him the tone of the story: "Greater Victoria's smoke police are about to take aim at their next target — the dying." Dr. Stanwick and the team were portrayed as unfeeling bureaucrats who were looking to arrest those who had only days to live, enjoying their last cigarette while in Hospice, the city's facility for the terminally ill.

To Dr. Stanwick it felt like a complete betrayal by another health care facility. He had known that Hospice and its new executive director David Cheperdak had not been entirely happy with requirements to obey the bylaw, but he'd thought that everything had been worked out satisfactorily. Even if some issues remained to be dealt with, he had never suspected Hospice would actually be party to such a devastating anti-bylaw piece.

Stevenson and the staff had included Hospice during their series of meetings with long-term care facilities for the previous 18 months. They'd discussed how Hospice, like the long-term care homes, could modify its facilities to comply while causing very little disruption to patients. Dr. Stanwick had personally met twice with the board of Hospice. He thought they had reached an acceptable compromise with the construction of a rooftop garden that Hospice said would also be for the smokers' use. He had left the discussions believing there had been a meeting of minds on the issue.

He had explained all that to *Times-Colonist* reporter Richard Watts when the subject of Hospice had been mentioned in an interview a couple of days earlier. He had told Watts that the indoor smoking room that was now located in the premises did not comply with the bylaw. In fact, it was not even separately ventilated, and non-smoking patients had sometimes complained about drifting second-hand smoke. However, Dr. Stanwick had said, over the next few months Hospice management would be developing a plan that would bring them into compliance.

Dr. Stanwick also knew that because of the bigger battles with the pubs and bars, it was most unlikely that enforcement would be targeted at Hospice, or any of the long-term care facilities, any time soon.

So how had Hospice suddenly become the rallying point for smokers' rights in Greater Victoria?

As Dr. Stanwick read the story, he found that the quotes he'd provided were included, but deeply buried below the comments from a dying patient and from Cheperdak, both bemoaning in emotional terms the mere possibility of moving Hospice smokers outdoors.

Dr. Stanwick didn't figure he could blame the patient, a woman named Sylvia Shandley who had said she — and by implication other smokers there — "would probably just tell them to get lost." Nothing they could do was worse than what was happening to her — a slow, miserable death from brain cancer. She doubtless had known nothing of the previous discussions or plans, but had just been approached by Watts asking provocative questions.

The health team suspected that Cheperdak had still been unhappy with the bylaw requirements, even though he had appeared to go along with the long-term plan. Cheperdak, in turn, told both Stevenson and Dr. Stanwick that he too felt sabotaged by the *Times-Colonist*. When he had talked to Watts, he said, he'd never expected the story to acquire the profile it did. However, Dr. Stanwick and his team realized that Watts could never have gained the access he had to Hospice's terminally ill patients without active co-operation from the facility's management. Health region rules normally made it next to impossible for reporters to visit wards or interview patients, except when they were specifically invited in. Those invitations were most often issued in rare cases of "good news" stories for the health care system itself.

In the news report, Cheperdak was quoted as saying he supported the principle of the bylaw, but that the politicians and health officials had to realize Hospice was "a special case," and there was no way staff could force patients to go outside in the last days of their lives.

Cheperdak had been at the Hospice board meetings at which the issue had been discussed. He knew that no immediate or strict enforcement campaign was in the works against Hospice and that his board had agreed to begin to work towards the compromise of a roof garden. None of that, though, was reflected in the story.

Dr. Stanwick knew at that point it didn't really matter who had been the primary source behind the story, Hospice itself or the *Times-Colonist*. What mattered was that the Hospice story needed to be neutralized quickly and successfully. Left to fester for even one day, it posed the risk of bringing huge amounts of sympathy to the bylaw opponents' cause.

Less immediate, but no less important, was Dr. Stanwick's conclusion that he and his team were going to have to acknowledge that some members of the media were active opponents of the bylaw. They would have to be considered in strategy plans just as much as the Freedom of Choice Coalition or the Oak Bay Lodge board. It wasn't an encouraging thought.

As Dr. Stanwick had expected from the moment he read the Hospice story, the cell phone started to ring before 9 a.m. The calls were from other media outlets in the city, across the province and even across the country, all wanting comments. Dr. Stanwick was glad that one of the strategy decisions the team had made was that he would be available to the media on the cell phone 24 hours a day, seven days a week during the tough implementation period. He had often found the constant late evening calls a struggle, and even more when outlets in eastern Canada confused the time difference to the west coast and phoned at 5 a.m. But the positive benefits had outweighed the inconvenience of constant phone calls: no reporter had ever been able to say that the bylaw proponents or enforcers could not be reached for comment. It was the best chance they had to defuse and deflect the sometimes absurd arguments that were made by the most outrageous of the bar owners and patrons.

That Saturday was probably the best instance of the need to have someone available for media calls at all times. From the tone of the first few calls, Dr. Stanwick realized that this was going to be the toughest battle yet to fight in the court of public opinion. This was a story that had emotional power, and in the news business, emotion will beat almost any logical argument. Even more than the seniors in long-term care homes, individuals who were within days or weeks of death attracted a natural sympathy from reporters — and from the public. More than any other news coverage, this was the story that painted Dr. Stanwick and the team as bureaucrats and zealots, rigid and inflexible.

As Dr. Stanwick had feared, the story generated some intensely negative publicity across the country. "This is the kind of cruelty that makes you wince and turn away when you hear of it, because it is so hard to believe anyone would stoop so low," wrote *Calgary Herald* columnist Naomi Lakritz,[34] in a piece that was also published in several other newspapers across the country.

"A certain Dr. Richard Stanwick of Victoria, B.C. celebrated [National Non-Smoking Week] by denying a bunch of people on their deathbeds the small comfort of a last cigarette," wrote Connie Woodcock in a column that also appeared in newspapers across Canada.[35]

Dr. Stanwick's repeated interviews and television appearances on the subject did much to deflect the worst of the criticism around "the Hospice issue." He was well aware that the logical arguments he needed could never compete with the emotional impact of the dying smokers. The arguments were complex and hard to explain in a simple soundbite. From a health viewpoint, the argument to be made was that even though the smoke from one dying person's last few cigarettes might not be much, the cumulative effect on the workers' health could be substantial. Over a period of months or years, the workers would care for hundreds or thousands of dying smokers, each contributing one more small cloud of second-hand smoke. It was even harder to explain the legal argument that McDannold and Stuart had made so forcefully to the team — the argument that allowing one "special case" in which some consideration beyond health would apply would open the gates for a flood of applications and possible court challenges, all asking for special-case exemptions as well.

Dr. Stanwick spent most of that Saturday consulting with the team and then preparing a news update that he could fax to all the media outlets he could reach. He wanted the tone to be conciliatory. He knew he must make it clear that the team wasn't going to give in to Hospice's desires, but neither were they going to take precipitate or insensitive enforcement actions. In the final version, he pointed out that "more than 83 per cent of facilities within the region providing care to fragile and vulnerable health populations had satisfactorily completed the transition to a smoke-free indoor worksite" before January 1.

He stressed again that "no immediate bylaw enforcement action is planned for any of the few health care facilities which have still been unable to plan and develop a suitable outdoor smoking area." Public health officials would continue to work with those facilities, including Hospice, to ensure satisfactory plans were developed, he said.

Most of all, he tried to emphasize that "the CRD and the Capital health region have no intention of stopping individuals in the last days of their lives from smoking. Only the location of the activity is being moved — for the health and safety of everyone."

It wasn't perfect, but the explanations were enough to take at least some of the lustre off the story for other media. A front-page story appeared in the *National Post*, but it looked at a variety of issues surrounding the bylaw and not just the situation at Hospice. Dr. Stanwick met again with Hospice's board, and by the end of the week, the issue had been resolved. The Hospice board had again committed itself to develop its rooftop garden for smokers or find an acceptable alternative. The meeting generated virtually no publicity at all. And Hospice disappeared off the agenda as a major public issue.

The successful resolution of that single issue, however, did not take away Dr. Stanwick's and Stevenson's overall concerns about the media. Day after day, it was becoming obvious that the oppositional stance of some media outlets and some individual reporters was, like the stance of some bars and pubs, hardening.

As with the bars, it was a minority of journalists that caused the team problems. But, also as with the bars, Dr. Stanwick and Stevenson were quickly concluding that the minority was causing difficulties far out of proportion to its numbers.

Some other reporters had made it clear, at least privately, that they supported the ban. Still others were as neutral as it was possible to be on such an emotional issue. Their reports accurately detailed what had occurred each day and what supporters and opponents were saying. The city's only major television station, CHEK,

Chapter 8 - Media Mania

fell into that camp, and gave the bylaw little attention. They had few crews working at night, which meant they were not usually available to cover the worst of the bar confrontations. For that, Dr. Stanwick and the team were thankful because constant TV footage of the yelling, Nazi-saluting patrons would have made the problems of implementation appear even more severe and widespread than they actually were.

The journalists who were, in the team's eyes, causing problems appeared to fall into two camps. For one group, the conflict and controversy appeared to be of much greater interest than either the health or the legal issues involved. Almost all their stories focused on the confrontations between enforcement personnel and hostile smokers and/or bartenders, the louder and more violent the better. For them, the power of emotion was again overshadowing the successful implementation in hundreds of other restaurants and bars. Their stories ended up painting an inaccurate picture of what was going on region-wide. Whether deliberately or inadvertently, these media outlets were providing ammunition for the opponents who were trying to argue that the bylaw was unenforceable and could never be used to provide a genuine level playing field in the hospitality industry.

An even smaller, but more vocal, minority of journalists appeared to be clearly on the side of the opponents. That set too, appeared divided into two sub-camps. One group included reporters who were known to be regular smokers and who obviously found the whole issue uncomfortable to deal with. The second group were those who had problems philosophically with issues of government interference in the lives of citizens. They were likely to be equally concerned about government efforts to impose any mandatory safety requirements on adults, such as moves to require the wearing of bicycle helmets or seatbelts in cars. Since debate on the bylaw had begun, the chief media spokesperson for that group had been Joe Easingwood, the provocative host of a morning talk show on C-FAX radio, the most popular radio station in the city.

However, since the day of implementation, Dr. Stanwick had begun to worry that the *Times-Colonist* — the city's only daily newspaper and its most influential media source — was moving into that latter camp. With the Saturday Hospice story, he was almost sure of it.

It was a significant change from the stance the *Times-Colonist* had taken at the time of the public hearings and the original debates about the bylaw at the regional board level. Then, the newspaper had been a strong supporter of the bylaw and had encouraged the board to stay strong every step of the way. An editorial in 1993 carried the heading "Smoking controls and political wimps." It urged the provincial government to take stronger action to try to prevent teens' access to tobacco. "Such stalling on a vitally important health issue represents a massive betrayal of responsibility," said the newspaper's editorial board.[36]

In the last few weeks before the bylaw was passed in 1996, the editorial headline read: "Smoke ban furore: stand firm, CRD." [37] The regional directors, it read, must resist the pressures from the hospitality and tobacco industries "for one very good reason — their responsibility to protect public health.

"Stripped of all the predictable rhetoric about smokers' 'rights,' this is first and foremost a health issue," it went on. At the time, Dr. Stanwick and Stevenson had been impressed with what they saw as the progressive and enlightened attitude the local newspaper was taking on the issue.

However, in the intervening five years, the *Times-Colonist* had gone through not only several changes of staff among its reporters and editorial writers, but even several changes of ownership. The views of its editorial board — presumed to reflect the views of its owners — had changed, and those changes were also reflected in its news pages.

The Canadian Broadcasting Corporation (CBC) radio station was new since the days of the bylaw debates, having opened in Victoria in September 1998. Across Canada, CBC was considered

Chapter 8 - Media Mania

generally to be sympathetic to progressive causes, and had not been considered to be a problem. But it had quickly become obvious that it was one of the outlets devoting a huge amount of its time to the conflicts and controversies rather than taking a broader view of events. One of its reporters was the journalist most likely to turn up at rowdy conflicts in defiant bars.

Between those CBC conflict stories, Easingwood's concerns about undue government interference and the change in viewpoint at the *Times-Colonist*, Dr. Stanwick was beginning to feel that the media as a whole were becoming an axis of opposition to the bylaw. The level of opposition the team was seeing in the press significantly exceeded the amount they'd expected when originally planning their strategy.

That Saturday also reinforced the message that in some ways, the media were in a position to cause them many more problems than were the obviously hostile protest groups. The taxpaying public expected the spokespersons for the smoking and drinking industries to be vehemently opposed to tobacco control measures. Public opinion was much more likely to be swayed if consistent media stories and columns were implying that the bylaw was unfair or was becoming unenforceable.

From the beginning of the implementation battles during the summer of 1998, the health officials had realized that the bylaw's opponents had also been developing a carefully crafted media strategy. They too had picked out the reporters and columnists most likely to espouse their views and had been providing them with information favourable to their cause. They found spokespersons from California and Toronto to insist loudly and publicly that clean-air legislation there wasn't working, wasn't being enforced and was causing serious economic harm in the few places where prosecutions had begun to occur. The inevitable conclusion for the media to draw was that such legislation just couldn't be made to work. The reporters were unlikely to do any independent research to check out the accuracy of the statements or "studies" cited to them — and in any case, few had the background to understand whether a study had been well crafted and was reliable or whether it was little more than a collection of anecdotes from the disgruntled. Many outlets were prepared to print or broadcast them as fact, even though in many cases the assumptions upon which they were based were seriously flawed.

The bylaw's opponents had also recognized that the media were more likely to write stories favourable to their cause if the "victims" of the bylaw were seen as deserving of sympathy in the public eye. That was one good reason for putting as much emphasis as possible on the problems with long-term care homes, rather than bars and casinos. The "freedom fighters" from the working-class bars would likely appeal to only a narrow segment of the population, mainly those who already hated government regulation in their lives. A greater number of ordinary citizens were likely to support senior citizens, especially veterans, who had already lost some dignity by having to end their days in an institution, and who now were going to find their pleasure of smoking severely restricted as well.

The Hospice story was the culmination of that strategy. Who could fail to sympathize with smokers who might have to live out the last days of their lives with no easy way to enjoy their last few cigarettes?

The elected officials on the regional board and health officials had anticipated that would be among the tactics of the opposition. What they had not expected was how receptive the media would be to these tactics.

Like the opponents, the politicians and the health authorities had begun to plan their media strategy in the fall of 1998. They wanted a strategy in place before the opposition began its campaign against the bylaw. From the beginning, Frank Leonard was convinced that the non-elected Stevenson and Dr. Stanwick should be the main spokespersons for the bylaw on issues surrounding implementation.

It was a lesson Leonard had learned from bitter experience several years earlier. He'd headed the CRD's environment committee at a

Chapter 8 - Media Mania

time when environmentalists across the U.S. decided to launch an aggressive attack on the region for the way it treated its sewage. Having the advantage of cold, deep, fast-flowing water in the ocean just off the city's coast, the region screened sewage, but then discharged it directly through a long outfall pipe without the need for chemical or settling treatment. Several scientific studies had shown that the sewage would dissipate without causing damage to the environment or risk to human health. But the Americans called it "discharging raw sewage into the ocean" and even threatened tourist boycotts of the city if it wouldn't start "properly treating" its sewage. Leonard had found himself having to defend the region's position in the media throughout Washington state and as far away as New York in the prestigious *New York Times*.

When the issue appeared to be getting out of hand, Leonard asked media consultants for advice — and received a surprising answer. "They told me to stop talking to the media," he says. The consultants explained that because Leonard was an elected official, whatever he was said was going to be seen as a political defence and was only going to fuel the fires of the controversy further. Leonard followed their advice. He asked Dr. Peck (the medical health officer at the time) and a regional engineer to begin responding to media questions, providing strictly factual and scientific answers to the allegations made. The tactics worked. The furore over sewage treatment died down within a matter of weeks.

As soon as the renewed opposition began to show itself on the smoking issue, Leonard concluded the same tactics should be applied. If he and other regional board members began taking on the bar owners in the media, he thought, it would again be seen as a political defence that would only inflame the controversy further. Stevenson and Dr. Stanwick, on the other hand, could provide the scientific data on the dangers of second-hand smoke, in a way that a politician never could. Every media appearance would subtly underscore the message that this bylaw was all about health and not about politics.

Dr. Stanwick and Stevenson thus knew early on that they would be acting as the main spokespersons in the early days of bylaw implementation. They agreed with Leonard that they should be able to reiterate the health message of the bylaw. They knew that Dr. Stanwick had, since his arrival in 1995, developed credibility as the key spokesperson on public health issues in the region, dealing with dozens of health-related topics that had nothing to do with tobacco.

Neither, they realized, should the health authorities or the CRD have a variety of spokespersons. That could lead to opponents or media outlets searching for tiny differences in interpretation and highlighting them in an effort to show a lack of unity and coherence.

The health authorities had, during those fall months, also spent time finding out which reporters, commentators and talk show hosts would most likely be sympathetic, or at least neutral, in their presentation of the upcoming controversies. What they found that they couldn't ensure, though, was that those reporters would be the ones sent by their editors to cover stories about the bylaw. And during the darker days of January, they sometimes wondered if the editors weren't deliberately sending out bylaw opponents to report on the confrontations.

Dr. Stanwick and Stevenson had also spent time during the fall providing the local and regional reporters with as much information as possible about the issues surrounding second-hand smoke and its health risks. As well, they had offered studies on the economic consequences of smoking bans, studies based on government reports of amounts of liquor sold, rather than reports based solely on opponent-supplied anecdotes. Although most of the reporters who had covered the public hearings and regional board meetings in 1995 and 1996 had become well versed in the topic, many of that group had moved on to new jobs in the intervening 30 months. As well, Stevenson noted, new and better studies had been published, documenting even greater health risks from second-hand smoke. With California's ban in place since

Chapter 8 - Media Mania

January 1998, the people involved were able to provide more detailed and accurate statistics of what happened economically after a ban was imposed.

After their successful trip to California, the Victoria team found two bar owners from that state who were prepared to travel to B.C. to share their positive experiences with both the hospitality industry and the media in Victoria. The pair met with bar and restaurant owners from Victoria, and also with many media members.

Carol Brookman and fellow bar owner Lou Moench, from Santa Monica, talked to reporters from *The Province* and the *Times-Colonist* and appeared on radio and television. *The Province* printed their stories much as they told them.[38] The *Times-Colonist* ran what they said, but included copious criticisms from local pub owner Gordon Card in the same article. He insisted that their experience was not typical of California bar owners.[39] Card, representing the Hospitality Industry Liquor Licensing Advisory Group, repeated the hospitality coalition's contention that bars and pubs in Victoria would lose "millions of dollars and 250 jobs in the first year." He insisted that those figures were based on reports his members had heard from their counterparts in California.

Dr. Stanwick and Stevenson also found some local hospitality businesses who had voluntarily gone smoke-free before the bylaw was implemented, and were finding no problems with the change. They too were encouraged to talk to the media, but it was difficult to persuade reporters that such successes were of as much interest as the predictions of doom that increasingly filled the news pages when the bylaw was up for discussion.

The autumn debates at the regional board, mainly dealing with Oak Bay Lodge and other nursing homes, had also led to colourful media coverage, most of it unfavourable. From the moment Oak Bay Lodge first raised the issue, its board received strong support on the editorial pages of the *Times-Colonist*.

"They may have survived the Depression and the Second World War, but there's no way Greater Victoria's seniors will evade the Smoking Police," began an editorial that appeared only days after Oak Bay council first decided to back the lodge board.[40] The editorial argued that the question was one of dignity for seniors. "The lodge is not just a workplace or place of business," the editorial writer argued. "It's a home and to be shoved around by bureaucracy in your own home is dehumanizing."

Just as he did later on the Hospice issue, Dr. Stanwick tried to explain that almost all the long-term care facilities in the region had found "collaborative and creative solutions" to the problem. They had come up with well-designed outdoor spaces that met all the terms of the bylaw but were still protected from the worst of the elements and were even heated. He tried to point out what a small proportion of residents in such facilities smoked. He tried to explain that second-hand smoke remained a serious hazard to frail seniors, even those who smoked themselves, let alone those who had come from smoke-free homes. He pointed out that the staff who would have to supervise them in their indoor smoking areas would be exposed, to a greater or lesser degree, to the toxic chemicals of second-hand smoke. He tried to point out that those seniors who moved to homes like Oak Bay Lodge had already given up many of the freedoms of living in one's home, such as pets and hobbies. He pointed out that some of the care homes that had already gone smoke-free found the exposure to fresh air actually appeared to improve the health of their smoking residents.

None of it seemed to matter. Even media members who were supportive to the bylaw overall found it much easier to sympathize with the 80-year-old who had been smoking for 60 years than with the authorities.

In the public's and media's view, the ban in long-term care facilities was much harder to defend than the one for the hospitality industry. The staff exposure to second-hand smoke was for much shorter time periods than that of the bartenders who would spend eight hours in a blue haze. The smokers were adults who had been

Smoking field must be level

The threat of a lawsuit by the Royal Canadian Legion's branch in Esquimalt is just the latest twist in the Capital Regional District's long fight to ban smoking in public places.

The legion is considering suing the CRD, accusing the region of unequal enforcement of its anti-smoking bylaw. The legion says it has been losing $1,000 a day since it started ensuring compliance with the CRD's Clean Air Bylaw a couple of months ago.

That enforcement only came after the legion was handed $100 tickets for not ensuring its patrons complied with the CRD regulations, which don't allow smoking in enclosed public places.

Now, the legion says, its customers have fled to other drinking establishments where the rules aren't being enforced. In other words, places where they can puff away to their heart's content while pouring back a cool one.

The legion says that if the anti-smoking rules were being enforced everywhere, the legion members would have had no reason to go elsewhere.

The basic theory behind the CRD regulation is a sound one — smoking is a health hazard. That's been proven, and proven again, for years and years.

But at the same time, tobacco is a legal product in B.C., and people have a right to use that product.

And don't forget that a legion, like a bar, has age restrictions. A child is not allowed to enter. Only adults are allowed — people who should have the right to do and say what they please (and some of whom fought in wars to protect that right) because they should be able to understand the possible consequences of their actions. It's a different story with a restaurant, or any other public place that allows the presence of children. We have a responsibility to ensure the health and safety of our young people.

As far as the legion's lawsuit is concerned, the CRD has been holding back on strict enforcement until it got the results of a test case on the bylaw's legality. It won that case, and we can now expect it will ensure that all public places comply — at least there will now be a level playing field.

But even if the playing field is now levelled, the CRD regulations should try to accommodate those who continue to use the evil weed (as the revised Workers' Compensation Board regulations do). We have to find compromises to enable smokers to feel like equal citizens, and to let businesses and clubs that wish to serve smokers do so.

Some drinking establishments say that a majority of their customers are smokers. Those businesses should be free to declare themselves to be smoke-filled areas — although these would be still have to be self-serve to protect employees — and could appeal to the people who want to light up while they drink. In time, the number of these smoker-friendly bars can be expected to drop, but that's something for the market to decide, not something to be legislated.

The idea has worked before, in reverse. Before the CRD instituted its smoking ban, several restaurant chains declared themselves smoke-free, and made it known that people could eat there without the inconvenience and health risks associated with smoking.

With the battle against smoking almost won, it's only fair to give the smokers who remain a chance to breathe the air of their choice.

Editorial in Times-Colonist, March 2001

accepting the risks of smoking for decades, and in the end, it was their home, albeit one where they had already given up many pleasures and freedoms.

The most serious reason for retaining the ban in long-term care institutions was the legal necessity to maintain uniformity on the basis of health. Because no safe levels had ever been determined for many of the chemicals in second-hand smoke, it wasn't possible to allow the staff at places like Oak Bay Lodge to be exposed to it, just because the time they were exposed was less than a bartender would be. But these arguments were too complex and in some ways too legalistic to appeal to the media. The human-interest stories of the seniors affected made much better TV clips.

Moreover, with Don Rittaler's lawsuit still pending, neither Dr. Stanwick nor McDannold could be up front about the legal problems that granting non-health related "exemptions" to the bylaw could cause. The last thing they wanted was for Rittaler and his supporters to know how worried they were about such a possibility.

When the regional board was about to cast the final vote on the issue in December 1998, the *Times-Colonist* editorial board weighed in again. "Seniors are consenting adults," its editorial concluded.[41] "If they want to smoke and no one else is harmed, surely that's their business. Our seniors will be gone from us soon enough. Let's not bury them in red tape while they're still alive."

The *Times-Colonist* did not, however, take an editorial stand on the parts of the bylaw dealing with the hospitality industry before it went into effect in January 1999. It remained even-handed in its reporting on the rowdy regional board meetings, the predictions of gloom and the emphasis on the improvement in public health. Like most media outlets in town, it gave prominent coverage to the Angus Reid poll that was completed less than a month before implementation day.

When the pre-implementation controversy was approaching its height in December, the *Times-Colonist* editorial board — instead

Chapter 8 - Media Mania

of writing its own piece — invited both sides to submit an 800-word article outlining their reasoning. Dr. Stanwick was approached to write the article from the "pro" bylaw side; Gordon Card and Grant Olson for the Age of Majority Business Coalition represented the opponents.

Dr. Stanwick quickly recognized that this would be one of the most important opportunities he would get to speak to the citizens directly through the media, before the bylaw was implemented. What he said would not be edited or abridged to fit into the space available. He put all his energy into writing the best possible article, given the tight time deadline he'd been offered for it. Neither side got to see what the other had written until it was printed, so he had to anticipate Olson and Card's criticisms as best he could, and try to deflect them. He stressed the public consultation process and the latest Angus Reid poll. He reiterated the health arguments to ensure they were well understood by as many citizens as possible. He emphasized the "level playing field" issue, arguing that the bylaw would actually work better in Victoria than it had elsewhere because all businesses would be treated equally whether they were serving liquor or only food. And he spent significant time dealing with the issue of ventilation, the option frequently proposed as an alternative in articles from the opponents. He cited the engineering studies on the impossibility of a realistic ventilation solution, and made the quote that got him the headline: "A ventilation system for second hand smoke makes as much sense as having peeing and non-peeing sections in swimming pools." [42]

He explained the benefits of the bylaw without attacking its opponents, but Card and Olson were not so kind.

"Why," they wrote, "are the elected officials allowing Dr. Richard Stanwick, an unelected official, to push his own personal agenda to make smoking history? ... Have local politicians lost control of a third level of government, the CRD?" [43]

The coalition estimated a loss in licensed establishments of $32.9 million in revenue after the bylaw went in — but didn't give any explanation of how that total had been calculated. Neither did it explain how it determined the prediction of a loss of 316 full-time jobs and 305 part-time jobs as a result of the decrease in business.

It stressed the freedom of choice argument, noting that: "We believe that all Canadians, including our adult customers, clients and staff, have the right to choose whether or not they patronize or work in an establishment which provides a smoking area which meets or exceeds WCB air standards."

At the very least, Card and Olson suggested, the CRD board should wait until the WCB had finalized and made public the details of its plans — a step which would likely have bought them another year of time in which smoking could continue in the bars and pubs.

As implementation day loomed, the team realized the task of handling the media was going to be even more difficult than expected. The rest of Canada had awoken to the fact that Victoria would soon become the first spot in the nation to try a 100 per cent smoke-free policy, and already the calls had begun to come in from national newspapers and television shows.

The strategy of using Dr. Stanwick as chief public spokesperson in the early days of implementation went into effect. He was not a "political" elected official. And if he were the one whose time was taken up with the countless rounds of interviews, Stevenson would be free to work with the team on innumerable other logistical details.

Dr. Stanwick would also make every effort to be available to deal with every media query and interview, 24 hours a day, if need be. He would share a media stage with any of the opponents who were invited. He and the rest of the team wanted to appear as open and accountable as possible — they had nothing to hide and did not want to give anyone any excuse for suggesting that they did. Even though it was the holiday season, they were well aware that

Chapter 8 - Media Mania

their opponents would still be out fighting for their cause. It was important to have someone ready to answer them at any time.

Right from New Year's Day, the importance of the media strategy was apparent. Dr. Stanwick took several media calls that day. An interview with the *National Post* led to a front page story in which the restrictions were described as "the toughest in North America." [44] During the weekend, some reporters passed on to Dr. Stanwick what, in the course of their research on the story, they had observed. He was told that on Sunday, January 2, the Esquimalt Inn had already posted its defiant signs reading: "This is a smoking area. Enter at your own risk." For the reporters, it was a quid pro quo. They knew they'd get a better interview if Dr. Stanwick had as much information as possible about what was going on.

Once the first enforcement efforts were started on Monday, the media interest was overwhelming. There was no way someone could have been out in the field and still managed to keep up with all the media calls. Some mornings that first week, Dr. Stanwick rushed from one interview to another, appearing on as many as half a dozen media outlets in the space of three hours. The "first in Canada" angle made it worthy of front page stories in both the *Globe and Mail* and *National Post*. He appeared on national television on each of the various networks, as well as on every local and regional radio and TV show. Sometimes he appeared by himself; sometimes it was a format of point-counterpoint with a bylaw opponent. His head-to-head encounters with Brian Mayzes made for amusing television simply because of the exceptional difference in their sizes — Mayzes was almost 30 centimetres (12 inches) taller than Dr. Stanwick and outweighed him by at least 75 kilograms (165 pounds). Sometimes Dr. Stanwick answered listeners' questions on radio talk shows. Some of the questions were hostile but more supporters called than one would have thought existed, based on some of the other media stories.

However, a problem quickly developed: some media outlets began thriving on the confrontations developing at places like the Esquimalt Inn. The enforcement team had made a deliberate decision not to invite the media along when they went out to monitor the situation and write the first tickets. Miles Drew and the others believed that the presence of notebooks and microphones, let alone TV cameras, would probably be enough to incite a hostile crowd still further, perhaps enough to put enforcement staff at risk of physical harm. Yet after a few days it became obvious that certain reporters, most often the CBC's Michael Tymchuk, were turning up anyway. The higher the level of confrontation, the greater the likelihood that the mikes would turn up on the scene.

Dr. Stanwick, Stevenson and Drew reluctantly concluded that some of the bar owners themselves must be calling their supporters in the media as soon as an inspection team drew up to the front door. It quickly became apparent that what they had feared was indeed coming true — a few of the more hostile smokers appeared to want to put on a show for the reporters, sometimes settling right down again as soon as the media had left. All the same, it was impossible to tell the reporters and photographers they couldn't be there, given that the activity was occurring in a public place. They could envision the stories and commentaries that would appear if it appeared that officials were refusing to allow journalists to cover incidents that would, in their view, show that the bylaw wasn't working.

It seemed that each day, the negative media focused even more on the few outlets that were refusing to comply, on the risk of violence, on the heightened level of confrontation. Reporters never seemed to turn up when the teams were visiting the restaurants or bars where compliance was high or where officials were treated with respect, even if the bylaw wasn't being fully implemented.

The culmination was the Hospice story almost exactly two weeks after implementation had started.

Aside from the outraged columnists, the issue did lead to some more unfavourable coverage from previously supportive media. By the Monday afternoon, Dr. Stanwick was able to tell *National Post*

Chapter 8 - Media Mania

reporter Mark Hume that the situation had been defused, but the next front page story that appeared in the *Post* was not nearly so sympathetic to the bylaw as the first one had been.[45] Not only did it stress the Hospice controversy, but it also printed Mayzes' highly coloured version of the confrontation at the Esquimalt Inn without getting any rebuttal at all from Dr. Stanwick or anyone else from public health.

Yet ironically, the Hospice story appeared to mark, at least for the time being, the end of the most inflammatory coverage of the issue. Because the controversy was settled so quickly, it hit the headlines for only two or three days. Moreover, the general issue of compliance and enforcement also began to get less media attention — at least until the decision several weeks later to change the law to allow the defiant bar operators themselves to be held liable and face a court injunction.

The coverage surrounding that decision provided the most overt support that the bars and pubs had been able to find from the media. The *National Post* went so far as to write an editorial fully embracing the "freedom of choice" issue — and not mentioning staff or workers' health at all.[46] "People have a right to choose a short life but a merry one," the editors wrote, suggesting that both smoking bars/restaurants and non-smoking ones be licensed.

"Our right to live our own lives — and to meet our responsibilities in doing so — is too important to be left to doctors," the editorial said.

Similar sentiments were echoed by Joe Easingwood, both on his talk show and in a weekly column he had started to write in the *Times-Colonist*.[47] He argued it was the same as expecting bank managers to deal with robbers without the help of police — even though the bylaw clearly stated that the process would go forward only for those who condoned or encouraged smoking, not for a manager who was unable to persuade the occasional recalcitrant customer to butt out.

"Is it any wonder bar and pub owners fighting the CRD bylaw say it's now 'total war' and plan to seal the doors to any CRD official who sniffs around?" Easingwood asked rhetorically. "This attempt at social engineering by the CRD goes over the top."

But when the CRD board held firm again, the uproar began to die down, in the media as well as in the community. To be sure, flare-ups continued until the final court injunctions were granted more than two years later. They usually centred around a specific event, such as a change in policy by the Workers' Compensation Board or an upcoming court case on the bylaw. Dr. Stanwick quickly realized he always had to be prepared to do another interview about the bylaw and how it was going, the information always fresh at his fingertips.

When the final cases went to court, they made barely a blip on the media's radar screen. The hostility had largely dissipated, the confrontations had ceased and the media had moved on to cover a more immediate topic. It's just the nature of the media business. Reporters always say they have short attention spans.

---

33. Watts, Richard. "Victoria's Smoke Enforcers Take Aim at the Dying," Victoria Times-Colonist, January 16, 1999.
34. Lakritz, Naomi. "A humane law would let hospice patients smoke," Calgary Herald, January 21, 1999.
35. Woodcock, Connie. "Another Tobacco War, Another Wasted Effort," Ottawa Sun, January 25, 1999.

Chapter 8 - Media Mania

36. Unsigned editorial, "Smoking controls and political wimps," Victoria *Times-Colonist*, November 27, 1993.
37. Moss, Paul. "Smoke ban furore: stand firm, CRD," Victoria Times-Colonist, May 18, 1996.
38. McLintock, Barbara. "California bar owners bring news on smoking," The Province, October 29, 1998.
39. Bell, Jeff. "Smoking ban 'good for business,'" Victoria Times-Colonist, October 28, 1998.
40. Unsigned editorial, "Let Lodge residents keep on smoking," Victoria Times-Colonist, August 20, 1998.
41. Unsigned editorial, "Smoking seniors deserve right to puff indoors," Victoria Times-Colonist, November 25, 1998.
42. Stanwick, Dr. Richard. "Carcinogen has no place in public areas," Victoria Times-Colonist, December 12, 1998.
43. Card, Gordon and Olson, Grant. "Businesses want right to freedom of choice," Victoria Times-Colonist, December 12, 1998.
44. Arnold, Tom. "Victoria begins ban on public smoking," National Post, January 2, 1999.
45. Hume, Mark. "Smoking ban applies to terminally ill patients," National Post, January 19, 1999.
46. Unsigned editorial, "Butting out in Victoria," National Post, March 16, 1999.
47. Easingwood, Joe. "It's not pub owners' job to enforce CRD's bylaw," Victoria Times-Colonist, March 21, 1999.

VOICES

A capital region bylaw extending smoking bans to such places as restaurants, bars and pubs comes into effect Jan. 1. Today, we offer the views of the regional medical health officer and of a group of adult-oriented businesses — such as bars and pubs — that oppose the bylaw.

Carcinogen has no place in public areas

By Dr. Richard S. Stanwick

CIGARETTE SMOKING is the leading cause of preventable death in Canada, claiming more than 40,000 lives every year. An additional 500 Canadians die annually from breathing second-hand smoke.

Second-hand smoke contains 43 chemicals known to cause cancers. For many of these harmful toxins, there is no acceptable safe level of exposure. The seriousness of the health risk is so great that the United States Environmental Protection Agency has categorized cigarette smoke as a Class 1 carcinogen, the highest of all possible risks.

Since the bylaw regulating smoking in the Capital Regional District was last updated in 1994, more than 300 articles in medical literature have restated the harmful health effects of second-hand smoke.

The medical literature and experts who have addressed the CRD also show that at present no ventilation system meets health standards for satisfactorily dispersing second-hand smoke. To ensure a safe indoor air environment, a wind tunnel of 20 kilometres per hour with continuous outside air exchange would be required. In essence, having a ventilation system addressing the second-hand smoke problem makes about as much sense as having peeing and non-peeing sections in swimming pools.

This bylaw is first and foremost about health.

PRIOR TO THE PASSAGE of Clean Air Bylaw 2401 in June 1996, the CRD board engaged in an extensive public consultation. Public hearings were held, letters were received from interested parties, and an Angus Reid poll was taken which showed more than 60 per cent of the residents of the CRD supported the principles of this bylaw.

Originally, we as health officials, hoped to have the bylaw in place on Jan 1, 1998; however the CRD board chose a compromise date of Jan. 1, 1999 to give businesses an extra year to prepare for the change.

In the two-year lead-up to the bylaw's implementation, many facilities, ranging from restaurants to golf clubs to long-term care facilities, have already implemented outdoor smoking policies or have designated suitable outdoor smoking spaces ready to go when the bylaw takes effect next month. We are convinced the region will see a high degree of compliance, thanks to the careful planning and organization of so many individuals and businesses.

We also know that a clear majority of CRD residents continue to support this bylaw. A new Angus Reid poll just last week found unflagging support for the bylaw since the last survey in 1996. In response to the same question that has been consistently posed in all three Angus Reid polls, the "strong" support for the bylaw increased from 38 per cent in 1996 to 44 per cent. Overall support was slightly up at 66 per cent.

We believe one of the reasons for that support is that the bylaw applies equally to all public premises in the entire Capital Region.

THE CRD HAS responded to the concerns of business that all premises have a level playing field. Unlike other jurisdictions in Canada which have applied smoke-free bylaws only to particular businesses such as restaurants, every business in the CRD will be subject to the same law. Fairness and consistency are key to the success of this bylaw, and no business will have an unfair advantage over others.

What are the average residents of the CRD to expect on Jan. 1, 1999?

After this date, there will be no indoor smoking in restaurants, bars, pubs, casinos, bingo halls and other businesses providing a wide-range of services, creating smoke-free public places and indoor worksites in the CRD.

THE BYLAW WILL BE enforced after that date. For example, individuals smoking in a restaurant in defiance of the bylaw are subject to fines that can increase from $200 to $1,000. Operators of businesses which defy the bylaw will be subject to fines ranging from $500 to $2,000. Enforcement of the bylaw will take place whenever businesses are open, not necessarily only during regular CRD office hours.

What do we expect from this bylaw?

☐ Significantly improved health for workers in the hospitality industry. An article in this week's *Journal of the American Medical Association* showed that in California, bartenders' respiratory health improved dramatically after only two months of moving to a smoke-free work environment.

☐ A high degree of compliance. The bylaw is no different from what is expected of individuals travelling on B.C. Ferries and certainly more accommodating than the policy on most airline flights, all of which changes have been achieved without major compliance problems.

☐ The potential for actual and significant improvements in business for those establishments affected. Last week's survey showed as many as 40 per cent of those surveyed said they are more likely to go to these establishments once they become smoke-free.

And everybody in the CRD will be able to breathe a little bit easier.

Dr. Richard S. Stanwick is the Capital Health Region's medical health officer.

A ventilation system for second-hand smoke makes as much sense as having peeing and non-peeing sections in swimming pools.

PAUL LACHINE

SATURDAY, DECEMBER 12, 1998

Businesses want right to freedom of choice

Here is the Victoria Age of Majority Business Coalition's position on the smoking ban in public places.

To CRD Chairman Geoff Young.

We rightfully request that you call an emergency meeting of the CRD board to hear the concerns of the Age of Majority Business Coalition, a group of concerned owners and representatives of age of majority establishments in the Capital Region.

We do not believe the board has appropriately considered our concerns. We are adults: Our customers and clients are adults. We believe our right to make reasonable business decisions which impact the way in which we meet the needs of our customers, and therefore maintain the sustainability of our revenues, will be significantly undermined by the enactment of this bylaw.

We have built our businesses, operated our establishments and employed our workers by providing hospitality — which clearly is based on accommodation, not discrimination. We believe that all Canadians, including our adult customers, clients and staff, have the right to choose whether or not they patronize or work in an establishment which provides a smoking area which meets or exceeds WCB air quality standards.

We do not believe that it is in the public interest for bylaw enforcement and/or police officers to focus their valuable time and attention on an adult (otherwise law abiding) who chooses to smoke a cigarette in an appropriate area of an adult establishment.

We respectfully demand the right to carry on business selling and facilitating the use of legal products. We respectfully demand that the CRD board exempt age of majority establishments from bylaw 2401.

Gordon Card, Monkey Tree Pub,
Grant Olson, Strathcona Hotel,
Coalition Co-Chairs

THE AGE OF MAJORITY Business Coalition has the following questions for the Capital Regional District:

☐ If the issue is really about the air quality of a workplace, why is the CRD focusing attention and resources on an issue more appropriately dealt with by the Workers' Compensation Board? Is this not a duplication of effort and taxpayers' expense?

☐ Why is the CRD ignoring the decision of other municipalities and regional districts of the province that are waiting for the WCB air quality guidelines in the year 2000?

☐ What is the real cost of this initiative including: program development, research, education, administration, advertising and enforcement? We calculate the total cost could be over $2 million.

☐ Why are the politicians allowing the CRD to hire and/or utilize more than 30 "smoking police" when other CRD budgets (health, garbage, roads) are being cut?

☐ How is this bylaw going to be enforced? We want to see the enforcement plan, who the key players are (both within the CRD and other partner agencies) and how the plan will be managed fairly throughout all adult establishments within the CRD.

☐ The politicians have jumped the gun on their anti-smoking bylaw. Do they understand the issues of our industry and choose to ignore them, or do they just not plainly understand them, or are they not being told the truth by CRD employees?

☐ Why are the elected officials allowing Dr. Richard Stanwick, an unelected official, to push his own personal agenda to make smoking history?

☐ The tourism and hospitality industry is a swiftly growing sector of our provincial economy. How do we maintain the viability of these sectors in a region that chooses to close the door on the portion of our adult visitors and locals who wish to enjoy a cigarette in an adult establishment?

☐ Our industry survey has indicated the potential for substantial job loss due to the smoking ban. Do CRD politicians have a plan to re-employ, relocate or subsidize these workers, as many of them have been employed in the service industry for years and have limited options?

☐ The B.C. government is spending millions of dollars on employment programs in the hospitality industry. If this sector shrinks instead of grows, these tax dollars will have been wasted! Does the CRD know something about the provincial government's plans that the rest of us don't?

☐ Have local politicians lost control of a third level of government, the CRD?

THE VICTORIA Age of Majority Business Coalition's platform is:

☐ To support in principle the Clean Air Quality Initiative for customers and employees as recommended by the Workers Compensation Board's provincewide initiative in the year 2000;

☐ To assist the CRD to develop and deliver youth and adult education programs on the hazards of smoking tobacco and approaches to smoking cessation;

☐ To demand the right to carry on business selling and facilitating the use of legal products;

☐ To uphold the freedom of choice for all Canadians.

Estimated annual impact on CRD licensed establishments

☐ A loss of **$32.9 million in revenue.**
☐ A loss of **316 full-time jobs.**
☐ A loss of **305 part-time jobs.**

9

Our Day in Court

*"All progress has resulted from people
who took unpopular positions."*
— Adlai Stevenson

The change in the bylaw in March 1999 gave the regional board and health department much-needed ammunition in the battle with the defiant bars and pubs. But by that time, no one in the health department was naïve enough to believe it would bring about compliance in most of the openly defiant establishments. Those operators had made it far too clear that they were not going to give in until they had no options left.

The Freedom of Choice Coalition's first step was to seek a meeting with the provincial minister of municipal affairs. Brian Mayzes and other spokespersons wanted to argue to minister Jenny Kwan that the regional board was exceeding its authority in its changes to the bylaw, and that it had based its decision on inaccurate information, ranging from the likely economic effects to the situation in California. Kwan agreed to a meeting, but made it clear from the beginning that she was most unlikely to side with the protesters. The New Democrat government to which she belonged was continuing its own crusade against Big Tobacco and had become the first Canadian province to launch its own lawsuit parallelling the U.S. experience in trying to get the tobacco industry to pay the health care costs of tobacco-caused illnesses. The NDP had also instituted numerous other anti-smoking initiatives, ranging from a Teen Tobacco Council (where young people learned peer leadership skills to try to discourage other youth from taking up the habit), to a requirement that the tobacco companies disclose the actual chemical composition of their cigarettes' smoke to government.

Behind the scenes, the provincial government had made it clear it supported the CRD initiative, although in public, government spokesmen said it was entirely a local decision. The meeting went nowhere. The actively defiant returned to defiance.

However, Stevenson and her enforcement team hoped that some who had been teetering on the brink between compliance and defiance would decide it was easier to obey the law than to devote large sums of time, money and energy to an ongoing legal battle. Even more importantly, they knew they could begin to work toward the goal of applying for an injunction in B.C. Supreme Court against the worst offenders if they still refused to comply.

In April, the enforcement team's efforts got a huge boost from another court decision, this one from the province's highest court, the B.C. Court of Appeal. It was one of those decisions written for lawyers and those involved in the complexities of municipal law. It attracted absolutely no public attention. But the five-page judgment made CRD lawyers McDannold and Stuart jubilant.

The use of injunctions was a time-honoured process in the B.C. courts, used more perhaps than in any other province. Most often they were used against protesters, especially protesters who wanted to save various provincial forests from clear-cut logging. To do so, they would physically prevent the logging, sometimes by blocking roads, sometimes by setting platforms in trees and occupying them, sometimes by chaining themselves to logging equipment and machinery with bicycle padlocks. The largest, in the summer of 1993, had seen a total of 856 demonstrators arrested at the Clayoquot Valley on Vancouver Island.

When a logging company found itself faced with such a protest, it would immediately go to the courts to obtain an injunction banning the protesters from disrupting the company's operations. But the applications to gain those injunctions were often long, drawn-out processes — and the companies had no guarantee of winning. The protesters were allowed to make numerous arguments as to why the injunction should not be granted, ranging from the company's own behaviour to the question of whether "irrevocable harm" would be done if the

Chapter 9 - Our Day in Court

injunction were not granted. The environmentalists would argue that the company would suffer only short-term economic harm if the injunction were delayed, whereas if the first-growth forest were cut down, the environment would indeed be irrevocably harmed. Judges had a great deal of discretion in deciding, in each individual circumstance, whether an injunction should be granted.

Until the April court decision, McDannold had feared that attempts to get injunctions against rebel bar owners would require the same process. He envisioned the possibility of lengthy, rancorous hearings at which the bar owners could make all sorts of arguments against the bylaw — and perhaps persuade a judge to delay granting an injunction to require them to obey it. He knew that that would be devastating to enforcement because the bar owners would consider it open season to defy the law.

But the April decision changed that. A three-member panel of the Appeals Court ruled that injunctions brought by local governments, such as a regional board, were not to be treated like other injunction applications. Rather, explained Mr. Justice George Cumming, they should be considered "statutory injunctions" because they were specifically permitted under the provincial Local Government Act.

"The court has no discretion to deny [the local government] an injunction once a breach [of a bylaw] is established...." said Cumming. "The court's only role is to determine whether a defendant had breached the bylaw the municipality seeks to enforce." [48]

That meant that bar owners couldn't argue the fairness of the bylaw in the first place. They couldn't argue that it was being unfairly enforced against some establishments and not others. They couldn't argue that the CRD board hadn't behaved fairly and didn't deserve an injunction, nor that the bar owners would suffer "irrevocable harm" economically if the injunction were granted. All McDannold had to do to get his injunction was to show the court that a valid bylaw was in place, and then to provide evidence that the establishment in question had been defying it. It was a huge benefit to the regional district.

The next step was to gather and organize the necessary evidence for the shortened process. Although inspectors and environmental health officers had been out regularly for the first weeks of bylaw enforcement, the long-term strategy had always been that enforcement would be a complaint-driven process, just as it was for other workplaces. The procedures for handling complaints of non-compliance from disgruntled staff or non-smoking patrons had been in place from January 4, and hundreds of complaints had already been received. A special telephone line had been installed on which complainants could leave messages, naming non-compliant facilities — and every morning when Stevenson and her staff came to work, they found dozens of complaints logged. Some came from citizen members of non-smokers' rights organizations who went out to check on compliance and reported their findings. But many more came from staff members who had hoped for a non-smoking environment, from patrons who had found the non-smoking atmosphere they'd anticipated to be non-existent, and even from operators of rival establishments, those who had decided to abide by the bylaw. They had been promised a level playing field, and they saw no reason why others should get away with defying the law — and, in their view, gaining a business advantage from it.

Now Stevenson and her staff added up the number of complaints received about individual establishments and descriptions of how staff and management were reacting. They added that data to the results of their own inspections to decide which individual establishments would be the first to face the new enforcement proceedings. They began sending out the warning letters as agreed in the new policy. To no one's surprise, the letters did nothing to bring any of those targeted into compliance. By June 1999, Stevenson had compiled a list of six of the worst offenders to bring back to the regional board. The board backed the decision to begin court action. It was agreed that applications for an injunction would be filed against six individual establishments. All six were ones who had blatantly disregarded the bylaw and encouraged their patrons to do so from the very beginning. Topping the list

Chapter 9 - Our Day in Court

were Mayzes' Esquimalt Inn and Thursday's Sports Pub, where the patron carrying the concealed daggers had been arrested.

When the court paperwork was filed, the health officials were optimistic that they were on the way to solving the problem of non-compliance. Injunction applications could usually be heard in the B.C. courts within a few months of being filed, and McDannold figured that with Justice Cumming's judgment in place, none should take more than an hour or two of court time. They had hopes that by the fall they would have the legal orders in place to force the rebel bar owners to comply.

However, it proved not to be that simple. The establishments got together and hired lawyer John Green to defend their interests in the proceedings. Green, a regular smoker himself, was well known in the city as a criminal defence lawyer, often taking on the cases of those accused of impaired driving or trafficking in drugs. He was a stickler for procedure and for ensuring that any government authority had correctly followed every step of law and process.

But Green never got to try the case in court. That autumn he was involved in a bad automobile crash and suffered a serious arm injury, which made it impossible for him to write for months. He began applying for adjournments on his cases, including the injunction issue. For the first few weeks, he was optimistic that the injury would heal quickly and he'd soon be back, but it didn't happen.

For the health officials the delay grew intolerable. Until those first court cases were settled, the regional board didn't want to put money into starting any new court cases. Although from the region's point of view, the goal of the court case was to obtain injunctions against establishments that were refusing to obey a duly passed bylaw, the operators had said publicly they were planning to challenge the validity of the bylaw as part of their defence. McDannold was convinced on the basis of the Cumming's decision that such a strategy wouldn't be upheld, but the delay still meant that any pub owners charged in future would merely ask the court to wait until the first cases were settled and the bylaw ruled valid or invalid, so identical cases weren't taking up valuable court time.

But the delays meant that effective enforcement for the small minority of establishments that were still defiant had stalled badly. Stevenson and her team still received complaints, monitored establishments, went out on inspections and even issued some tickets to individual smokers. But without the power of heavy fines against the recalcitrant operators, defiance in the bar community became, if anything, worse. Operators were well aware that no new court actions were going to be started, so they considered that they had, for all practical purposes, a free ride to defy the law for a while without consequences. The health officials hadn't expected the case to drag out for months. Although nearly all restaurants and many bars remained compliant, piles of inspection reports and complaints on the hotline built up relating to the defiant operators. Nothing more could be done until the case made its way to court. In many bars, the situation was even worse than it had been before the 100 per cent ban was implemented. While they were required to keep 50 or 60 per cent of their space non-smoking, most of the bars had at least come close to meeting the rules. But now the defiant ones weren't even bothering doing that. The smokers had completely taken over, and there was no way to avoid the blue haze.

Throughout the waiting period, the hospitality industry played a constant game of words, often in the media, with Dr. Stanwick and Stevenson. At one point Mayzes insisted that he believed he had now worked out a policy which met the letter of the law.[49] He explained that he told his customers that the bylaw prohibited him from serving them while they were smoking. So, he said, "they put their cigarettes out, I serve them." If they lit up again mere seconds later, he said, it wasn't his problem; he had not disobeyed the bylaw. It would, Stevenson said, be up to the courts to decide whether that piece of equivocation met the requirements of the legislation.

Mayzes, the other bars awaiting their court date and some of their supporters put up new signs in their establishments. "Under threat of injunction," they read, "the proprietors cannot encourage, condone and/or assist our valued customers in violating the Clean Air Bylaw."

At another point in the waiting game, the defiant bars took to deluging Stevenson's office every afternoon with faxes. They had a form printed up in which they complained that people were smoking in their establishment, and they requested help from the health office's enforcement personnel. The number of smokers with whom the proprietors couldn't deal varied from day to day and from bar to bar, ranging anywhere from three to 30 on any given day. Their apparent hope was that they would be able to argue in court that it wasn't fair or reasonable for them to be held responsible for smokers in their establishments, if the officials wouldn't come to assist them when they asked. Nowhere on the form, however, did it ever say that they had genuinely refused service to the smoking patrons — the step that the judge in Vancouver's Doll and Penny's case had predicted would actually deal with the problem behaviour.

An enforcement officer sometimes would try to respond immediately to the complaints, either on the phone or in person. They usually reported back to Stevenson that the bar's managers were never actually very pleased to see them on those days when they did show up.

The hospitality lobby also continued to try to convince the public that the bylaw was unnecessary, impractical and unenforceable. They brought to town John Luik, who was co-author of a book entitled *Passive Smoke: The EPA's Betrayal of Science and Policy*. The book was published by the Fraser Institute, a right-wing British Columbia-based think tank. It concentrated on the decision by a judge in the tobacco-farming state of North Carolina that threw out the U.S. Environmental Protection Agency's assertion that second-hand smoke should be categorized as a Class A carcinogen, claiming that the process the EPA used to come to this conclusion was faulty. Victoria media wrote about the book, and Luik appeared on television to reiterate his views that second-hand smoke posed a negligible health risk to non-smokers, and that if governments wanted to regulate it, they should do so solely on the basis that it was a nuisance, not a health danger.[50]

The book and the Victoria appearance garnered widespread criticism from both medical personnel and anti-smoking groups. AirSpace noted that both Luik and his co-author, Dr. Gio Gori, had a long history of being paid by the tobacco industry. As well, they pointed out that Luik's doctorate was actually in philosophy, and had nothing to do with medicine or any of the health professions. (Later, an investigation by the CBC's highly regarded investigative show *The Fifth Estate* would show that Luik had also been fired from two Canadian post-secondary institutions for misrepresenting his academic credentials. *The Fifth Estate* also discovered that the tobacco industry had provided funding to the Fraser Institute for a project that included the publication of Luik and Gori's book.[51])

Dr. Stanwick was backed by the B.C. Medical Association when he pointed out that Luik was ignoring hundreds of studies that showed a variety of health risks from second-hand smoke. He pointed out that even if one accepted the judge's logic, he had dealt solely with the links to lung cancer in his decision, and had not dealt with the many other ailments brought on or exacerbated by second-hand smoke, ranging from asthma to heart disease.

Ventilation expert James Repace wrote the most scathing review of the book for Canada's Non-Smokers' Rights Association. "The polemic by Gori and Luik," he concluded, "like second-hand smoke itself, is toxic waste. It should be disposed of safely in a sealed container."

It was January 1, 2000, before Stevenson and her team finally received some respite from their enforcement battles. On that day, the province-wide Workers' Compensation Board regulations were implemented. The net result was that rules very similar to the Victoria bylaw came into effect in every hospitality establishment in British Columbia. The difference was that the

Chapter 9 - Our Day in Court

WCB had wide-ranging enforcement powers, powers that very few businesses were ever keen to run afoul of. If the WCB had to progress to actual enforcement action, the fine would not be $100. It was much more likely to start at anywhere between $1,500 and $4,000 — and go up for repeated offences. Moreover, the reputation of the WCB was that once its inspectors had decided a business appeared to be defying board orders, it was likely to keep inspecting until it had checked everything from the safety provisions for the window washers to the training manuals provided for employees.

Weeks before the WCB smoking bans went into effect, Stevenson and the local inspectors had negotiated a procedure for joint enforcement. Since the WCB system was also expected to be complaint-driven, the two agencies agreed they would share complaints and inspection reports.

The level of compliance rose somewhat when the WCB ban took effect, with only a handful of defiant bars continuing to defy the rules. But several of those establishments had still managed to acquire enough complaints in the first two months of the new regulations to receive formal warning letters from the WCB. The letters promised further enforcement action shortly if the situation didn't change.

Across the province the hospitality industry was even more furious at the WCB rules than the Victoria establishments had been at the CRD bylaw. Widespread civil disobedience of the regulations caused the WCB to admit that the compliance rate in the first few weeks was only about 65 per cent. Vance Campbell, president of the B.C. Cabaret Owners' Association — one of the groups most vigorously opposing the rules — acquired copious media attention through issuing all his bartending staff gas masks and white paper suits to wear while on the job. He said he figured that by doing so, the workers were genuinely protected from any risk from second-hand smoke while patrons continued to be free to smoke as they wanted.[52] But the system didn't last long and Campbell was soon hit with fines totalling more than $10,000 for breaking the rules.

Another bar in Vancouver tried to get around the new system by insisting all its bartenders were "independent contractors," and not employees at all, and therefore weren't covered by the Workers' Compensation Board legislation. Out in Sooke, Don Rittaler tried a similar tack, laying off all 10 staff in his pub, and replacing them with family members, another group not within the jurisdiction of the WCB.[53]

Vance Campbell and other hospitality organizations also kept what they called a running total of jobs lost because of the ban, and released the list to the media regularly. The numbers had topped 600, according to Campbell's statistics,[54] before the ban had been in place two months — but he could never provide any independent confirmation of that.

The most important thing that Campbell and other hospitality coalition members did was to launch a lawsuit challenging the legality of the new rules. Lawyer Tim Williamson argued that the legislation establishing the WCB system required the board to hold public hearings before making any changes to workplace health and safety regulations. He said that although the board had held hearings on the general question of smoking in the workplace, at the time when they did so, hospitality establishments were exempted. He argued that they could not legally be brought into the fold without a new round of public hearings.

In the middle of March, the B.C. Supreme Court justice who had heard the case, Madame Justice Sunni Stromberg-Stein, handed down her ruling. She agreed with the bar owners. The process was flawed, she said, and so the regulations were of no legal force.[55]

The WCB was forced to go back to square one and begin work to schedule a whole new round of public hearings before it could consider reinstituting the regulations.

There was jubilation in bars across the province on the night the judgment was announced. But not in Victoria. Within hours of the judgment, Dr. Stanwick had gone public to make it clear that nothing was going to change with the CRD bylaw as a result of the

WCB decision.[56] In fact, he pointed out, "we did in fact engage in exactly the kind of consultation process that the judge criticized the Workers' Compensation Board for omitting." Not for the first time, Dr. Stanwick was glad he was adamant that the CRD have its own bylaw and that the regional board had not been persuaded by the lobbying efforts to wait until 2000 and use the Workers' Compensation Board rules as their own. Had they done that, the region would have been left with no regulations for bars and pubs at all, as was now the case in much of the rest of the province.

Dr. Stanwick and Stevenson realized the urgency of getting their own court case back on track. Without the WCB's enforcement powers, the small minority of non-compliant bars were returning to open defiance within a matter of days. The health officials worried that if a genuine level playing field couldn't be established, other bars might feel they had no choice but to defy the bylaw too, since the non-compliant were using smoking as a way to gain a competitive advantage.

Yet it was still several more weeks before a court date could finally be found. The region received an interim injunction, requiring the establishments to obey the bylaw until a full hearing of the case could be held. But that was only the first step for Stevenson and the enforcement team. To proceed further, they had to be able to provide evidence that would stand up in court to show that an establishment was continuing to defy the bylaw. Only then could lawyers McDannold and Stuart argue that the establishments were in contempt of the court order — the decision they needed in order to have the fines high enough to serve as a sufficient deterrent. Any lower fine and the owners were likely to conclude that the money to be made from smoking patrons exceeded the costs of the penalties.

Throughout the summer and fall of 2000, Stevenson's team gathered evidence in the small number of defiant bars. It was no longer any good for Stevenson herself, or others who had been key in enforcement from the outset, to visit bars for this purpose. They were well known to staff and even to regular patrons, and the threat of the injunction was enough to ensure that the bartenders would see that the rules were obeyed for the short time in which the personnel were inside.

Instead the team used environmental health officers, who were less likely to be recognized, to take up the undercover roles as ordinary patrons. They carefully noted what signs were present, whether ashtrays were visible, whether staff would bring patrons ashtrays or cigarettes on request. They watched to see how the staff treated people who were smoking, whether they were reminded about the bylaw, or told they'd be cut off if they continued to disobey. They checked to see if the staff themselves were smoking or were cheerfully serving patrons who continued to smoke. The reports left no doubt that the managers and staff were active participants in encouraging patrons to break the law.

Stevenson had said both publicly and privately from the beginning that her goal was not to make operators pay hefty fines, but rather to get them to abide by the bylaw. The ongoing and protracted process took its toll on the accused establishments as well. One by one, they agreed to sign voluntary (but legally binding) agreements promising they would ensure the bylaw was obeyed in their premises if the lawsuit was dropped. In some cases, like that of the Esquimalt Inn, the new attitude was the result of a change of ownership. In others, the owners simply tired of paying lawyers for what was beginning to appear to be a never-ending process, especially as it seemed likely the Workers' Compensation Board would eventually make similar demands, even if the inevitable had been delayed a year or so. Some were warned by their lawyers that in light of Justice Cumming's decision about local government injunctions, their chances of winning were slim.

Dr. Stanwick and Stevenson took time out during the summer of 2000 to put together a team to travel to the Workers' Compensation Board hearings to try to convince the board not to weaken its stance. The WCB itself had hired a statistical team from Pacific Analytics to look at the likely economic impacts of its move to smoke-free hospitality facilities, and that team had used the CRD example as its case study. Their findings mirrored those found

Chapter 9 - Our Day in Court

in most other places which had introduced similar legislation.[57] They found that the bylaw had had no quantifiable impact in the first three months of 1999 because a huge exhibit at the Royal B.C. Museum in Victoria had attracted so many tourists that the results were skewed. In the second quarter of the year, though, the hospitality industry did experience a 6.4 per cent downturn in sales, a number the researchers called "significant."

By the middle of the year, though, everyone had apparently become used to the new rules. No impact was shown for the time from mid-1999 to August 2000. The report's conclusion was that "within the CRD there are no long-term impacts associated with the no-smoking bylaw . . . long-run tourism activity in the CRD was not negatively affected by the introduction of the no-smoking bylaw" [emphasis theirs].

By the time the court case on the first potential contempt charge arrived, only a single bar was left to contest it. That was Thursday's Sports Pub. The Logan brothers made no secret of the fact that they felt abandoned and even betrayed by their fellow entrepreneurs. When the coalition had begun, they said, they had always assumed that it would be a case of one for all and all for one. They had hoped for legal, financial or even just emotional support from the owners and operators of the other establishments which had been involved.

It hadn't turned out that way. Fourteen months later, the Logans were in the courthouse all alone. Even worse, they were also facing the fine and the lawyers' fees on their own. When the case began on February 13, 2001, McDannold and Stuart presented to Justice John Bouck the evidence the staff had carefully gathered to show that Thursday's was doing nothing to discourage smoking. They had documented numerous instances in which staff served people who were smoking, or even smoked themselves at the bar.

Then it fell to Stuart to suggest what the CRD thought would be an appropriate penalty. She suggested a total of $75,000 — a fine of $25,000 for John Logan and for each of the two corporate entities that own the business. Disobeying a court order is far more serious than a simple bylaw breach, she noted, and this disobedience had been repeated, prolonged and obviously intentional. Although the sum seemed huge, it fell within the range possible, given B.C.'s history of enforcing contempt proceedings against demonstrators who had breached injunction in their protests. Indeed, many of those demonstrators had been required by the courts not only to pay large fines, but also to spend time in jail.

Thursday's lawyer Peter Klassen (who had eventually taken over from Green) barely had time to start his argument before the court day ended. He just had time to make his first argument — that it was unfair for the CRD to be going after Thursday's alone when it was well known in the community that several dozen bars throughout the region were equally defiant. Because the level playing field had never been made to work, he argued, Thursday's staff couldn't afford to be tough on smokers either, or the clients would simply take their business to another non-compliant establishment.

Klassen had been scheduled to continue his arguments the next morning, but instead he approached McDannold and Stuart before the second day of the hearing ever began. His clients, he said, wanted to work out a deal.

The Logan brothers later admitted frankly that the possibility of a $75,000 fine had horrified them — it was more than they'd ever dreamed they might be required to pay, and far more than they could afford. Bouck was a judge who had a reputation of being particularly tough in contempt of court cases, based primarily on how he handled some of those environmental protest cases.

McDannold and Stuart were happy to negotiate — and happy to reduce the amount of money they were asking for, provided a full agreement could be reached. But they had some preconditions upon which they insisted. Thursday's would have to agree to a permanent injunction, requiring them to obey the bylaw in perpetuity. They would have to agree that it be legally registered as a binding document in open court. And they would have to agree to a monetary penalty substantial enough that it would show other

Chapter 9 - Our Day in Court

non-compliant establishments that the injunction process was not to be trifled with. Fine, Klassen said. For almost the full morning, the lawyers worked out the precise details of the agreement. In the end, Thursday's agreed to pay a total of $20,000 — a $15,000 fine plus $5,000 in costs.

"I hope it will resolve all the problems," said Justice Bouck as he formalized the order, "but I don't think it will in this city."

Dr. Stanwick and Stevenson were delighted. The size of the fine should be enough to make the most defiant bylaw operator nervous, they believed, and, even more important, the permanent injunction was now registered and on file as a Supreme Court judgment.

But Justice Bouck was right. The judgment didn't have the immediate chill on the outright defiance that they had expected. Over the next few weeks, the complaints continued to come in. The *Times-Colonist* sent columnist Jack Knox out one evening to check the bars to see how many were now genuinely 100 per cent non-smoking. "Right now the playing field is about as level as the Himalayas," Knox wrote.[58] He found that only about 50 per cent of the bars were obeying the bylaw, even yet.

However, the judgment did give Dr. Stanwick and Stevenson a powerful new weapon. They returned to the regional board and were given permission to begin the process of preparing to take the worst offenders to court, yet again. That meant more undercover visits by environmental health officers, more detailed reports, more negotiations with those operators who received the first round of court documents and realized they had now reached that point where they had little choice but to obey. Despite the added work, they believed it was now just a matter of putting the final pieces in the puzzle.

In some cases, the health region staff found themselves facing a difficult challenge. In establishments such as Rittaler's Sooke River Hotel, all the EHOs and bylaw officers were too well known by the bar management and staff for them to monitor the situation incognito. After overcoming initial reluctance by the team, Dr. Stanwick changed enforcement tactics and hired private investigators (PIs). McDannold had worked with such agencies on cases requiring discrete surveillance and made the necessary arrangements. The PIs visited the bars undercover as customers and checked on the same things as the EHOs had done. In some cases they were able to make surreptitious videotapes of activity within the premises, something that is legal in Canada although audiotapes made in the same circumstances would not be permissible. Whether staff members or private investigators carried out the inspections, they wrote up detailed reports each day on their findings, a report that could later be easily turned into an affidavit for court.

The team was taken completely by surprise when, in March 2001 — one month after the successful Thursday's court case — Oak Bay mayor Christopher Causton moved that the regional board should revisit the issue once again. The reason, Causton explained, was that the Workers' Compensation Board had provided its new recommendations on what should happen province-wide. After hearing more than 600 submissions, the WCB had ended up with a policy that was very similar to the one the courts had tossed out, but with one big difference for drinking establishments. The WCB was recommending that these premises be allowed to have designated smoking rooms — provided employees would normally never have to enter them. It suggested that establishments could, if the Liquor Control and Licensing Board would allow it, establish separate self-serve rooms; a person could walk into the main bar and order their beer, then take it back to the smoking room to consume it. The rooms would have to be designed and ventilated so that the smoke from them would never end up in the portion of the establishment where the workers spent their time.

Causton again suggested the region should use the WCB standards instead of having different ones of its own. He never, he said, had been comfortable with the idea that bars and restaurants in Victoria had to deal with a different set of rules from those in the rest of the province.

Chapter 9 - Our Day in Court

It was enough to get the whole debate re-ignited. Although the hospitality industry wasn't thrilled with the new WCB proposal, the smoking rooms made it more acceptable to them than an all-out smoking ban. They were happy to encourage CRD directors to make the change to that format.

Some CRD directors were also beginning to worry about the ongoing costs of enforcing the region's own bylaw. They knew that court cases ate up budgets, and they feared an unending string of court cases against defiant bar owners. Indeed by the time the issue came to the board, Stevenson had sent 27 establishments formal letters explaining Thursday's decision to them and warning them that they could be next if they didn't fall into line.

In this, Dr. Stanwick got a boost from the Capital health region, a new structure created in a government reorganization of the health system, and by which both Dr. Stanwick and Stevenson were now both formally employed — even though the elected CRD board remained the legal "board of health." Dr. Stanwick was now a senior executive with the new health region and directly reported to the CEO. He made the case to the health region board in support of the enforcement of healthy public policy. The health region's new CEO, Rick Roger, recommended the region should support the effort, and committed $50,000 to cover that amount in enforcement costs for the ensuing year. That amount had been approximately the court and lawyers' costs to date of the battle against the first six. Roger also attended the CRD board meeting when the resource issue was discussed in a show of support.

Dr. Stanwick breathed a sigh of relief. He had had visions of the CRD board maintaining the bylaw, but refusing to provide the resources to fund the necessary enforcement actions properly. He and Stevenson were both convinced that the stream of court cases would not in fact be never-ending. They suspected that once the courts had validated the bylaw one more time, court challenges would fade away.

Even the promise of $50,000 didn't much impress some of the bylaw's opponents, such as Stew Young, mayor of the suburb of

Langford. "So he throws $50,000 in there?" snorted Young. "Well, the next court case that they face isn't going to be $56,000. Wait until one of the big guys decides to fight."[59] He was still sending the subtle message to the unhappy owners and operators that they needn't worry much about obeying the bylaw, because it was still somehow going to disappear.

The CRD board members wanted a detailed report on how the regional bylaw would differ from the WCB system before they made a decision. Dr. Stanwick and Stevenson pulled together a lengthy comparison in which they noted the confusion that would be caused if the CRD went back to a system in which only workplaces would be covered. What, for instance, would they do about schoolyards, elevators and the concourses of shopping malls — all of which were now smoke-free in Victoria, but wouldn't be covered by the new WCB regulations. Dr. Stanwick also warned the board that the WCB system would reintroduce smoking as a competitive factor in the industry in the region, because many smaller establishments were unlikely to have either the space or the money to install a complex smoking room of the sort the WCB had described.

After another heated debate, the CRD board voted to stay with the existing bylaw by a vote of 12 to 9. It was too close for comfort, but it allowed the health officials to move on towards the final enforcement measures that were needed.

Of the 27 establishments that had received warning letters, formal court proceedings were started against 12. Just as the first time, as the date drew closer to the actual court hearing, a large majority decided they would rather sign voluntary declarations of compliance. The court case proceeded against only two: Don Rittaler and his Sooke River Hotel, and the Tudor House in Esquimalt, both long-time leaders in the anti-bylaw crusade.

For this court case, the owners hired Tim Williamson, the lawyer who had successfully represented the hospitality industry against the Workers' Compensation Board. Throughout the summer, McDannold and Williamson exchanged documents and discussed procedures. Williamson, like Green, was very thorough procedurally and wanted to see all the documents related to the bylaw's history.

The exchange of documents made McDannold realize he had a problem, potentially a major problem. All bylaws passed by local boards of health had to be signed off by the provincial ministry to be deemed effective. In this case, the person to sign off the bylaw was, ironically, Dr. Peck — and he'd done so one day too early, just hours before he had the legal authorization to do so. Theoretically such a tiny misstep could have been enough to allow the bars to win their court case and require the whole bylaw to be debated and passed again. The clear solution to the problem was to have passed another MEVA (under the Municipalities Enabling and Validating Act), as had been done to remedy the lack of clarity in the authorizing legislation back in 1998. Because the legislature was in session, it would be possible to have the MEVA passed quickly and quietly. But McDannold and Dr. Stanwick were very anxious about the whole proceeding.

By this point, the supportive New Democrat government had been replaced by the less sympathetic Liberal administration and no one was quite sure whether the legislation would be passed in time. When it was finally introduced in the legislature just three days before the summer session ended, McDannold, Dr. Stanwick and the rest of the team, who felt as if they had been holding their breath for six weeks, were able to breathe freely again.

Williamson was offended by the MEVA but there was nothing he could do about it. By the time the case reached court in October, it was the official law of the land.

The case came before Justice Allen Melvin, one of the longest-sitting judges in the province. Again McDannold presented evidence gathered from the undercover expeditions.

Williamson got more of a chance to argue for the defence than Klassen had. He argued that it was unfair for the regional board to move immediately to an injunction proceeding rather than laying a charge of breaching the bylaw. An injunction application, he noted, didn't provide for several checks and balances in the system that can be used if someone is facing a criminal or quasi-criminal charge. However, Justice Melvin, who had previously admitted he didn't like losing his discretion in such cases, followed the Court of Appeal decision and ruled that provincial legislation made it quite clear that a local government body could choose which route of enforcement it wished to take.

Justice Melvin also had no trouble in finding that both establishments had been in breach. "I have no hesitation concluding on the evidence presented that there is an abundance of evidence which would demonstrate that customers of the Tudor House and the Sooke River Hotel were smoking cigarettes or other tobacco combustibles on the premises," he said in his written judgment.[60] "Further, I find that the staff, by providing cigarettes and ashtrays, and continuing to serve customers who smoke, were encouraging the consumption of tobacco in violation of the bylaw, rather than discouraging that practice."

He issued an injunction in very specific terms. The two establishments were required to post specific signage and to let customers know they'd be refused service if they continued to light up indoors. They also had to follow through and refuse to serve anyone who was still smoking. The bars did not have to pay any monetary penalty as they had never received a formal injunction.

As Dr. Stanwick had suspected, that judgment was the end of the organized defiance. If Tim Williamson couldn't win them a court case, most bar operators figured, then probably no one ever could. As far as smoking was concerned, the region had become something very close to a level playing field. It had taken six years, almost to the day, from the time that Dr. Stanwick had first come to town and suggested moving so quickly to a full smoking ban.

Chapter 9 - Our Day in Court

48. Judgment of the B.C. Court of Appeal in Langley (Township) vs Wood, 1999, BCCA 260.

49. Cleverley, Bill. "Inn agrees to pay smoking fine," Victoria Times-Colonist, August 11, 1999.

50. Watts, Richard. "Book refuting health hazard of smoking causes flap," Victoria Times Colonist, April 28, 1999.

51. Tremonti, Anna Marie et al. Fifth Estate, CBC National, June 21, 2001.

52. Vallis, Mary. "Pub workers don respirators," The Province, January 3, 2000.

53. Cleverley, Bill. "Sooke pub continues to condone smoking," Victoria Times-Colonist, January 21, 2000.

54. "660 layoffs blamed on 'smoke police,'" The Province, March 2, 2000.

55. Judgment of Mme Justice Sunni Stromberg-Stein in B.C. Liquor Licencees vs WCB, 2000 BCSC 505

56. Cleverley, Bill. "Regional butt bylaw unaffected by ruling," Victoria Times-Colonist, March 23, 2000.

57. Pacific Analytics Inc. "Economic Impacts of the Proposed Amendments to the ETS Regulations," February 2001.

58. Knox, Jack. "Phony war smoulders in bars," Victoria Times-Colonist, February 26, 2001.

59. Cleverley, Bill. "CRD sets aside $50,000 to defend smoking bylaw," Victoria Times-Colonist, April 27, 2001.

60. Judgment of Mr. Justice Allen Melvin in CRD vs. Sooke River Hotel and Jadwiga Holdings et al., 2001 BCSC 1373.

DON'T SMOKE OUR BYLAW!

To: The Residents of the Capital Regional District

The Capital Regional District Clean Air Bylaw is in jeopardy.

TODAY, Wednesday, April 25th, the Capital Regional District (CRD) Board will be debating a proposal to weaken the Clean Air Bylaw which has provided all citizens of the Capital Region smoke-free indoor public places for the past 2 ½ years. The weaker secondhand smoke regulation of the Workers' Compensation Board (WCB) is being actively promoted as an alternative to the Clean Air Bylaw.

The Clean Air Coalition of B.C. urges you to oppose this backwards step.

Here's why:

THE CURRENT BYLAW...requires all indoor public places in the CRD to be free of secondhand tobacco smoke.
THE WCB PROPOSAL...would allow all businesses to construct "smoking rooms" for their customers. No age restrictions for entry would apply. Entry by staff would be limited.

THE CURRENT BYLAW...provides a level playing field among businesses, with smoking removed as a competitive factor.
THE WCB PROPOSAL...would give a competitive advantage to businesses that could afford to construct and operate a "smoking room."

THE CURRENT BYLAW...recognizes the latest (1999) ventilation engineering standards which specify that there is no safe level of exposure to secondhand smoke.
THE WCB PROPOSAL...relies on an old (1989) standard which does not protect health but makes the smoking environment more comfortable.

THE CURRENT BYLAW... bans smoking in schools and on school property.
THE WCB PROPOSAL...would allow schools to reinstitute smoking rooms for staff and create smoking rooms for students.

THE CURRENT BYLAW...provides one set of clear, easy-to-understand rules for everyone. Indoor air is smoke-free.
THE WCB PROPOSAL...is not comprehensive enough to protect the public as it is responsible only for workers' health.

A combination of the Clean Air Bylaw and WCB Regulations can only result in greater complexity for both administration and enforcement. This mix would be confusing for business operators, employees, the public, and visitors to the region. For instance, would smoking be allowed on elevators and in public restrooms?

We know the majority of residents of the CRD have supported the Clean Air Bylaw since 1996. The most recent IPSOS-Reid poll showed that 77 percent of adults in the Capital Region favoured the Bylaw – including the majority of smokers.

We know the Bylaw works. The three healthiest regions in B.C. are Richmond, North Shore, and the CRD. It is no coincidence that they are also the three areas with bylaws which provide for all indoor public places being smoke-free.

We know that tobacco products are not illegal. We recognize the right of adults to choose to smoke. However, the purpose of the Clean Air Bylaw is to protect the health of all people living within the CRD by determining where smoking occurs.

We urge you to support your local Clean Air Bylaw by sending an e-mail through the CRD's website at (http://www.crd.bc.ca/cro/response.htm), faxing the CRD Board members at (360-3130), or dropping off a letter at 524 Yates St. Otherwise, call the CRD at (360-3128) to register your support for the Clean Air Bylaw. If you want to read more about the issue, you can find the report of the Region's Medical Health Officer at (http://www.caphealth.org/mho.html).

Scott McDonald,
Executive Director,
British Columbia Lung Association

+ BRITISH COLUMBIA LUNG ASSOCIATION

Bobbe Wood,
Chief Executive Officer
Heart and Stroke Foundation of B.C. & Yukon

Barbara Kaminsky,
Chief Executive Officer
Canadian Cancer Society
British Columbia and Yukon Division

A full page ad in the Times-Colonist (2001) asking for continued public support of the bylaw.

10
LESSONS LEARNED

"History never looks like history when you are living through it. It always looks confusing and messy, and it always feels uncomfortable."
— John W. Gardner

During the past two decades, health authorities and local politicians in Greater Victoria have moved from the first steps smoke-free indoor workplaces to successful implementation of the first local bylaw in Canada to ban smoking completely from all indoor public spaces, including bars, pubs and bingo halls. During this time, they have also watched numerous other jurisdictions follow the same path. Some have also been successful. Some have managed to get bylaws enacted, but have learned to live with lower compliance rates, particularly in pubs and bars. In others, the hospitality and/or tobacco industry lobbies have managed to persuade the authorities to pass less demanding laws, or to revoke stringent bylaws weeks or months after they took effect.

From their own experiences, and from watching the experiences of others, the health authorities from the Capital regional district have learned numerous lessons about how best to implement a clean-air bylaw. By sharing their experiences, hopefully others will not have to re-invent the wheel as they move towards smoke-free spaces.

Do not expect this to be a process that leads to immediate results. When beginning the work towards developing a 100 per cent smoke-free bylaw, be prepared for it to take a number of years to have the bylaw passed and implemented, and with a high level of compliance. As more and more communities, and even states and countries, adopt clean-air bylaws, the process does appear to be becoming smoother and shorter. A succession of court decisions confirming the legality of the laws should also reduce the time necessary for implementation.

Yet it should still be noted that a time frame of five years may not be unreasonable, depending upon a variety of factors, including the laws prevailing in neighbouring communities and the level of resistance.

In Greater Victoria, it took a total of eight years from the time that the bylaw was proposed to the time that it could genuinely be said that the goal had been achieved in more than 99 per cent of public places. That, however, was the first clean-air law to be successfully implemented in Canada. Given the growing number of studies that now conclusively show that such legislation has no long-term business impact, many health boards and elected officials should now be able to push ahead more quickly. On the other hand, it could take even longer if the process is beginning in a community that had been relying on voluntary controls and had had no legislation mandating the size of non-smoking sections.

A lengthy time frame itself provides a subtle advantage to opponents of a bylaw. In that time, an election will almost invariably take place. The campaign gives the hospitality and/or tobacco industry the opportunity to work against the bylaw and try to have new officials elected, ones who oppose the legislation. Even if they fail in getting blatant opponents elected, a group of new electees are likely not to know all the background of the issue and may therefore be more ready to reconsider the legislation if pressured by industry. Bylaw opponents will almost invariably take advantage of any signs of weakness among the elected officials.

Referring to the California experience, University of California tobacco control expert Dr. Stanton Glantz wrote: "Throughout these battles, the industry tried to create a positive feedback loop in which smokers would be encouraged to ignore the law because it was going to be repealed, and the industry then used the non-compliance as an argument in the legislature for repeal.

Chapter 10 - Lessons Learned

Although this strategy failed to get the law repealed, however it did create compliance issues."[61]

In Victoria, health officials were amazed to see the lengths to which elected officials who opposed the bylaw but had regularly lost the votes at the regional board would take this process. They persuaded their fellow board members to reconsider repealing the bylaw once again, even after the province's Supreme Court had agreed to grant injunctions against non-compliant establishments and the first such establishment had agreed to pay a fine of $15,000 plus $5,000 court costs.

The length of the process can also create other problems. Staff members come and go; resources and budgets come under increasing pressures; whole governmental or public health administrative structures may be reorganized. All of these can lead to a process that is thwarted, even after several years of steady progress.

From the very beginning, a long-term plan needs to be in place to ensure that the necessary structures, personnel and resources will be in place until the goals have been achieved. In the best of all possible worlds, key personnel will be in place throughout the length of the process.

The passage of a bylaw or similar legislation is not the end of the process. It is, in fact, only the beginning. For many who begin work on a strategy to achieve a smoke-free community, be they public health officials or non-smokers' rights groups, the passage of legislation becomes the ultimate goal. They concentrate on developing the necessary alliances and finding the necessary data to convince the elected officials to adopt a bylaw mandating 100 per cent smoke-free indoor public spaces. They ensure that large numbers of supporters of a bylaw sign petitions, write letters and attend meetings. They search the research literature to find good evidence to defeat the spurious arguments put forward by the hospitality and/or tobacco industries. All of these are extremely important activities, for without them, few local councils or local boards of health would be likely to move ahead on the legislative front.

When this work has been done and the local elected officials have passed the necessary legislation, it is tempting for those who have instituted the idea to assume the worst is over. However, the experience in Victoria and in many other jurisdictions has shown that this is not the case. Issues of implementation, of continuing public education and of enforcing compliance are at least as time-consuming and as difficult as is getting the bylaw passed in the first place.

Throughout the period between passage of the legislation and its implementation, education must be carried out with employers, hospitality establishments, consumers and the general public. Once the date for implementation arrives, considerable resources and staff time will need to be devoted to dealing with the media, to further education (especially of those establishments seen not to be obeying the new rules), to monitoring of compliance and, in the toughest cases, to enforcing the regulations. To a greater or lesser degree, monitoring and education become long-term, ongoing projects. Enforcement may take considerable time, money and energy, especially if it leads to drawn-out, complex and hard-fought court cases as was the case in Greater Victoria.

A steady pace needs to be developed from the beginning. If one has spent all one's staff time, resources and volunteer energy just in getting the legislation passed, there will be far too little for the equally important latter phases of the project. Budgeting needs to be considered as part of a long-term, multi-year process.

Leadership needs to be strong, with the ability to inspire others to keep going through what may be very difficult times. Some staff, particularly those charged with enforcing the bylaw, may find this the most arduous assignment they have ever undertaken, especially if their normal jobs don't put them

Chapter 10 - Lessons Learned

in positions of confrontation. Likewise, some local politicians, used to mediating and working out compromises in cases of community conflict, may find the level of bitterness and hostility unlike anything they have ever experienced. These individuals will need strong support from leaders in their organizations to stay the course.

Those preparing to undertake those leadership positions must realize from the beginning that the process is likely to be both emotionally and mentally challenging. "In this battle, attacks will not be restricted to ideas, but very often will take place at a very personal level," Dr. Stanwick notes in looking back on the experience. During the most emotional days of implementation, both Dr. Stanwick and Frank Leonard, the bylaw's champion on the regional board, received anonymous and harassing middle-of-the-night phone calls at their homes, sometimes even reaching the level of death threats.

They had to put those experiences aside to support staff members who were also facing threats of violence on the job while visiting the openly defiant bars and pubs. Dr. Stanwick admits now that there were a few moments when the potential for violence was so palpable that he wondered whether they should back off, rather than continue running the risk of injury to staff. Instead, they worked with their lawyers to devise the alternative enforcement methods that eventually proved to be so effective. In doing so, they were able to promise the staff that the worst would be over. Those who are not prepared to struggle through those darkest moments, and to give ongoing support to staff and fellow bylaw proponents, should not take up leadership roles in the process in the first place.

In looking at leadership, it is important that one person have the final authority to make decisions on implementation tactics. This is not a case where collegial decision-making or decision-making by committee will always prove successful. The medical health officer on a number of occasions exercised his authority and made decisions contrary to the wishes of the team; ones for which he ultimately accepted accountability and responsibility.

Resources, resources, resources. It is essential to have the necessary financial resources available for all phases of the project — bylaw development, implementation, education and enforcement. This is not a project that can be successfully tackled without adequate dedicated resources. Sufficient personnel must be in place to undertake the many tasks that go into successful passage and implementation of legislation. Lawyers' fees can be considerable. Money will be needed for development and distribution of educational materials, staff overtime for late-night pub monitoring and a host of other special projects. From the first days of the development stage, for instance, Greater Victoria spent money on conducting a regular series of public opinion polls asking citizens their views on the bylaw and how it might affect their restaurant- and pub-going behaviour. The polls were undertaken by one of Canada's top pollsters, the Angus Reid Group (now Ipsos-Reid). Dr. Stanwick insisted on retaining such a prestigious firm, even though it was more expensive than others, because "the polls had to be unassailable, from either a political or a legal point of view." Other jurisdictions may find similar examples where extra money must be spent for political or legal reasons.

Administrative staff need to be adept at obtaining added resources. Although core costs will normally be funded by the local government, funding for some of the extraordinary expenses may be found elsewhere. Greater Victoria found that some of the major health organizations, such as the Cancer Society and the Heart and Stroke Foundation, were prepared to provide funding to develop educational materials about the dangers of second-hand smoke. They had received provincial funding for such educational programs in general, and agreed to funnel it to a community which was taking the lead in developing smoke-free spaces. If several jurisdictions are involved in closely related tobacco lawsuits, it may be possible to share some of the lawyers' costs.

Above all, those involved must realize that elected officials opposed to the bylaw, unable to actually get legislation defeated or repealed, may weaken it substantially by underfunding implementation and especially enforcement efforts. Greater Victoria came close to losing its ability to work through the final court case it needed to achieve virtually full compliance because regional board directors were reluctant to provide the necessary funding for more legal proceedings. The day was saved only when Rick Roger, the CEO of the Capital health region (which oversees health care in the region, but has no legal authority to itself pass bylaws), stepped up to provide $50,000 for enforcement and personally was present at the CRD during critical discussions.

Media availability is crucial to maintaining public credibility, especially during times when confrontation is common and emotions are running high. This means a spokesperson needs to be available to the media 24 hours a day, seven days a week. The cell phone should never be turned off (although it can be passed among various individuals sharing a leadership role, if each of them is clear exactly what the message is). Individuals leading opposition to the bylaw often are on the job at times that are outside the "normal business hours" worked by most government and health department staff. They will often use that timing strategically to provide information and opinions to media outlets; what they say will most often be printed or broadcast unchallenged if no one is available from the pro-clean-air side to comment immediately. One favourite tactic was for the hospitality industry to stage demonstrations or other shows of opposition on weekends when news tended to be scarce, and the opponents hoped that proponents of the bylaw would be hard for reporters to find as well.

Dr. Glantz and his team noted in their history of the California experience that opposition factions were highly successful in garnering media coverage. "The tobacco industry dominated early media coverage of the impact and popularity of smoke-free bars," he wrote. "Articles that were published the week before the smoke-free bar provisions went into effect, and until three months afterward, emphasized opposition to the law and claims of lost business, lost jobs, and problems with enforcement, as well as the probability that the law would be repealed."[62]

Greater Victoria's experience was identical to that found by Dr. Glantz in California. The only way to achieve even a modicum of balance in the coverage was to ensure that reporters were never able to write the line that "the health department could not be reached for comment."

(From Left) Dianne Stevenson and Dr. Stanton Glantz at the University of California, San Francisco discussing the implementation plan

Chapter 10 - Lessons Learned

Never assume the position any individual or organization will take on legislation to mandate 100 per cent smoke-free indoor public places. One of the greatest surprises to many of those involved in developing and implementing Victoria's bylaw was discovering who turned out to be friends and who turned out to be opponents. Issues ranging from individuals' personal experience with smoking to their philosophic views on freedom of choice could, and did, influence how they approached the bylaw. The implementation team had expected full co-operation from local police forces — but found, instead, a mixed response. While individual officers most often readily provided whatever backup was needed, some senior police managers were reluctant to commit resources to aid in enforcement and were even unwilling to acknowledge that the bylaw enforcement officers were themselves legal "peace officers" with the rights that that designation implied. The implementation team had also expected backup from the provincial Liquor Control and Licensing Branch as a condition of every drinking establishments' licence was that they complied with all local legislation. But the Branch was also loathe to become involved, insisting its job was not to enforce municipal or regional bylaws.

And though the team had expected everyone involved in the health care field to be on side with the bylaw, they soon realized that wasn't the case either. Not only did some long-term care home managers and the Hospice director come out clearly and publicly against the bylaw, but even some staff within the public health department said privately they thought the bylaw was going too far or wasn't workable. Some refused to work the necessary overtime to monitor bars late at night. Managers realized that others were so uncommitted that it was best they not be assigned to enforcement teams. Although it was never proven, there were suspicions within the enforcement team that a staff member in the health department itself may have been tipping off the bars as to the team's schedule of inspections.

"The important thing is to have an open enough mind to be prepared to think the unthinkable" if the evidence is clear that someone believed to be an ally is in fact an opponent, says Dr. Stanwick.

Equally important is to search out individuals who are in support of the legislation, even if the industry group to which they belong is opposing it. Some bar and pub owners are likely to express their support for a bylaw; it is crucial to ensure that their views are also made public to show the elected officials and citizens that opposition is not uniform. In Victoria, a critical step was taken when Don Monsour and the restaurant sector agreed to support the bylaw, provided it guaranteed the "level playing field," with restaurants, bars and pubs all treated exactly the same way. Other allies may be found, for instance, among environmentalists concerned about the huge use of fossil fuels to run ventilation systems. It's important to think "outside the box" in considering who may prove valuable allies.

It's also important to realize that people's positions may change over time. Bar owner Gordon Card, for instance, was a strong opponent of the Victoria bylaw when it was first proposed and introduced, but within a few years of implementation, had become a supporter. He had realized that the bylaw could be made to work and wasn't going to be the economic disaster that had been feared.

When developing alliances, the acute-care sector of the health system is crucial. The acute-care sector will, in the long term, be the primary benefactor of the reduced burden of illness that result from smoke-free legislation. Not only will such laws decrease the number of patients suffering from ailments caused or exacerbated by second-hand smoke, but the shrinking number of smokers that normally accompany the legislation will also lead to a reduction in pressure on the acute-care sector. Leaders in the acute-care sector must, if necessary, be educated about these benefits and must be encouraged to be active participants in the process of developing health-promoting public policies. This could range from testifying at public hearings about the consequences of tobacco-related illnesses, to advocating with political decision makers, to committing funding for bylaw promotion activities as the Capital health region administration did in Victoria.

Analyze the prevailing political and social climate before deciding how best to proceed to achieve the ultimate goal of smoke-free indoor public spaces. Greater Victoria was fortunate in that during much of the time it was developing and implementing its bylaw, the New Democratic provincial government was also waging a major war on Big Tobacco. The provincial government, for instance, became the first in Canada to launch a U.S.-style lawsuit to try to force the tobacco companies to pay for health care costs of smoking-related illnesses. Although it had little direct involvement in local bylaw development or enforcement, provincial health ministers made it clear they supported the route the Capital regional board was taking. Less than a year before implementation date, NDP cabinet ministers told reporters they were hoping the province would follow Victoria's example at the same time or shortly thereafter. The string of provincial pronouncements against the tobacco industry reinforced public support for moves like Victoria's bylaw.

By contrast, the Liberal provincial government, which was elected in a landslide in 2001, prides itself on its anti-regulatory and pro-business stance. One of the Liberal MLAs had previously headed a hospitality coalition strenuously opposed to similar bylaws in Vancouver, and the industry had made donations to the Liberal party. As a result, the cabinet overruled the Workers' Compensation Board's plans for strict second-hand smoke regulations in the hospitality industry and also has weakened employee standards in other areas. One suspects it would be much harder to have a bylaw developed, passed and implemented in such a climate. It's not easy to be an island in a sea of opposition to such strategies.

If the climate does not appear to be conducive to the passage and/or implementation of legislation, it is often much better to move more slowly and build the necessary climate of support than to risk losing the battle. Opponents gain much more in the public eye from having a bylaw defeated at a council table or, worse, repealed a few weeks after implementation, than they do by having a slightly slower process invoked to begin with.

Never lose sight of the reason for the legislation — improved health for workers and for the population at large. Only the most obdurate opponents of smoke-free places will argue any longer that second-hand smoke has not been proven to be a health hazard. The scientific evidence is simply too overwhelming for this argument to hold any water. Rather, opponents will focus on non-health arguments — that legislation will devastate business, especially in the hospitality industry; and that adults who have the right to choose to smoke also should have the right to enter public spaces contaminated by second-hand smoke. Both these arguments may be rebutted: as to the first, numerous scientific studies have shown no long-term deleterious effects on business from smoke-free legislation; as to the second, no one is trying to ban smoking, merely regulate where the product may be consumed for the betterment of the health of all.

However, in Victoria, it was found to be much more successful to concentrate on the health arguments and avoid the minefield that the economic arguments can become. It is worth noting that employees would not be allowed to "voluntarily" work in other contaminated areas, such as those riddled with asbestos. To exempt one group of workers from clean-air legislation, such as those in the hospitality industry, is basically to say that those workers are second-class citizens as far as protection of their health and safety is concerned.

Because one of the other arguments that opponents are likely to make is that suitable ventilation systems can achieve the same goals as smoke-free laws, it's important to be prepared with evidence to show that such solutions may reduce the dose of contaminants to which workers are exposed but won't eliminate them. For some of the toxins in second-hand smoke, there is no proven safe level of exposure.

Be prepared to counter unreliable and biased "surveys" and "polls" which are likely to be produced by the hospitality industry and their allies. Bylaw opponents will use their own polls and surveys to argue that smoke-free legislation does not enjoy widespread support among the public, and to show that short-term economic consequences of any legislation are devastating. Most of these surveys have serious methodological problems, such as drawing their samples from persons visiting establishments whose operators are encouraging defiance of the legislation, or basing their argument of business losses from a small sample of self-reports from irate bar owners and operators. In Victoria, the Freedom of Choice Coalition produced a "survey" of economic effects, based on self-reports from only one-quarter of its own members. This "estimate" for a three-month period from only about 150 businesses was then extrapolated to an entire year and then to the entire business community of Greater Victoria, resulting in a claim of a $6 million loss as a result of the legislation. When official government liquor sales figures for the period were compiled, they showed that no such business losses occurred. Yet the $6 million-loss figure is still being touted as accurate by opponents of similar bylaws at public hearings in other Canadian cities. It is important for bylaw proponents to have available the services of an expert in survey methods to combat these types of figures, which may otherwise discourage elected officials from passing or keeping a bylaw.

Never descend to the low level of insults and personal attacks likely to be offered up by bylaw opponents. Knowing just what to say in public and how best to say it in the midst of confrontation is a complex job. Those who become spokespersons for clean-air legislation should develop as strong a team of advisers as possible to help work out these messages. These could include anyone from members of their agency's public relations department to supportive media members (who wouldn't put themselves in a conflict of interest position) to people who have served as spokespersons in similar battles in other communities. It is invaluable for the spokesperson to have someone "rehearse" the possibly difficult questions and answers before a major public presentation or media appearance. It is far better to realize there is an awkward question in a private rehearsal when there is time to prepare a response than to be caught flat-footed in front of half a dozen TV cameras.

The most basic principle, however, must be to stick to the key health issues and not descend to the level of opponents, who will often launch personal attacks and hurl insults at anyone seen as the "public face" of a bylaw. A spokesperson who loses his or her temper in public and retorts with an equal insult will lose large amounts of credibility in the eyes of the public.

When developing a bylaw, don't forget the issue of "smoking pits" in high schools, even if they are located outdoors. Greater Victoria's efforts to ban "smoke pits" by making all school grounds smoke-free zones also created significant controversy, including some from principals and parents' advisory councils. Even though it was illegal for almost all students to buy cigarettes, the parents and administrators feared students would simply slip off school property to smoke, likely causing trouble with the neighbours and possibly putting themselves at risk by smoking in unsupervised or unsafe surroundings. However, these problems did not materialize to any significant degree and the value of the ruling has been more than amply demonstrated by the smoking rates among high school aged teenagers in the region. The rates are currently hovering around 17 per cent, which is as much as 50 per cent lower than the smoking rates in school districts which still allow students to light up on school property.

Ensure staff are adequately trained, administrative systems put in place, and logistics worked out before implementation day for smoke-free legislation. Even highly skilled staff are likely to need enhanced training to look at not only the legal specifics of the bylaw, but also the sorts of situations that staff may face, ranging from trying to write tickets in a dark and noisy bar to dealing with hostile and confrontational patrons. Greater Victoria's enforcement teams received conflict-management training from a police expert only after two weeks of stressful nights in pubs and bars; staff now agree it should have been undertaken before enforcement started. It is helpful for the individual enforcement teams to be identified early so they can become accustomed to working as partners.

Other systems also need to be in place for implementation. These range from internal communication mechanisms to ensure everyone stays in the loop and receives the same information, to systems for tracking statistics and ones for collecting, monitoring and handling complaints.

Determine what backup will be in place from other law enforcement agencies in cases where problems develop. Victoria faced a difficult problem when the police departments backed out of their commitment to providing proactive support to enforcement teams just weeks before implementation day. The details of the relationship with law enforcement need to be clearly spelled out, probably in writing, beforehand.

---

61. Magazem, Sheryl and Glantz, Dr. Stanton. "The New Battleground: California's Experience with Smoke-free Bars," American Journal of Public Health, 91 (2) 245-252, 2001.

62. Magazem et al. "Print Media Coverage of California's Smokefree Bar Law," Tobacco Control, 10(2) 154-160, 2001.

EPILOGUE

The court victories against the Sooke River Hotel and the Tudor House signalled the end of organized defiance to the bylaw in Greater Victoria. Compliance rates immediately stabilized at more than 99 per cent, where they remain to this day. The Capital regional district is unaware of any communities where the compliance rate is higher for a bylaw mandating 100 per cent smoke-free indoor public places.

The rate of smoking also continues to drop throughout the region and remains one of the lowest in Canada. The last survey undertaken showed that fewer than 14 per cent of adults over the age of 15 are current smokers, compared to a Canadian average of 21 per cent.

The rate of teen smoking has also continued to decline. Only about 17 per cent of students aged 15 to 19 in the region now identify themselves as current smokers. In some other British Columbia school districts where, interestingly, "smoke pits" are still allowed on school grounds, the smoking rates are double that number.

The growth in popularity of the bylaw continues. The health department continues to use Ipsos-Reid to undertake regular polling on the issue. In the most recent poll, conducted in 2001, a total of 81 per cent of those surveyed approved of the law, including, for the first time, a majority of smokers themselves.

In 2002, the Capital Health Region/Vancouver Island Health Authority won the Alexander Officer Award from the Canadian Institute of Public Health Inspectors for outstanding and meritorious achievements in the field of public health, largely due to work done in the field of tobacco control.

The business losses feared by the hospitality industry have not occurred. Liquor sales statistics showed that during the second quarter after the bylaw was implemented, sales decreased by a significant six per cent, but they rebounded and stabilized after that. Neither did tourism nor employment decrease as the result of the bylaw.

However, some of the bylaw opponents continue to insist that the bylaw did significant harm to individual businesses and specific sectors of the hospitality industry, most notably beer parlours. Don Rittaler maintains to this day that the $6 million in annual losses predicted by opponents early in 1999 really did occur, despite all the statistics to the contrary. He says his Sooke River Inn alone would have lost some $500,000 a year, had it remained in its old beer parlour format.

However, soon after the injunctions were granted, Rittaler took advantage of new rules allowing hospitality establishments to establish full-service privatized liquor stores. Rittaler has turned about half the space formerly devoted to the beer parlour into an upscale liquor store. The success of this project has been so great he is now expanding the liquor store further.

Rittaler has hired Brian Mayzes to run the new liquor store for him. Mayzes has become more philosophical about the results of the bylaw. He now says that the beer parlour sector of the hospitality industry was hard-hit — but adds that that sector was probably a dying one anyway. He figures drinking and driving laws have as much to do with it as smoking rules, and so does a general increase in health awareness in the population. "The days of the blue-collar guys stopping after work at the beer parlour for six, seven beer and then driving home are just coming to an end," he says. "And when that's gone, so is the smoking."

Others of the bylaw's previous opponents have now come to embrace it. The Great Canadian Casino company, one of the strongest opponents of the idea during the public hearings in 1996, has chosen, based on its Victoria experience, to make all its casinos throughout British Columbia smoke-free indoors — even where the law does not require them to do so. Casino managers say the customers and staff both appreciate the cleaner air, and patrons are happy to take short breaks in comfortable and well-designed outdoor smoking spaces.

Bar owner Gordon Card readily admits publicly that he has changed his mind about the bylaw. When it was first proposed, he says now, he genuinely feared the loss of business he believed the bylaw would bring, and he also believed that owners should be allowed to decide based on the marketplace whether or not to go smoke-free. However, he says, once the bylaw was implemented, business went down for only about three months and then bounced back to pre-bylaw levels.

What he hadn't expected, he says, was the improvement in the atmosphere. Staff are happier and customers are happier. "It's just a better, more pleasant environment."

Card went so far as to appear on a radio show in 2004 in Saskatoon, Saskatchewan when that city's council was considering a bylaw. His message to bar owners there: don't be afraid of it. In the end, it won't hurt your business and it will improve the atmosphere for your staff. (Saskatoon council later passed the bylaw, modelled closely on Victoria's.)

The New Democrat government of British Columbia that was so supportive of the region's bylaw efforts was voted out of office by the electorate in May 2001. The new Liberal government under premier Gordon Campbell refused to allow the Workers' Compensation Board to go ahead with its plans to ban smoking in hospitality establishments, except in "self-serve" rooms which employees would normally not be required to enter. The provincial cabinet invoked a rarely used power to overrule the independent board and allow all hospitality establishments, including restaurants, to designate as much as 45 per cent of their space as smoking. The smoking areas must be separate from non-smoking areas, and vented to the outside, and workers must not work in the smoking areas for more than 20 per cent of each shift. Theoretically workers can refuse to work in the smoking sections, but labour minister Graham Bruce said it would be lawful for employers to screen job applicants to ensure all employees were willing to expose themselves to the second-hand smoke. However, the Liberals' rules don't apply in Greater Victoria or other areas which have enacted smoke-free bylaws.

Christy Clark serves as deputy premier in the Campbell government. Her brother Bruce moved on to become a top fund-raiser for the successful campaign to get Paul Martin elected leader of the federal Liberal Party and hence Prime Minister of Canada. However, in 2003 he was one of a number of Martin operatives in B.C. whose home-offices were searched by RCMP officers. The search warrant was one of a series executed, including two on offices of ministerial aides in the B.C. legislature, as part of a probe into possible influence-peddling or corruption. The investigation continues, and no criminal charges have yet been laid. It is still not clear where Clark may fit into the probe.

The provincial Liberal government also reorganized the health care management system, making all of Vancouver Island a single health management region, rather than just Greater Victoria. Rick Roger, CEO of the Capital health region, was appointed CEO of the new island-wide health authority. Roger's most recent community initiative has been the creation of a much needed and highly praised sobering centre in downtown Victoria. Dr. Stanwick has now taken over as chief medical health officer for all of Vancouver Island, and Dianne Stevenson is head of tobacco control programs for the entire Island as well. Among their future projects will be efforts to enact the same type of bylaw as Greater Victoria's in other Island communities. They are also spearheading an effort to make all hospital and health facility grounds smoke-free, both inside and out.

Eugene and Rhoda Kaellis moved to the Lower Mainland of B.C. in 1988, where they continue to pursue social justice projects. Much of their energy is now focused on the need to provide more affordable housing for lower-income British Columbians. Rhoda Kaellis still says their efforts to have smoking restrictions in the Capital regional district was one of her easiest, most successful and most satisfying campaigns.

Christopher Causton remains as mayor of Oak Bay, but after two terms as chair of the Capital regional district board, was defeated in a vote of fellow board members in 2002.

Joyce Westcott took early retirement in 2003 as executive director of Oak Bay Lodge. After ongoing struggles over shrinking revenues from the provincial government and ongoing

Epilogue

investigations with licensing officials over standards, the board of the lodge decided in early 2004 to cease running the lodge as an independent operation. They turned it over to the Vancouver Island Health Authority, which is now running it as a long-term care facility within the island's overall hospital system. The indoor smoking room is gone and an outdoor shelter has replaced it.

David Cheperdak has left Hospice to head up the Lodge at Broadmead, the second-largest long-term care facility in Greater Victoria.

Frank Leonard took over as mayor of Saanich in November 1996 after Murray Coell had been elected an MLA in the Gordon Campbell government, where he serves as minister of human resources. Leonard this year is serving as president of Union of B.C. Municipalities.

In the winter of 1999, Brian Mayzes ran against Leonard for the mayoralty in the civic elections. The final vote count: Leonard, 14,602; Mayzes, 1,003.

Dr. Stanwick was given the award of "Jackass of the Week" by Forces International, one of the most passionately pro-tobacco sites on the worldwide web (http://www.forces.org/usa/files/jack.htm). Describing him as a "perky anti-tobacco cheerleader," they went on to say that "Stanwick dons his pompoms and leaps into frenetic fact-defying acrobatic capers whenever anti-tobacco needs to pull the wool over people's eyes."

But just a few weeks later, he was also given the Norman C. Delarue Award, the top award of the group Physicians for a Smoke-Free Canada, for his work over the previous two decades in tobacco control, with a special emphasis on this work in developing and implementing the bylaw in Victoria.

Dr. Stanwick says, however, that he gets more satisfaction from the enthusiastic thanks he continues to receive from many area residents. Shortly after the bylaw went into effect, most of those who congratulated him were non-smokers who suffered from sensitivities and/or allergies to cigarette smoke. They were pleased because they could enjoy entertainment venues that heretofore had to be off limits to them.

In the last year or two, however, he has also received thanks from former smokers who say the bylaw was the last impetus they needed to quit the habit. They tell him how much better they're feeling now, and how they can take part in activities which were previously too strenuous for them. That, he says, is a big part of what makes it all worthwhile.

Thank You

The Clean Air Coalition of BC congratulates the Capital Regional District (CRD) Board for their continued support of the Clean Air Bylaw. All citizens in the Region remain protected from sechondhand smoke in indoor public places while a level playing field is maintained in the hospitality industry. **The Clean Air Bylaw remains in place and intact; it has not been changed.**

The Clean Air Coalition acknowledges the contribution of the hundreds of CRD residents who took the time to e-mail, fax, and phone the CRD Board to voice their support for the Bylaw.

The Clean Air Coalition of BC, which includes the Heart and Stroke Foundation of BC and Yukon, the BC Lung Association, and the Canadian Cancer Society, BC and Yukon Division, believe the original slogan in the CRD best describes the reason for the Bylaw - "Just for the health of it."

Scott McDonald,
Executive Director,
British Columbia Lung Association

Bobbe Wood,
Chief Executive Officer
Heart and Stroke Foundation of B.C. & Yukon

Barbara Kaminsky,
Chief Executive Officer
Canadian Cancer Society
British Columbia and Yukon Division

✝ BRITISH COLUMBIA LUNG ASSOCIATION

HEART AND STROKE FOUNDATION OF B.C. & YUKON

BRITISH COLUMBIA AND YUKON DIVISION

An ad in the Times-Colonist (2001) thanking the public for their continued support of the bylaw.

A BRIEF CHRONOLOGY

October 23, 1984 — Greater Victoria's first smoking regulations take effect, banning smoking in such places as elevators, service line-ups and buses.

1986 — Amendments to the bylaw strengthen it, especially for workplaces, but still allow places like shopping malls to designate half their space as smoking zones.

January 1, 1992 — Further changes to the bylaw go into effect, making almost all indoor workplaces 100 per cent smoke free. The sole remaining exceptions were hospitality establishments and smoking lounges in long-term care and seniors' homes. However, restaurants and bars were required to provide 50 per cent of their seating for non-smokers.

June 1992 — Regional medical health officer Dr. Shaun Peck proposes a move to 100 per cent smoke-free hospitality establishments as well, but the opposition from the industry is so great that the idea is put on hold.

October 1995 — The region's new medical health officer, Dr. Richard Stanwick, again raises the issue of requiring all public indoor spaces to be 100 per cent smoke free, including the hospitality industry.

April 1996 — Three days of "smoking summit" talks between health department staff, health advocates and the hospitality industry fail to reach a consensus on when or how the change should take effect.

May 1996 — Ten hours of public hearings are held to let both those with vested interests and the general public air their views.

June 1996 — The Capital regional district's health committee recommends the hospitality establishments all be required to go smoke-free on January 1, 1998, but the whole board agrees to a delay of one year. The bylaw will take effect on January 1, 1999.

September 1996 — A portion of the bylaw that bans smoking anywhere on school properties, indoors or out, takes effect.

March 1998 — The CRD board votes to take Sooke hotelier Don Rittaler to court for failing to obey the bylaw requiring 60 per cent non-smoking seating in his pub.

May 1998 — Rittaler launches a constitutional challenge in B.C. Supreme Court against the moves to make the hospitality industry 100 per cent non-smoking.

August 1998 — The board of Oak Bay Lodge first proposes that long-term care facilities be allowed to be exempt from the ban because it serves as the "home" of its residents.

October 1998 — Bars and pubs unhappy with the bylaw band together to form the Age of Majority Business Coalition, later renamed the Freedom of Choice Coalition.

November 1998 — Rittaler adjourns his constitutional challenge lawsuit with no new date set for a hearing of it.

December 1998 — The CRD board votes to implement the bylaw as planned in 1999 for both the hospitality industry and the long-term care facilities.

January 1999 — The bylaw requiring all indoor public spaces to go smoke-free goes into effect as planned.

March 1999 — The regional board approves a change in the bylaw to allow operators of establishments to be held liable if they continue to condone and encourage smoking in their premises.

June 1999 — The first court case is launched against six recalcitrant bars.

January 2000 — New Workers' Compensation Board regulations go into effect province-wide, requiring all workplaces to be smoke-free, including in the hospitality industry.

March 2000 — A B.C. Supreme Court judge rules the new WCB rules are not valid because the legally required consultations with industry have not taken place.

April 2000 — The first temporary injunctions are issued against non-compliant bars in the CRD.

February 2001 — After one day of a planned two-day court case, Thursday's Sports Bar agrees to a permanent court injunction against it and to pay fines and court costs totalling $20,000.

October 2001 — A B.C. Supreme Court judge issues an injunction against two of the last remaining hold-out bars, marking the end of any organized defiance of the bylaw.

INDEX

A

Acts (of legislatures)
  Health Act, 4
  Local Government Act, 169
  Municipal Act, 81, 82, 112
  Municipalities Enabling and Validating Act, 84, 112, 185
addiction(s), harm-reduction model, 107
Age of Majority Business Coalition, 93, 110
  on economic effects of tobacco-control, 157–158
  opposes tobacco-control laws, 88
air-quality standards, 40–41, 48
AirSpace, 4–5, 21, 134, 174
Allen, Brian, 10
Amchitka Island, nuclear testing at, 3–4
American Conference of Governmental Industrial Hygienists, 41
American Society of Heating, Refrigerating and Air-Conditioning Engineers, 31
  air-quality standards of, 40–41
Anderson, Gerry, 100
Angus Reid Group
  polls on attitudes to tobacco control, 27, 30, 56–57, 76, 90, 156, 196
Anorexia's Fallen Angel (by Barbara McLintock), xiv
Anthony, Rick, 132
Arizona smoking-control laws, 2
Arneil, Allan, 6–8, 10
Arvay, Joe, 79, 89–90, 102
Ashes to Ashes (by Richard Kluger), 9
Avison, Claire, xix, 73

B

BAT Industries, ix
B.C. Cabaret Owners' Association, 175–176
B.C. Cancer Agency, 58
B.C. Hotels Association, 30
B.C. Lung Association, 12, 58, 91
  on health consequences of second-hand smoke, 62
B.C. Restaurant and Food Services Association, 30
B.C. Society of Respiratory Therapists, 58
Bender, Christine, 44
bingo. *SEE UNDER* gaming establishments
Bird of Paradise (pub), 125–126
Blatherwick, John, 27, 29, 33, 45
Bouck, John, 179–181
Bourree, Frank, 60
Boyd, Wendy, xx–xxi, 10, 14
breweries and tobacco-control, 89
Brigden, Linda, 15
British American Tobacco (corporation), 79
Brookman, Carol, 90, 153
Brown & Williamson Tobacco Corporation, ix, xi
Bruce, Graham, 209

C

California tobacco-control laws, 3
  opposition to, 192–193
  public support for, 76
  success of, 85–88, 90
Campbell, Gordon, 209
Campbell, Vance, 175–176
Canadian Broadcasting Corporation
  coverage of bylaw implementation by, 148–149

219

Canadian Cancer Society,
    12, 58, 60, 196
Canadian Hotels' Association
    Courtesy of Choice
        program and, 79
Canadian Tobacco
    Manufacturers' Council, 80
    ventilation solution
        standards and, 39–40
Capital regional district, 4–5
carcinogens, xi, 24, 63, 173–174
Card, Gordon, 17, 34, 43,
    46, 49, 76, 88, 119,
    157–158, 200, 208–209
    on economic effects of
        tobacco-control laws, 153
Casino Management
    Council of B.C., 36
casinos. *SEE UNDER* gaming
    establishments
Causton, Christopher, 17, 104,
    105–106, 138, 181, 210
Charland, Philip, 64–65
Charter of Rights and Freedoms
    constitutionality of anti-
        smoking laws and, 32
Cheperdak, David, 141–143, 211
children, safety of, 21
choice, freedom of, 55, 57,
    60, 62, 64, 78, 158
    SEE ALSO Freedom of
        Choice Coalition
Clark, Bruce, 30, 34, 40,
    43, 44, 63, 209–210
Clark, Christy, 30, 209
Clayoquot Valley
    injunctions against anti-
        logging demonstration
        at, 168–169
Clean Air Bylaw
    Age of Majority Business
        Coalition opposes, 165
    government campaign
        for, 56–59
    public hearing on, 58–61
    public support for, 53, 56–59
    Stanwick's defense of, 164
Clifford, Russ, 80
Coell, Murray, 27, 50, 51, 55, 211

Commonwealth Games
    (1994), 1, 16
compliance rates, 207
Corbeil, Cary, 43
Court of appeals, B.C.
    position of against non-
        compliance, 168–169
Courtesy of Choice program, 79
    and Rittaler lawsuit, 89
Coy, Peter, 49, 82
CRD. *SEE* Capital
    regional district
Cull, Elizabeth, 82–84
Cumming, George, 169

D

de Wolf, John, 31, 128
death(s)
    tobacco-related, ix, 32
Doll & Penny's Cafe,
    135–136, 173
Drew, Miles, xvii–xix, 122, 160

E

earthquake, 63
Easingwood, Joe, 147, 149
Eaton, Rex, 93
economic effects of
    tobacco-control, x, 17,
        30–32, 34, 49, 60–61, 76,
        88–90, 127–128, 149, 153,
        157–158, 178–179, 208
EHOs. *SEE* environmental
    health officers
Elephant and Castle
    economic effects of tobacco-
        control at, 127–128
enforcement of tobacco-
    control laws, xviii–xx,
    6–7, 10, 120–134
    in high schools, 72–73
    media reporting of, 141–163
environmental health
    officers, 178
    recognized as peace
        officers, 123

Index

Environmental Protection Agency (U.S.), 24, 173–174
environmental tobacco smoke (ETS). *SEE* second-hand smoke
Esquimalt Inn, 119, 138, 178
   enforcement attempts at, 121–123
   non-compliance of, xvii–xxi, 120
   targeted for, 171
Esquimalt Legion
   non-compliance news conference at, 126–127
ETS (environmental tobacco smoke). *SEE* second-hand smoke
exemptions from anti-smoking laws, 14, 108, 117, 156

F

Field Research Corporation
   poll on economic effects of tobacco-control, 76
The Fifth Estate
   investigation of John Luik by, 174
Forces International
   "Jackass of the Week" award, 211
Fraser Institute, 173–174
Freedom of Choice Coalition, 137
   announces court challenge, 126–127
   opposes tobacco-control laws, 119, 167
   study by, 203

G

gaming establishments
   bingo, 46–47
   casinos, 46–47, 208
   level playing field approach and, 46–47
Gillespie, Bob, 105
Glantz, Stanton, 86, 192, 197
Gould, Ed, 4
Great Canadian Casino, 208
Green, John, 171
gypsy-moth spray program, 125

H

Harrigan, Dennis, 74
health care facilities, 16, 200-201
   exemptions from anti-smoking laws, 14, 108, 117
   long-term, 97–100, 199
   SEE ALSO Hospice; Oak Bay Lodge
Health Promotion Conference (Chile, 2002), xiii–xiv
Healthy 2000 (B.C. special projects), 11
Heart and Stroke foundation, 12, 58, 60, 91, 196
Heinold's First and Last Chance Saloon, 90
high schools, smoking in, 63, 66
Hirschfield, Rob
   study on ventilation solution, 41–44
Hospice, 104, 141–142, 199, 211
   media coverage of implementation at, 160–161
hospitality industry
   adult only argument of, 45–46
   effect of smoking bans on, x
   exemptions from tobacco-control laws in, 14, 24–25
   and freedom of choice argument, 55
   level playing field approach and, 16, 46–47, 61
   opposes tobacco-control, 16–18, 25–27, 29–34, 39–51, 55, 66
   California, 192–193
   Vancouver, 135–136
   supports tobacco-control laws, 64–65
   ventilation solution and, 31
Hospitality Industry Group
   ventilation solution and, 31

Hospitality Industry
    Liquor Licensing
    Advisory Group, 17
hospitals. *SEE* health
    care facilities
Hume, Mark, 161
Hunter, Wayne, 137
Hutchinson, Bill, 36

I

injunctions against non-
    compliance, 168–169
The Insider (Disney movie), 74
Ipsos-Reid, 56, 196

J

Jackson, Geoff, 122–123
Johannessen, Don, 7
Johnny's Cafe, 128
Johnstone, Tim, 22–23
Jordan, Bill, 22

K

Kaellis, Eugene, 3–4, 8, 210
Kaellis, Rhoda, 3–4, 5–6, 8, 210
Keep, Everett, 9
King, Jim, 105, 115, 135–136
Klassen, Peter, 180–181
Kluge, Eike, 114
    on additions, 110
    on ethics of tobacco-
        control, 106–109
Kluger, Richard, 9
Knox, Jack, 181
Kwan, Jenny, 84, 167

L

Lakritz, Naomi, 143
Laundy, Dave, 80
Laur, Darren, 126, 132
legislation, anti-smoking, 6, 8
    Arizona, 2
    California, 3, 76
    economic effects of, 8,
        30–31, 59–61, 76
    Minnesota, 2
    North York, ON, 75
    Ottawa, ON, 3
    public opinion on, 63–64
    public support for, 27–28, 30
    Saskatoon, SK, 209
    Sweden, 2
    Vancouver, B.C., 24–27
    Victoria, B.C., 13
        Bylaw 1440, 10
        Bylaw 2401, 164
        compliance rate, 11
    Winnipeg, MB, 22
Leonard, Frank, 26–27, 106,
    114, 116, 150–151, 211
    threats against, 195
level playing field approach to
    air-quality standards, xx,
        16, 41, 45–47, 61, 120, 170
    cost of ventilation
        solution and, 41
Lewis, Lynn, 71
Liberal government, 185
    position of on tobacco-
        control, 209
Liquor Control and Licensing
    Board, 77, 199
Local Government Act, 169
Locke, Brenda, 25
Logan, Stewart
    challenges WCB position, 127
Logan brothers, 179
Lower Mainland
    poll on anti-smoking
        laws, 27–28
Lower Mainland Hospitality
    Industry Group, 29–30, 34
Luik, John, 173–174
lung cancer, 3, 9

M

Marchenski, Maxine, 86
Martin, Paul, 210
Maxwell, Andrew, 104,
    110, 114, 115
Mayzes, Brian, xviii, 138,
    159, 172, 208, 211
    argues against tobacco-
        control bylaw, 167

court challenge of
bylaw and, 127
supports smokers'
rights, 119, 120
targeted for non-
compliance, 171
McCloy, Scott, 93
McDannold, Guy, 81
McKinley, Michael, 73
McLean, David, 106, 115
McLintock, Barbara, xiv–xv
media
importance of coverage
by, 197
reporting of tobacco-control
enforcement by, 141–163
Melvin, Allen, 185–186
Minnesota
smoking-control laws in, 2
Moench, Lou, 153
Monsour, Don, 17–18, 36, 43–44,
47, 60, 66–67, 85, 200
supports
level playing field
approach, 47
tobacco-control laws, 75–76
Montreaux Clinic, 125
Mount Edward Court
(nursing home), 100
Municipal Act, 112–114
Municipalities Enabling and
Validating Act, 84, 185

N

Native reserves
casinos on, 46–47
Neighbourhood Pub
Owners of B.C., 25
New Democratic government
(B.C.), 185
sues "Big Tobacco," 167, 201
tobacco-control and,
82–84, 98, 167–168
non-compliance, 128–133
injunctions used against, 137
penalties for, 134–135,
179–180
targeted establishments,
170–171

threats against health
workers, 124
Non-Partisan Association, 32
Non-Smokers' Rights
Association, 174
North York, ON
tobacco-control
compliance in, 75
nuclear testing
opposition to, 3–4

O

Oak Bay Lodge, 210–211
media coverage of bylaw
implementation
at, 153–156
opposes tobacco-control
laws, 100–117
Olson, Grant, 34, 88, 119,
133, 157–158
opposition to tobacco-
control laws
SEE UNDER hospitality
industry; Tourism
Victoria
Orr, Sheila, 83
Ottawa, ON
smoking-control laws in, 3

P

Pacific Analytics
economic impact of tobacco-
control laws and, 178–179
Palmer, Malcolm
economic effects of tobacco-
control laws and, 127–128
Pan American Health
Organization
Health Promotion Conference
(Chile, 2002), xiii–xiv
Parklands Secondary School
tobacco-control and, 72, 73
Passive Smoke (by John Luik
and Gio Gori), 173–174
Peck, Shaun, 1–2, 11–19
passim, 56, 151, 185
Perry, Alan, 59

Peterson, Jody, 78
Philip Morris (corporation), 79
   ventilation solution
      standards and, 39=40
police and bylaw
      enforcement, 123
Potter, Les, 91–93, 132–133
private investigators, 182
Progressive Democratic
      Alliance, 84

R

Registered Nurses' Association
      of B.C., 58
Repace, James, 3, 174
Research for International
      Tobacco Control, 15
respiratory disease(s), 3
Restaurant and Food
      Services Association
   level playing field
      approach and, 46
Restaurant Association
      of B.C., 36
   supports ventilation
      solution, 45
restaurateurs
   level playing field
      approach and, 45, 61
rights
   of non-smokers, 2
   of smokers, 55, 57
Rittaler, Don, 80, 108,
      117, 156, 176, 181
   challenges constitutionality
      of tobacco-control
      laws, 78–79
   court proceedings
      against, 184–186
   on economic impact of
      tobacco-control laws, 208
   opposes tobacco-control
      laws, 76–82
Roger, Rick, 183, 197
Royal B.C. Museum, 179
Royal Canadian Legion, 30
Royal Canadian Mounted Police
   refuse to enforce tobacco-
      control laws, 92–93

S

Saskatoon tobacco-control
      bylaw, 209
schools, high
      tobacco-control in, 69–75
Scott, Mark, 50
Scraba, Cindy, 12
second-hand smoke
   classified as Class A
      carcinogen, 24, 173–174
   deaths from, 32
   health consequences of, 62
   studies on hazards of, 3,
      8–9, 11, 152–153, 174
Seniors' Homes. *SEE* health
      care facilities
Shandley, Sylvia, 142–145
Smoke-Free Task Force
      (CRD), 42–48
Sooke River Hotel, 181
   court proceedings
      against, 184–186
Steinfeld, Jesse, 2
Stelly's Secondary School
      and tobacco-control, 71, 74
Stonehouse Pub, 64–65
Strathcona Hotel, 133
Stromberg-Stein, Sunni
   decision on WCB anti-
      smoking regulations, 176
Stuart, Kathryn, 81, 134
studies
   air-quality standards, 41–42
   second-hand smoke hazards,
      3, 8–9, 11, 152–153, 174
   unreliability of, 203
Sweanor, David, 111
   on constitutionality of anti-
      smoking laws, 32, 33

Index

Sweden
  smoking-control laws in, 2
Swiftsure Lounge, 133

T

Tally-Ho bar, 134
Teen Tobacco council, 167
Thackray, Allan, 135–136
Thursday's Sports Bar, 179–180
  non-compliance of, 127, 130–133
  targeted, 171
Times-Colonist (newspaper)
  coverage of bylaw implementation by, 156–157
  supports Oak Bay Lodge exemption, 153–154, 156
tobacco industry
  B.C. government suit against, 167, 201
  Courtesy of Choice program of, 79
Tobacco Manufacturers' Council of Canada, 39–40, 80
Tobacco-Free Task Force, 12, 46, 49, 58, 82
  on health consequences of second-hand smoke, 62
Toronto, ON
  tobacco-control laws in, 3, 75
  public support for, 57
tourism industry
  effect of tobacco-control on, 179
Tourism Victoria, 43
  opposes tobacco-control laws, 26, 44, 49, 61–62
toxoplasmosis, 22–23
Tudor House pub
  court proceedings against, 184–186
  economic effects of tobacco-control on, 125–125
Tymchuk, Michael, 160

V

Vancouver, B.C.
  tobacco-control laws in, 24–27
  challenges to, 135–136
ventilation solution to second-hand smoke, 9, 17, 26, 31, 39–44, 49
  objections to, 33
  systems for, 202
Verbrugge, Natexa, 62
Victoria High School
  tobacco-control and, 72, 74–75
Victoria Medical Society, 58

W

Walton, Ken, 104
water, drinking
  toxoplasmosis and, 22–23
Watts, Richard, 143
Westcott, Joyce, 104, 210
Whyte, Lorne, 26, 43, 50–51, 62
Wigand, Jeffrey, 74
Williamson, Tim, 176, 184–186
Wilson, Gordon, 84
Winnipeg, MB
  anti-smoking laws in, 22
Woodcock, Connie, 143
Workers' Compensation Board, 28, 65, 93
  air-quality standards of, 44, 49, 103
  regulation on workplace smoking implemented, 174–175

Y

Yak and Yeti Hotel (Nepal), 79
Young, Stew, 183–184

Barbara McLintock is an award-winning journalist, author and broadcaster. In addition, she now serves as a coroner's agent in Greater Victoria. In 2002 she was named an Honourary Citizen of the City of Victoria in recognition of her many years of extensive community service. In 2004 she was given the Victoria YM-YWCA's Woman of Distinction Award for Communication.

She spent more than 20 years as reporter, columnist and Victoria Bureau Chief for The Province newspaper, where she won a number of awards, including the Canadian Association of Journalists' national award for best investigative newspaper reporting for 1996.

Her first book, *Anorexia's Fallen Angel: The Untold Story of Peggy Claude-Pierre and the Controversial Montreux Clinic* was published by Harper Collins Canada in 2002 and was named runner-up for the VanCity Book Prize in 2003.

McLintock was born in Regina, Saskatchewan, grew up in Winnipeg, Manitoba and has resided in Victoria, B.C. for the past thirty years. *(Photo courtesy of Esther Parker)*